Angela Merici's Journey of the Heart

The Rule, the Way

Mary-Cabrini Durkin

Angela Merici's Journey of the Heart

The Rule, the Way

Mary-Cabrini Durkin

Cover photograph: At the Brudazzo, this road passes a small shrine (left of camera) commemorating the traditional site of Angela's vision. Photo by Mary-Cabrini Durkin

Published by WovenWord Press
www.wovenword.com

Cover and book design © 2005 by Vicki McVey

Hard cover ISBN: 0-9678428-6-7; soft cover ISBN: 0-9658137-2-X
Durkin, Mary-Cabrini
        Angela Merici's Journey of the Heart: The Rule, The Way/Mary-Cabrini Durkin

1. Merici, Angela 2. Women's spiritual life—Rule, Company of Saint Ursula
3. Biography 4. Women's history 5. Catholic Church

Library of Congress Control Number: 2005929940

Grateful acknowledgment is made to the following.
For permission to incorporate images:
Hector Bedolla for his photographs of viniculture from Handal-Bedolla Vineyards (pp. 24, 183, 221),
The Centro Mericiano, Brescia, for *St. Ursula and Companions* by Alessandro Bonvicino, Il Moretto (p. 280), for *Blessed Mother Angela opens her Rule and founds the Company on St. Catherine's Day, 1535* (p. 70), and for the photograph of *Blessed Angela, Brescian Virgin, Foundress of the new Congregation of Virgins called the Company of St. Ursula* (p. xiv).
The Civic Museums of Art and History of Brescia for *Portrait of a Lady* by Luca Mombella (1518 - after 1588) and for *The Seamstress* by Antonio Cifrondi (1657-1731), both in the Pinacoteca Tosio-Martinengo, Brescia (pp. 116 & 117).
Madeline Kelly, OSU, and Dianne Baumunk, OSU, for their photograph of a detail of a statue of St. Angela Merici in St. Angela Merici Parish church, Desenzano, designed by Benedetto Pietrogrande and sculpted by Peter Kostner (p. 16).
The Memphis Brooks Museum for *The Mystic Marriage of St. Catherine* by Girolamo Romanino (1484/87 - after 1559). Memphis Brooks Museum of Art, Memphis, TN; Gift of the Samuel H. Kress Foundation 61.202 (pp. 96, 288.).
Stiftsbibliothek, St. Gallen for *hl. Ursula with companions*, Timber panel pressure 5, NR. 21 (facsimile edition) (p. 140).
Cesare Vecellio's woodcuts appear in *Vecellio's Renaissance Costume Book*, Dover Publications, Inc. (www.doverpublications.com) (pp. 22, 191, 195, 198).
To the Ursulines of the Roman Union for access to the Trivulsian text (Italian), first published as Appendix 1 of *Angela Merici: Contribution towards a Biography*.
To the archives of the St. John the Baptist Province, Order of Friars Minor, for Secular Franciscan documents.

Dedicated to
Angela Merici,
Mother and Sister,
with deep gratitude
for her vivid spirit
shining through the pages of the Rule,
for her creativity on behalf of women
and for her loving voice.

Contents

Acknowledgments

This book represents a confluence of many streams, flowing through people who have shared their insights into Angela Merici's words and spirit.

Women of both the Company of St. Ursula and the Order of St. Ursula embody the living tradition of Angela's vision. Several groups have made particular contributions to this work through their spirit and encouragement. Of special note are the Ursulines of Cincinnati, among whom I learned to know and love Angela. The inter-Ursuline "Way of Life Committee" called forth the seeds of the reflections found here. The Company of St. Ursula in Canada has made me at home, sharing the graces and challenges of their lived experience.

Luciana Mariani, Elisa Tarroli and Marie Seynaeve have presented the fruits of their archival research in *Angela Merici: Contribution towards a Biography*. Their service of scholarship is unequalled.

The Ursulines of the Roman Union have graciously allowed me to include the original Trivulsian text, first published as Appendix 1 of *Angela Merici: Contribution towards a Biography*.

Other Ursulines, associates and friends have, through the years, sparked ideas that I cannot adequately attribute. I hope that they will accept my gratitude as genuinely intended for all of them. Members of Women Writing for (a) Change have listened and critiqued and offered their own fresh perspectives.

Some individuals have been integral to the development of this work: Nettina Gullo Eckert, whose skills in translation helped me hear "the voice of the Madre" in the Rule; Maria Teresa Pezzotti (Daughter of St. Angela, Brescia), who introduced me to art in Brescia; Kathleen Hallinan (Company of St. Ursula in the United States), whose insights contributed to the book's reflection questions; Liliane Dozois (Company of St. Ursula in Canada), whose encouragement has been a great support; my sister Sheila Durkin Dierks of WovenWord Press, to whose capable and generous hands I have entrusted this book; and designer Vicki McVey, whose care and creativity bring it to the page immensely enhanced by her own blend of spirit, eye and skill.

Jacqueline Morin, US (Company of St. Ursula in Canada), Anne Curry, OSU (Eastern United States Province of the Roman Union of the Order of St. Ursula), and Dr. Heather Arden were kind enough to read the manuscript, and I appreciate their thoughtful responses and suggestions.

Of course, I bear responsibility for the book's limitations and any errors.

The companionship of all these grace-full people has been a rich blessing. I offer to them a deeply felt "Thank you," and for them an earnest "Deo gratias!"

Blessed Angela, Brescian Virgin, Foundress of the new Congregation of Virgins called the Company of St. Ursula. Photograph of original which was destroyed in the bombing of the Church of St. Afra, Brescia, by American forces on March 2, 1945; artist unknown. Courtesy of the Centro Mericiano, Brescia.

Preface

Treasuring the "Trivulsian" Rule

One hand touches the book on her lap. The other points to the monogram symbol for Christ, an IHS.

This woman is Angela Merici. The book is the Rule of the Company of Saint Ursula. Its central meaning lies in that gesture. Like Angela herself, the Rule points always to Christ.

The painting is titled *The Blessed Angela, Brescian Virgin, Foundress of the New Congregation of Virgins Called the Company of Saint Ursula.* Painted in the sixteenth century, it is visible today only through black and white photographs taken before bombs destroyed it during World War II. With Angela are six Ursulines, each also holding the Rule. They have embraced the life it outlines. The hands over their hearts reflect her words (seen backwards, as proceeding from her lips), "*Hic est amor meus,*" "This is my love."

Today we are in the very moment of listening once again to that lesson, in the words of the Madre herself dictating her Rule, which has just been rediscovered. It is an exciting moment. Ursulines, whose spiritual genetics have always carried her spirit, are now once again able to listen to her voice. This book seeks to open twenty-first-century ears to its accents, in the hope that her voice may echo in other hearts, pointing them, too, toward God.

How is it that Angela's Rule, composed in the early sixteenth century, is so new today? How did it get lost?

The Rule Through History

Early art associated with Angela Merici almost always includes the book of her Rule, which she had dictated to her friend and confidante Gabriele Cozzano. Diocesan approval was granted in her lifetime (1536) and papal approval in 1546. Yet history has played fast and loose with it. Damiano Turlino produced an edition in 1569, slightly modifying the original oral style and sacrificing its spontaneous and impassioned tone for a cooler, more polished rhetoric. Saint Charles Borromeo oversaw a revision, printed in 1582, which he circulated throughout his ecclesiastical province in Northern Italy. He spread Ursuline life. He also integrated it more formally into Church hierarchy. Borromeo's revision launched many Companies, which multiplied exponentially.

The Company of Ferrara, however, began with an edition closer to the original and added a chapter on Christian Doctrine. This Rule of Ferrara spread to France at the end of the sixteenth century through Sybille de Mazan and Françoise de Bermond.

Cultural, ecclesiastical, and spiritual factors influenced the shift from the Company to the Order of Saint Ursula in France and then much of Europe in the seventeenth century. That meant adopting monasticism, long considered the only acceptable setting for conse-crated women. Upon this new form of Ursuline life, an ancient Rule was conferred: The Rule of Saint Augustine, replacing Angela Merici's. Possessed of an apostolic spirit for religious education, Ursuline nuns initiated schools within their monasteries. Thus began the schools for girls that were eventually to have a profound impact on the women of every continent.

Only in Italy did the original way of Ursuline life, the Company, sur-vive. But Napoleon suppressed it, among many religious groups, in 1810 after his conquest of much of the Italian peninsula. Except in Bologna (where he did not prevail), the Company seemingly ceased to exist. Maddalena and Elisabetta Girelli brought it back to life in Brescia in 1866. Encouraged by Brescia's Bishop Girolamo Verzeri, they adopt-ed the Borromean version of the Rule used before the suppression, which at first they supposed to be original.

Angela's original Rule was apparently lost. Twentieth-century schol-arship has rediscovered the precious treasure. Turlino's edition came to light in the1920s. It seemed largely a matter of historic and spiritual interest. By mid-century most of the Companies accepted canon law's definition as secular institutes and adopted documents reflecting that structure. Then the Second Vatican Council challenged all religious fam-ilies to get back in touch with their "founding charism," their founders' original spiritual gift. Historians began to retrieve an authentic under-standing of the Ursulines' foundress, who had been interpreted in the Order through the lenses of religious life and a school-based educa-tional mission.

Teresa Ledochowska, OSU (following in the footsteps of her aunt, Cecylja Lubienska, OSU), carried forward the work and shared it through publications and speaking tours. A further generation of scholars carried the study forward in the 1980s. Luciana Mariani, OSU, and Marie Seynaeve, OSU, of the Roman Union and Elisa Tarolli of the Company of Brescia shared their archival research in *Angela Merici: Contribution towards a Biography,* first published in Italian in 1986.

Among their ground-breaking discoveries was a long-forgotten text in the Trivulsian Library in Milan. It was a 1545/46 manuscript of the Rule of the Company of Saint Ursula, which can be dated by internal evidence. It appears here as Appendix 2. The text includes one line in Chapter II which was clearly interpolated between late 1545 and May 1546. Other than that, the text reflects an oral style predating the Turlino edition. Its written technique links it with Cozzano, to whom Angela Merici had dictated. Here at last was the Rule as Angela had spoken it. At last we can listen to the voice of the Madre!

Several English translations have been made: in 1993 by Olga Lombardi (Melaragno), in 1997 by a group of Ursulines of the Roman Union. A meticulous and rich line-by-line study by M. Ignatius Stone, OSU, was published in 1996, titled *Commentary on the Writings of Saint Angela Merici.* Nettina Gullo Eckert and Mary-Cabrini Durkin also concluded a translation in 1997. With slight revision, it is included here as Appendix 1 and in references throughout this work.

The Voice of the Madre

Nettina Gullo Eckert and I approached the translation process with this objective: "to hear the voice of the Madre." This focus guided our choices. We sought to be fairly literal, as close as English could get to the original. When we began the process, the Trivulsian text was a new landscape for English readers, and we thought the original usages should be known first, before being adapted.

The result echoes the oral style of this dictated work, although we cannot truly represent in English the regional dialect which both Angela and Cozzano used. The sometimes rough constructions, with fragments and parenthetical asides, tell of a woman who spoke from the heart, with simple directness, not formally.

We hear the speaker—Angela—searching for the right word or rephrasing a thought. Her redundancies illustrate the evolution of an idea or emphasize it with escalating intensity. One such climax occurs in her prayer: *...so many errors, so much ugliness and blame, so many monstrous* *and frightening beasts and shapes!* Similarly, she urges reliance on *God alone, on the kind and ineffable providence that is his alone.*

Cumulative transitions, such as the oft-repeated "again" which opens new chapters or thoughts, show us the process of moving on from topic to topic, perhaps on subsequent occasions of dictation. There are aborted sentences and shifts in grammatical structure. Exclamations escape her lips. Superlatives reflect intense feelings, such as her affection for her *most beloved daughters and sisters.*

Damiano Turlino must have considered the oral style of the Rule a flaw. His 1569 edition has been polished according to literary norms. However, recovering Angela's spoken word is a great gift of the Trivulsian edition. Far from being flaws, her idiosyncrasies show the mind at work and the passion driving the words.

Nettina Gullo Eckert and I sought to render the voice that we heard in the Trivulsian manuscript—that of a woman practical, well-balanced and realistic, yet large-spirited and confident; a woman respectful of others and filled with a joy that she wishes to share with them; above all a woman deeply in love with the Christ who has first loved her.

So important is Angela's voice—spoken and transcribed—that I have sought to use her exact words as much as possible in this book, to allow us to listen to her. Words and phrases directly quoted from the Rule or from her Counsels and Testament (Legacies) appear throughout in italics.

Working with the Trivulsian text has been an occasion of grace. This text offers an intimate association with the Madre. Her spirit is so alive as to glow though the words, vibrant today as when she dictated them to Gabriele Cozzano.

A Passionate Heart

Warmth pervades the Rule, the warmth of Angela's impassioned personality, which expressed itself often in extremes. In her life and in her words, she achieved a certain balance. Yet hers is a balance created not by a smooth, even temperament but by her capacity to hold opposites in dynamic tension. It is not motionless. It is an exchange of energy between the poles—positive and negative, enthusiasm and prudence, passion and pragmatism.

Angela could *cry out and shout to Heaven* and *lament the fact that I have been so late to begin serving.... Alas!* (Chapter V:22, 27, 28) and could also speak practically of *the means and ways that are necessary to persevere and prosper till the end* (Prologue:10). We may live in the light of eternity, but our road passes through all the daily-ness of the here-and-now.

Having faced hardships and sin, Angela sometimes felt as though there were a devil *like a roaring lion* (Prologue:21) outside her and *monstrous...beasts* (Chapter V:21) prowling inside. The creative tension between fear and trust appears in the words, *However, my very own sisters, you must not be afraid of this because if you strive with all your might, ...I have this undaunted and firm faith and hope in the infinite divine goodness...that not only will we easily overcome all dangers and adversities, but we will conquer them, and with great glory and jubilation* (Prologue:22, 23, 25).

Warmth flows also from the relational framework of the Company, formed out of Angela's own relationships. Of course she was passionate about the happiness of the people she loved! Her blood rose over what she cared about. This Rule is not about trivialities. It is about our eternal well-being. She cherished her *most beloved daughters and sisters* (Prologue:4). *My very own sisters*, she liked to call us. She spoke with urgency, inviting us to *strive with all your might* (Prologue:23) and to *be alert with great and longing heart* (Prologue:32). When we encounter these vivid feelings, we glimpse her heart.

Life, yes, our Ursuline life, is for living intensely, for enjoying, for drinking deeply, and Angela Merici could not describe it in any other way.

A Woman's Experience

The Rule of the Company of Saint Ursula is very nearly unique in having been authored by a woman. That in itself is intriguing and invites exploration. The Rule is distinctive for its complete originality, based on no models. The deeper we go, the clearer it becomes that the pattern for Ursuline life is the product of Angela's lived experience intersecting with God's grace.

Angela is quite specific about social and spiritual practices. Her teaching is very concrete, very contextualized in the life and culture of sixteenth-century Italy. Herein lies a grace but also a stumbling block. Many of these details are so remote as to cast doubt on her relevance for us. But let us explore more closely the significance of these points in her surroundings. We will find an authentic way for her insights and challenges to illuminate our own day. Angela had found the way to God in the sacred here-and-now. In that sense, she invites us to do the same. Yet we must understand her context, seeing how she addressed the issues of her day, in order to address the issues of our time and culture in her spirit.

Rule as Guideline

The word *rule* has not been popular for quite a few decades. Laws, rules, and regulations have often felt oppressive, have been the tools of oppression, or have seemed like chains binding us to concepts befitting a bygone era. This document is not about regulations. It embodied liberation for sixteenth-century women. Its implications for today lie in a clear understanding of the word *rule*.

If a Rule does not mean "rules," what does it mean? As a foundational document, it is not legislative. Not a law, but a guide. The related word *ruler*, as applied to a measuring stick, clarifies the difference. We use a ruler to measure. It offers a standard by which to evaluate (in its case, length). We also use a ruler as a guide when we want to draw a line or cut material according to a desired pattern. It is in this sense that Angela's Rule can be understood. It offers criteria and guidelines, leading the Ursuline through practical measures to a *golden and brilliant virginal crown.*

Rule as Invitation

Most essentially, the Rule is an invitation. God invites us to this life. Those who answer sincerely by taking this path will freely embrace *the means and ways that are necessary to persevere and prosper to the end* (Pr:10).

Our whole life is based on a free response to God's invitation. Angela would not command. She invites others to experience the blessings and joys that she has found. She offers reminders about how to act, such as *remember that each one should want to embrace bodily fasting too as something indeed necessary* (Ch. IV:1). She stresses that we should *want* to fast, to pray, to care for each other. Or she *exhorts* us to *make a practice of confession* (Ch. VII:1) or to *embrace poverty* (Ch. X:1). Angela's repetition of *let* (in Italian, the subjunctive mood of a verb) is the language of gentle encouragement: *let each one go to Mass* (Ch. VI:1) or *let each one strive...* (Ch. X:8).

The Italian word *voglia* appears often. It could be translated (and is frequently used) as "please." In the Rule it often suggests a polite command, in the subjunctive rather than the imperative. Yet the word is so clearly a part of the verb meaning "to will" or "to want" that we have preserved that sense: *each one should want to....* The individual member's commitment motivates her actions.

Leaping the Hurdles

A few hurdles arise from the differing consciousness of our different centuries. Properly sensitive to gender-inclusiveness in language, we may feel uncomfortable with Angela's masculine pronouns for people in general. (She always used feminine pronouns in referring to the women of her Company.) She had such a visionary sense of women's dignity! Why did she not conform to the practices of the—twenty-first—century? Of course, we cannot expect that. But why have we not made those adjustments in translation? The answer is our effort to hew closely to her modes of expression in this work. For other uses, adaptation is appropriate.

A further issue results from a misunderstanding about readership. A quick look at the first three chapters has led some to dismiss the Rule as though it were intended for teenagers. Rather, Chapters I to III are directed to the women who will introduce new members to Ursuline life. They describe first steps about admission and behaviors that will help new members put their good intentions into action. Later chapters plunge deeply into a way of life for mature women.

Another hurdle for contemporary readers is the many detailed warnings of what "not" to do. Despite her passion about the eternal meaning of it all, Angela sounds very realistic, even cautious at times. The Rule grew out of her experience through more than forty years, from her late teens. It was not easy to be single, to belong to God and to herself. But she had learned how to handle the problems and to enjoy the beauty. So, yes, the Rule has plenty of practical advice, mostly about living with integrity.

Further Dialogue

Finally, exploration of the Rule invites further dialogue. This book applies a very particular lens, that of a member of the Company of Saint Ursula in the United States of America, for whom the Rule is life-shaping. The Ursuline spiritual family is far more extensive.

Angela's daughters in the Order of Saint Ursula now constitute the majority of Ursulines. Ursuline religious have profoundly explored her words and deeds, especially since the Second Vatican Council. Their graced lives prove the multi-faceted dynamic of her vision. *Angela Merici: Contribution towards a Biography* resulted from collaboration among Ursulines of the Order and of the Company.

Several autonomous Companies and those in the Secular Institute of Saint Angela Merici probe similar topics: how to understand and apply Angela's founding vision in today's world. It still invigorates the Companies that have grown, been suppressed and grown again in her native soil. In more recent years Companies have sprouted on nearly every continent. Thus more culturally varied voices are chiming in. In offering this volume, I must acknowledge the Western, Euro-American limitations of my own perspectives. Other cultures have fresh insights to offer, which I am eager to learn.

From the very beginning, Angela's spiritual family embraced lay men and women connected with the Company. Her appeal still draws such followers. The late twentieth century saw lay (and some clerical) associates gather around religious congregations. Angela's attraction for such groups was natural. Associates find that her spirituality enriches their Christian vocations.

This historical moment is especially exciting. New initiatives are emerging, exploring new forms of spiritual community inspired by Angela. Those who call Angela "Madre" carry her spiritual legacy. They approach her Rule from richly variegated vantage points, even from different vocations. The Rule speaks of life with and for and touched by God, the deepest reality of all Christian paths. People in ever wider circles are interested in her spiritual initiative and have insights to share.

It is only beginning. A rich and exciting "new" text has burst upon our sight. We are still in the moment of discovery. Our on-going conversations mine the Rule's significance, as we engage with Angela's words through both scholarship and experience. This work seeks to contribute to the conversation, welcoming responses and further discussion.

May these pages introduce readers to Angela's spiritual vision and invite her old friends to an even deeper sharing in her spirit!

Mary-Cabrini Durkin
January 27, 2005

Introduction
Exploring the Rule

Honoring the Madre's Voice

The Rule of the Company of Saint Ursula treats matters of equal importance to people who are five centuries apart. Angela Merici's vast spiritual family drinks from the same fountain, but in very different eras and cultures. How can we explore her words with respect for her and for all her hearers? Challenges arise.

Angela urged us to think of her as present, even in the twenty-first century. She spoke in the present tense when she pledged to be with the Company after her death: *Also, tell them that now I am more alive than I was when they saw me in the flesh, and that now I see them and know them better. And can and want to help them more. And that I am continually among them...* (Fifth Counsel:35-38).[1] Honoring her promise, this book assumes that she still speaks to us. It generally uses the present tense about her teachings. Yet some situations referred to in the Rule are so clearly historic, not current, that the past tense is more appropriate.

The Trivulsian text has made audible again the voice of the Madre, spoken directly to people she loves. One way to honor the relational quality of the Rule is to engage with its author, not stand at a distance. Therefore, this book speaks often in the first person, as we listen to Angela's words through the ears of her followers.

Treasuring Angela's personal, oral style, we savor words quoted directly from her Rule, Counsels and Testament (Legacies), indicated by italic type. (Italics are also used, as is typical, for foreign words and for certain titles.) Part 1, "Angela's Story," incorporates her own words as much as possible. It is essential to appreciating the Rule.

Context

Angela's story and an understanding of the Church, society, and women's life in sixteenth-century Italy are necessary starting points for comprehending her full message. However, the reader can omit the historical "Context" sections and still appreciate the way of life outlined in the "Rule" sections. The reader who finds the "Context" distracting is urged to skip it.

Recognizing the significance of context, Youngstown Ursuline Mary McCormick, OSU, has applied principles of biblical exegesis to Angela's writings. Drawing upon Sandra Schneiders' *The Revelatory Text*, Mary McCormick identifies the "world behind the text," sixteenth-century Renaissance Italy; the "world of the text," that is, "the text as it stands now"; and "the world in front of the text," which is "the ideal meaning which the reader is invited to enter."[2] This book will follow her example, seeking to enter into "dialogue with the text"[3] with a "transformative interpretation."[4]

The reader is also invited to follow what Sandra Schneiders calls a "trajectory." How did a particular detail relate to Angela's historical moment? If it stood ahead of contemporary practice, then we ask ourselves to follow the trajectory and to hear those words as invitation and challenge. Where might the trajectory take us today, ahead of the practices around us? "Reflection" points following each chapter will lead in this direction.

The Language of Beauty

A poetic and creative genius like Angela's is closely akin to art, which opens the spirit. Beauty speaks more deeply than words. Works of art incorporated into these pages can open us to the wordless spirit between the lines.

Angela may have known Saint Ursula as much by paintings as by words. Although she did not explain why she chose the patron of her Company, much can be deduced. Part 6, "Saint Ursula," looks at how visual and literary arts may shed light on her choice and its meaning for Ursulines.

The conclusion of this book contemplates the splendid altarpiece *The Mystic Marriage of St. Catherine, with Sts. Lawrence, Ursula and Angela Merici* by Angela's contemporary, Girolamo Romanino. Painted to commemorate the Company's founding, it synthesizes the Company's spirit as surely as does the Rule itself.

Spiraling Toward the Heart

With artistic unity, the Rule takes a member from entrance to death and heavenly glory. Chapter groupings treat integration into the Company, spiritual practices, the evangelical counsels and community.

Angela Merici began her Rule with a Prologue in the form of a letter, treated here in Part 2, "A Letter from the Madre." She wanted to speak directly to her daughters, from her heart. In the Prologue she set out the whole meaning of Ursuline life, from the point of God's invitation, through years of joy and suffering and of mundane activities, to a glorious conclusion in heaven. Each chapter develops a particular aspect of this life, in stages along the way.

Chapters I to III help to bring new members into the Company, showing practical ways for integrating their commitment into daily life. Each of these first three chapters also supports one of the core Gospel values that are developed later. For example, Chapter I stresses the new member's freedom as being essential in her choice to become an Ursuline. That freedom is the basis of her capacity for *obedience*. Chapter II, on clothing, supports the spirit of joyful *poverty*. And Chapter III is about interactions with others that demonstrate the single-hearted-ness of her celibate calling.

In Chapters IV to VII, Angela recommended spiritual practices to nourish the women in their vocation. Each of these practices also nourishes a particular element of the Gospel core. Fasting helps us to be emptied of all gods but God, and to feast on the good things God gives. That is *true poverty of spirit*. Prayer and the Mass deepen the relationship with Christ at the heart of an Ursuline's heart, what Angela called *sacred virginity*. Confession helps us clarify our own truth, the better to hear and obey the Holy Spirit. That is Angela's *holy obedience*. A spiral shapes this arrangement of chapters. They wind in toward the Gospel center in Chapters VIII to X, which treat obedience, virginity and poverty respectively and are dealt with in Part 3 of this book, "At the Heart of the Rule."

Angela called the last chapter "About Governance." Another name might have been "community." It is really about how this spiritual family translates into action the relationships that support each Ursuline in living her call. It describes the ever-practical Madre's creative organizational structure to make it all work. In the process, Angela had created a countercultural network to empower the oppressed. Like the Prologue, this chapter ends after death, in heaven. It is the subject of Part 4, "A Spiritual Family."

Part 5, "The Trellis," treats the chapters on integration and spiritual practices (Chs. I-VII) separately. It is to be hoped that the areas of overlap will take the reader deeper rather than being repetitious, but some repetitions necessarily occur.

The Rule as a whole and each chapter within it have this single purpose: to support the members of the Company in living their vocation.

Guidebook for a Journey

Angela liked to call Ursuline life and this Rule *via*, a "path" or "road." The Prologue is a snapshot of the route. The whole Rule is a guidebook for the journey. Both the Prologue and the body of the Rule begin with answering God's call, and both end in heaven.

Far from being dry or legislative, the Rule's vocabulary is vivid and picturesque. We can almost see Angela's images and feel her emotions as she responds to the beauty of nature or the ugliness of evil. This image-filled style is not surprising if we remember that the Rule is really a guidebook. Of course Angela describes the scenery along the way! Sometimes it seems like an actual landscape beside the *thorny and rocky roads* which *we will find flower-strewn for us, paved with finest gold* (Prologue:27). Her lively tone encourages us forward.

Often her words echo personal experience. When the army of Charles V was approaching Brescia in 1529, she may well have felt that *armed against us are water, air, and earth with all of hell* (Prologue:20). Years of working in vineyards had taught Angela the energy that we need to *lop off vices and errors* (Chapter IV:2), just as she would lop a diseased branch from a healthy vine. *[L]ords* in the spectacular parades winding though the streets at carnival time gave her a picture of how the devil swaggers around, *lord[ing] it over the world* (Chapter IV:10).

As these lines show, Angela was a poet, not a theorist. She proceeded by images and experiences, not by concepts. She gazed upon the earth and its people and took them into her heart. She reached their innermost reality by an intuition blended with common sense and fueled by love. Her poetic language allows us to visualize the world as she saw it.

How beautiful our world is, in Angela's imagery! In the shouting crowd celebrating a victory, she heard the people we love, cheering us on, *where from all those in Heaven and on earth great glory and triumph will arise* (Prologue:31). She evoked the lovely sight of a procession, *going two by two in charity and each one with a candle in her hand* (Chapter XI:32). The traveler who had stood on the Adriatic shore, had sailed the Mediterranean to the Holy Land and back, sensed the vastness of God, whose name she *blessed beyond the ocean's grains of sand, beyond the drops of the waters, beyond the multitude of stars* (Chapter V:26).

Ursuline life is a journey of the heart. No wonder that its guide-book glows!

At the Brudazzo, this road passes through the place traditionally associated with Angela's vision.

---

[1] This and all subsequent quotations from the English translation of Angela Merici's Counsels are quoted from *Writings: Rule, Counsels, Testament*, translation by a team of Ursulines of the Roman Union (Rome: Ursulines of the Roman Union, 1995).
[2] Mary McCormick, OSU. "Interpretation of Angela's Writings," Address to the Ursuline Society (Youngstown, April 1995), p. 6.
[3] McCormick, p. 2.
[4] McCormick, p. 6.

Part 1

Angela's Story

The young Angela Merici. Detail of statue in St. Angela Merici Parish church, Desenzano, designed by Benedetto Pietrogrande and sculpted by Peter Kostner. Photo by Madeline Kelly, OSU. Courtesy of Dianne Baumunk, OSU

Angela's Story

Personal experience is the matrix not only of political systems but of spiritual ones as well. Feminist scholarship has explored this reality in many fields. Angela Merici constructed a company of women based upon her interior and exterior experiences: of herself, God, family, society in general and women's situations in particular, Church, economy, personal relationships, etc. The Rule of the Company of Saint Ursula outlines an alternative life for women which is rooted in her self-understanding and religious experience and takes shape in practices and relationships. The following imagined dialogue sets forth her life experience as best we can trace it. This foundation is essential to the rest of the book because it was essential to the Company.

The biographical and historical information on which this chapter is based can be found in several sources, but primarily in *Angela Merici: Contribution towards a Biography* by Luciana Mariani, Elisa Tarolli and Marie Seynaeve. Their informational treasure-trove also includes appendices. One of the most valuable for this book is the record of sworn testimony by those who knew Angela. Taken by a notary named Giovan Batista Nazari as a preliminary to the canonization process, it is generally known as the *Processo Nazari*. Though documentary references are not used here, lest they interrupt the flow of the conversation, the same information is documented when it reappears in later chapters.

Here and throughout the book, italic type indicates words from Angela's own mouth, in her Rule, Counsels and Testament.

Let us take a quick trip from the twenty-first century to the sixteenth, to an afternoon late in 1539. Sit down at the kitchen table in a small apartment next to St. Afra Church. Sipping the hot vegetable soup that Barbara Fontana has just served before going out on an errand, we think about what we would like to ask our hostess, Angela Merici. Angela breaks the loaf of bread. Over sixty, she seems to glow as she smiles across the table.

Q: Angela, what was it like to grow up in your world? The Renaissance in Italy! We think of it as an exciting period and place of creativity. Even though you're over sixty now, I'm sure you remember being young in the late 1400s.

Angela: My memories are fresh, even after all these years. To tell the truth, life on our farm was probably pretty much the way it had been for centuries there. We all shared the work.

I was born right in the heart of Desenzano, on the first floor of a house on the Vicolo Castello. That was 1474. When I was about two years old, Papa and Mama persuaded Uncle Carlo Merici to turn over Mama's dower—he'd been holding onto it—and they bought the farm at Le Grezze. They moved our family out there. We grew up helping with the animals. My sister and I would drive our cows and goats to the common pasture to graze and home again. We had fun together and we learned responsibility, sometimes by our mistakes. We got into trouble when Papa had to pay a fine for our carelessness, like when our animals trampled part of a neighbor's field. Now and again we just picked fruit to nibble and realized too late that we had stepped onto our neighbor's land.

Gradually Papa and Mama bought more fields—like the one we call the Machet—and hired other farmworkers, but we all worked together. Neighbors helped each other at certain times of the year. During the olive harvest, all the girls and young women would work together. My sister and I enjoyed that.

Farm life took up most of our time and attention. But we weren't at all isolated. It takes only half an hour to walk along the road to town, to the shore of Lake Garda itself. Garda is the largest lake in Italy, stretching north of Desenzano for miles and miles. All kinds of traffic and trade and news come to Desenzano. Grain from Mantua and Cremona gets shipped out; metals and merchandise get shipped in. Why, Desenzano is on the commercial route to Trent, and Venice is just ninety-eight miles away. Even though we're in Lombardy, they call it Venetian Lombardy. And with Papa having come to Desenzano from Brescia—he was actually a Brescian citizen—by way of Nuvolento, and Mama from Salò, we had relatives in different places. Maybe that's why I've been so interested in traveling.

Whether we were at church or market or working together in the fields, we were always hearing about the rest of the world, as well as the local gossip. You can hardly imagine how excited we were to hear about that Genovese sailor, Cristoforo Columbo, sailing to India. I was almost twenty then. Of course, now that forty more years have passed, we know that it wasn't really India, and we've also realized that the earth really is round. Some people were saying that all along. It turns out that the world is a much bigger place than anyone thought.

Now we have new ways of knowing about it, and of knowing about other people. In our very own home at Le Grezze we had a book! It was a great treasure. It told the lives of the saints. And Papa could read! Every evening he would read to the whole family. He showed us how to read the words, too.

The stories were about the special saint of each day. They were exciting. We learned about holy people, men and women. Some were quiet and hidden, and others were great leaders or heroic martyrs. That's how I learned about heroines like Saint Ursula and her companions, who were true to Christ *even to the shedding of their blood*. We celebrated the feasts of our own special patron saints, like Mama's, Saint Catherine of Alexandria, on November 25.

Hearing about the saints, I wanted to be like them. My brother and I played saint games, like pretending to go out to the desert. As I got a bit older, imitating the saints led me to serious spiritual practices and the beginnings of contemplation.

Mama taught my sister and me how to *be useful* in the house and farmyard, so that we would always know how to take care of our responsibilities when we grew up.

Q: It sounds as though you had a happy childhood.

Angela: Oh, I did! We all did. I was in my late teens when my world turned cold and dark for what seemed like forever. First Mama died. How we cried! We cooked and tried to keep things up the way she had, but the house seemed empty and dim without her. Papa was our strength to keep going. It must have been hard for him, though. It wasn't long before he joined her in heaven, but not before we had suffered another blow, a terrible and unexpected loss.

My dear sister died. She was so full of fun, and we were so close, that I felt as though all the sunshine had left my soul. Not only that! I was worried about her. Was she in heaven? Was her soul ready? I longed to know. Now I realize that she was a good girl, and none of her foolishness or mischief could separate her from God's love, but I was very young and very sad, and nothing seemed sure. I wore myself out with tears and prayers. This worry haunted me.

Losing these dear ones seemed to have cut all my moorings. I felt like a small boat adrift on Lake Garda in a storm, tossed about by loss and confusion. Feeling that I had nothing, no one left, I leaned back on God. Faith told me that God was still there, even when I could not feel any presence at all. My heart was too heavy. But in my deepest sadness, *our kind and loving God* took pity on my grief-stricken heart. This is how it happened.

Life, of course, went on, and so did my responsibilities at the farm. One noontime, I was in our field at the Machet. Suddenly, there in the air above the trees, was a row of angels, *angels of eternal life*! Among them was my dear sister, smiling at me, assuring me that she was happy in *celestial glory*. Sweet peace entered my soul. Heavenly light bathed me. It still draws me heavenward. Nothing is more sure than the promise of this *light and joyful splendor* of heaven, where *a new crown of glory and joy is prepared for all*, and where we will all be together once again.

Q: That was in the 1490s? You were a teenager, weren't you? Without parents?

Angela: Yes, and you know how alone an unmarried girl is. My brothers Giovanni Maria and Lodovico were still trying to manage the family farm. Later Giovanni had to go to work at the docks. Mama's brother Uncle Biancosi and his wife invited my little brother Merico and me to live with them in Salò. That's Mama's hometown, just a few miles north of Desenzano along the shore of Lake Garda. Mama used to take us there to visit when we were young. Once Papa had mediated a dispute between Mama's brothers in the mayor's court there. Aunt and Uncle's son, my cousin Bartolomeo, was very young when Merico and I moved there. They were all so loving and good to us! In fact, Cousin Bartolomeo and I are still quite close. We made a pilgrimage together a few years ago.

Uncle Biancosi was a prominent person in Salò. People called him "Ser." Later, he was on the city council. Salò is a much more splendid town than Desenzano. Life in the Biancosi home was very, very different from what my brother and I were used to on the farm. There my bedroom window looked out on the fields. In Salò the high, shuttered houses in the San Bernardino district peer at each other across narrow, stone-cobbled streets. No more fields or olive groves! I shared the housework with the other women, the normal things like laundry, baking, cooking, carrying water and so on. Mama had taught me well. But the Biancosi linens were finer, the fabrics softer. They make beautiful, soft yarns in Salò.

There were books in the house. I loved to practice reading, as Papa had taught me to do. Aunt had new clothes made for me and taught me how to act at parties. She and Uncle loved me and had one goal in mind: a husband. They thought this was their most important responsibility to me and to the memory of Mama and Papa.

Q: How did you feel about getting married, about having a family of your own? You had grown up in such a happy family! Surely partnership with a good husband and mothering your own children would have been wonderful for you.

Angela: Yes, my family had been joyful and loving. But my call was different. My heart was steady. I belonged to God alone and I told Aunt and Uncle this. They were kind, but they were very sure that they knew what was best for me. I didn't know how to convince them. To tell the truth, I sometimes went to extremes. People used to say that my blond hair would surely attract a man. Blond hair was all the fashion in Venice, and girls copied the fashion by washing their hair with chamomile shampoo. Then they would draw their locks through special hats to bleach them in the sun. So I did the opposite! I tried to darken my hair with ashes. I can laugh about that now, but then I was confused and impetuous.

There were other confusions inside me, too. I didn't know how to fit together my sexual feelings and God's call. There were young men willing to take advantage of that confusion, though I was protected as a niece in the house, not a servant. Once a tempter appeared in my room, beautiful as an angel—a very attractive apparition, beyond imagining! Was he the stable boy? Was he the devil? Was he the figment of my own desires or pride? I threw myself down, with my face to the floor so as not to see him, and screamed at him, "Go to hell!" Deep inside I realized that, attractive or not, he didn't represent my deepest heart. There was another desire on which I would build my life. This tempter could not turn me aside from it.

Physical attractions didn't magically go away. After all, *the flesh and our sensuality are not yet dead!* But I find that they do point to the source of all that is desirable, if I let them lead me forward in that direction. The stirrings of my heart and body are like a magnet, drawing me toward a thrilling unity. What I have already tasted of my God completely satisfies me. And yet, it also tantalizes me with the sure hope of being completely immersed in Someone divine. That will happen!

Venetian woman bleaching her hair in the sun on a rooftop gallery. Woodcut by Cesare Vecellio (1521-1601), #112 in *Vecellio's Renaissance Costume Book*, Dover Publications, Inc. (www.doverpublications.com).

Q: But you speak about families so often, so warmly. Haven't you ever wished for your own children, your own home and family?

Angela: Many times I have held a little niece or nephew and felt a yearning for someone whose life came out of my own life and would carry it on. It would be heart-warming, now that I'm old, to have a circle of grandchildren. When I was in my teens in Salò, I honestly didn't realize what I would be missing in terms of children. But a yearning is not a regret. There is nothing I would wish to change. I have the great happiness of many spiritual daughters and sons. All love given comes back as love.

Q: How did you strengthen and nourish yourself along the way, as you tried to follow your own call?

Angela: With the help of the Franciscans. The friars said Mass at the church "della Disciplina," near Aunt and Uncle's house in Salò. They were from San Bernardino Convent. There were friars on the Isola, the Island in Lake Garda, too. I used to visit the friars for guidance and the sacraments. I also began to meet a group of wonderful lay people, women and men, mostly married, who were part of the Franciscan family, in the Third Order of St. Francis. They followed a Rule that guided them along a spiritual path and had special opportunities to receive Holy Communion. Their Rule outlines practices like fasting and abstinence, prayer, the Divine Office, Mass, visiting the sick and being peacemakers. Their life attracted me. So did Saint Francis, with his spirit of joyful poverty. He shared so deeply in the sacred Passion of our Lord! With him we came to feel close to Jesus' human life!

When I was close to twenty, I became a secular Franciscan of the Third Order too and made a commitment to follow this spiritual path as a lay person. Members have the right to wear the Franciscan clothing made of coarse gray cloth, and to be buried in it, in a Franciscan cemetery. Not many choose to dress this way throughout their lives, but I have for many years.

Q: How did your aunt and uncle react?

Angela: Even though they were pious people, they didn't always encourage my devotions and fasting. They were afraid that I would go to extremes. And they wanted me to cooperate with their marriage plans, go to parties and public entertainments, chaperoned, naturally. My aunt saw no harm in some innocent flirtation from the balcony. All the girls did it, just to make it clear that they were available, from a safe distance, of course. But I wasn't really available, not in my heart. Finally, they began to see that my direction was steady. And the friars could assure them that my way of life was spiritually sound.

Eventually we all came to an agreement. I would return to Desenzano. Instead of a dowry that would have been mine at marriage, I would have a vineyard as my own property, in the Caser area near Monte Zorzo.

Soon I was home again, living and working on the land! It was a simple life, a good life. I tended the *vines entrusted* to me, *cultivating* them, loosening the soil, pruning, *lopping off* diseased branches, gathering the grapes and marketing them. I kept ownership of the vineyard even after I moved to Brescia and could no longer work on it. But its crop has provided some income for me, and I kept paying the five lire plan-ete property taxes each year.

Angela cultivated the vines entrusted to her. Photograph
courtesy of Hector Bedolla

I was a farmworker again, busy in the vineyard and fields. There in my workplace God once again reached my heart. During the olive harvest, people from all around the area work together in the groves. The girls climb ladders set against the trees and shake the branches to drop the olives. Everybody sings and has fun. I always enjoyed harvest days.

One day, when we had finished eating our noon meal there in the grove at the Brudazzo, most of us settled down quietly for a little siesta. I was dozing and praying. Suddenly I heard music and heavenly voices. I opened my eyes, and there among the olive trees I saw a ladder rising all the way to heaven. There were angels on it, playing instruments, and young women among them, singing. I can still sing their song, it entered so deeply into my heart. It was only a moment. Then it was over. It has never really been over, though.

Somehow, in that moment God showed me that I was to help other women and girls to live here on earth in ways that would lead them heavenward. At the same time, I saw that there is no distance between our life here and eternal life, between earth and heaven, between us and God.

Q: Did you know then that you would begin a company of women?

Angela: I understood something of the sort. It took many years though, a lot of living, before a company began to take shape, even in my mind. But I did realize that God was inviting me to belong to him forever.

Q: Did your life change?

Angela: Not exteriorly. The difference was inside. I knew that everything around me was connected with heaven, luminous with God's light. What peace and joy spread through me!

Q: How did people treat you? Most twenty-year-old women were wives and mothers.

Angela: I was very fortunate. Many a single woman must either go out to find work as a household servant or live in her brother's home, pretty much as a servant to his wife.

Q: What about the neighbors?

Angela: At first they didn't know what to make of a single woman like me. I didn't try to change anyone's mind, just thanked God, who is so loving to me, and tried to share God's love with them. Here and there an old person needed special care, or a family with a new baby.

I received *great consolation* and strength *every day in going to Mass*. There I *participate in the blessed merits of Jesus' passion* and in *a communion of the spirit* with *my Lover, who is the Lover of us all*. From the moment of my vision in the olive grove, I knew that I belonged to him alone. My daily prayer became a more and more intimate conversation with God in the *secret recesses of my heart*.

Gradually my neighbors came to accept me. The curiosity and kindly matchmaking faded away. Many people began to call me their sister, "Suor Angela." Young people would ask me to teach them how to pray. Some neighbors began to confide their spiritual questions or family problems, and we would talk about how God's words might light their path.

Q: What sorts of questions?

Angela: Mostly about daily concerns or fears about death. But questions of conscience and religion became more and more frequent. Many of my neighbors didn't know what to think when we heard arguments from Church reformers. Desenzano has a lot of communication with Germany, where people like Martin Luther were criticizing some of our beliefs as well as calling for reforms. The Dutchman Erasmus spent time nearby, in Venice. The area around Desenzano had a history with these ideas. The monastery of Leno, close to town, had long ago been a center for Church reformers. Some of the neighboring landowners have town homes in Brescia too, people like the Patengola family. Naturally, these ideas circulate widely. Erasmus has ardent followers here in Brescia, who are publishing his writings.

Most of our parish priests were good men, but with little more knowledge than their parishioners. There was no one to lead them, either. Why, even here in Brescia, our bishop, Cardinal Andrea Cornaro, doesn't live here. Neither did his uncle, Cardinal Francesco Cornaro, before him. We must continue to *pray for the reform of the Church!*

Occasionally I would take a boat up the lake coast to Salò to visit Aunt and Uncle Biancosi and Bartolomeo, and the Franciscan friars. A friar there was still my spiritual father, and I learned much from his guidance. Third Order members gathered there, too, many dear friends.

That's how I met Caterina Patengola. She had ties at Padenghe, the home of her husband's family, near Lake Garda. The Franciscan friars knew her. She was just a little older than I.

Q: I know that you went to Brescia to be with her. Why?

Angela: Poor Caterina! She was suffering so horribly that our Franciscan friars were afraid for her. She was already a widow when, in the space of four terrible years, Caterina lost all three of her children, first Costanzo in 1513, then Gandolfo in 1516, and her daughter Monica, all fine young people just beginning their adulthood. When Monica died, Caterina's grief seemed unbearable. Just a year before that loss, Suor Candida had died in 1515. She was a saintly Augustinian nun on whom Caterina had relied for spiritual support. She had been Caterina's servant—called Giustina then—and had entered the Monastery of Santa Croce.

Q: How did you come to Caterina's house in Brescia?

Angela: The friars asked me to go there in 1516 to be with Caterina for a while. I remembered the suddenness, the emptiness of my own losses. Of course I would go! I was just over forty then. Little did I expect to be starting a whole new life.

Q: What was it like in Brescia?

Angela: The Patengola household reminded me of the Biancosis' in Salò, large, comfortable, kept up by the household staff. But there were no parties, no laughter. I tried to lend a hand with the housework. When Caterina felt like talking, I listened. When she needed comfort, I tried to offer what I could. We prayed together. Some of the penitential psalms seemed to give voice to her distress. Often we went to St. Alexander the Martyr, her parish church. At Mass we felt close to the suffering Christ and his Blessed Mother, who watched him die.

Caterina is a generous woman with a loving extended family. No one could take the place of her dead, of course, but she was not completely alone. She had taken in her orphaned granddaughter Isabella, Monica's little girl. Isabella was three and a half. A nephew, too, was close to her, Giralomo, who was twenty-two years old then. He visited his aunt and tried to console her. One afternoon he brought along a young friend, Giovan Antonio Romano. I still smile to remember that meeting. Antonio can still tell you what I was wearing that day. Of course, that is Antonio's business. He is a cloth merchant. I'll tell you more about him later. Antonio came often to talk.

Q: So you weren't isolated while Caterina was in mourning?

Angela: Oh no! She had many friends among Brescia's nobility and other prosperous business and professional people. Some I knew slightly from their ties to land-owning families around Desenzano. Others I met through Caterina. They are good people, many of them deeply prayerful and concerned about others. Their city was in deep distress, and they wanted to help.

So many lives had been shattered by war! When mercenaries in the pay of the French had penetrated Brescia's Castello on February 19, 1512, they massacred not only the army but thousands of civilians — 10,000 people or more. Children orphaned! Girls ravished! Women widowed! Men and boys wounded or corrupted! When the French left, class warfare followed, with reprisals, torture and executions. In four years the city was battered back and forth, conquered and reconquered three times. The Venetians besieged and bombarded Brescia for ten days in May of 1516 and finally took it back from the Spanish. I arrived here a little later that year. At last there was hope for peace, but the wounds of war were deep and festering.

Brescia was demoralized. The needs were overwhelming — spiritual and material. In 1521 Girolamo Patengola was one of the zealous laymen who were starting a Hospital for Incurables to care for dying sick people. My friend Agostino Gallo is now the hospital's treasurer, and my neighbor Giacomo Chizzola is one of its trustees. Most of the incurables are infected by the "French disease" [syphilis, supposedly introduced to Italy by the invading soldiers] and have no family to help them, or no family who will.

Dying women leave little ones orphaned. Isabetta Prato and other good women of Brescia have gathered orphaned girls to care for them. Laura Gambara takes in women who wish to turn away from prostitution. Isabetta and Laura are leaders. They have enlisted other devout citizens in this effort and have really made a home for the homeless. Laura Gambara devoted her own house to sheltering them. It is now called the Carità.

They are remarkable people. Some say that our Church is corrupt. To be sure, here in Brescia we never see our Cardinal bishop. Many pastors are also absentees; many others have concubines. Agostino says he's going to talk about it in the book he's writing. Devout lay men and women are the Church here in Brescia.

Q: It must take courage and commitment to face all those problems. Where do they get it?

Angela: From faith and from prayer—from God. Most of the women are devout widows who have already reared their own children. They have experience and resources. A circle of dedicated women working together for God's children can accomplish wonders.

Several of the men belong to a brotherhood called Divino Amore. It was started in the 1490s in Genoa. The members don't talk much about it, but they encourage each other in good works.

These good men and women befriended me. I was eager to support them in their good works. When they need encouragement or are worried about family problems, we sit down together, talk things over, consider God's word and pray for the Holy Spirit's guidance. I came to realize that I had been drawn to Brescia as my place to do God's work.

Q: You said that you would tell me more about Antonio. Is he one of these devout men?

Angela: Oh yes! The first day we met, we struck a chord of friendship with each other. Antonio was only twenty-three then, not yet married, just beginning his business life. He was part of a whole generation coming to adulthood in the awful aftermath of the war. So many were cynical, caring about nothing. They were victims of war, too. But some, like Antonio, had looked at the devil's work and wanted a path through

29

the ruins, God's path, to a better life. Antonio loved to talk, question, listen. He was searching.

After a few months, some measure of peace had returned to Caterina's heart and it was time for me to leave the Patengola household. Antonio extended an invitation—persuaded me, actually. His large house in the Vicolo Santa Agata, with his cloth business in the shop at street level, had a small but comfortable room which he offered me. He said that he would be honored if I would be his guest there. He called me his spiritual "Madre." That arrangement lasted about fourteen years.

Q: How did you spend your days there?

Angela: Each morning I went to Mass at Santa Agata. I loved to gaze at the new fresco of the Crucifixion. It is right above the altar, making it clear that in the Mass we can share the graces won for us by Christ's Passion, *his blood shed for love of us*. On some occasions I went to San Francesco, the Franciscan church, for Confession and spiritual guidance, and to meet with other members of the Franciscan family. The friars' choir is so inspiring! Fra Bonaventura conducts simple, beautiful music during the Mass.

In Antonio's home I earned my living by the work of my hands, following St. Paul's example. Not that Antonio expected that, but I did. I helped the serving women with the housework. Though Antonio always treated them well, I soon saw how hard life was for poor girls like the servants in the neighborhood.

Many of them were orphans. Others had come from the country to the city for employment. Most were trying to save enough money for a dowry so they would be considered marriageable. Some had brothers or uncles who had refused to pay their dowry after their parents' death, so they could not marry. Some employers refused to pay their wages. Meanwhile, few had any protection in their households or on the streets. No wonder they came to Antonio's "Madre" for consolation! Many of these girls had not grown up in homes where they could learn to *be useful*. Few knew how to pray. Hardly anyone had been kind to them.

Often my widow friends could advise them or find them a better job, even take them into their own homes or the Carità. The men of

Divino Amore could represent them in court to obtain their dowries and wages. In those cases I was mostly a bridge. Even if little could be done to change their situations, they could find their dignity by experiencing God's love.

Q: It sounds as though some of these women and girls had very little love in their lives.

Angela: Exactly! But God is always with us, loving each one, caring for each one. Those who are *servants of Jesus Christ* must show that love. That is usually how God touches and speaks to us and provides for us, through the care of others. But God is also present *in the deepest recesses of our hearts*. When we pray we are talking and listening to our most intimate friend. The words of the Holy Scriptures are God's word to us, too. This is what I try to teach: how to pray, how to be aware of God's Spirit, how to love.

Q: From the number of men who visit you, they must want this teaching, too, like Antonio.

Angela: Everyone is hungry for God. Yes, even well-educated men! Even powerful men!

Q: Like Duke Francesco Sforza of Milan? Didn't he ask you to accept him as your spiritual son?

Angela: Ah! Francesco has suffered! When he asked to meet me in Brescia in 1528, he and his court were refugees from Milan, staying at St. Barnabas Convent. Yes, he sought my prayers. His life had never been peaceful since he was eight years old. The Swiss and the French and the Spanish! Back and forth! I visited him soon afterwards on my way home from Varallo. We met again in Cremona, when we were all in exile there in 1529.

Q: Why do preachers and theologians seek you out?

Angela: Together we seek God's Truth in the Holy Scriptures.

Q: Surely Francesco Martinengo and Filippo Sala are not in that category!

Angela: No, but they needed God's word just as much, or more! Their wives came to me in tears. Francesco and Filippo had quarreled over a debt and were determined to settle their score by a duel. Surely one would kill the other! The Duke of Urbino and city leaders had tried to intervene, but to no avail. Their wives' pleas had fallen on deaf ears. There was no room for forgiveness in either man's heart. Each one thought that his honor required him to fight, no matter what became of himself or his family. Their duel might have sparked a bloodbath. Yes, I went out to talk with them. Eventually, God softened their hearts, and the duel was cancelled.

Q: Is that what happened with Lord Luigi Gonzaga when he had punished your relative so harshly? Was Gonzaga's heart softened?

Angela: Yes, at least a little. Lord Luigi Gonzaga is known to be severe. My relative had committed an offense, but to lose all his possessions and be exiled! That was excessive punishment. On the way home from a trip to Mantua, I stopped in Solferino to see Lord Gonzaga and asked him to relent. I urged him to realize that he could forgive without excusing what had been a very real offense. Forgiving is not the same as excusing. He agreed to recall the offender from banishment and restore his goods.

Q: That pilgrimage to Mantua was one of many, wasn't it? If you were so at home in Brescia, why did you travel so often? Travel was so hard and dangerous!

Angela: Even so, I relish the different sights and places, especially ones that help me to experience God's presence and guidance more deeply. Two holy women, Osanna Andreasi and Stefana Quinzani, inspired me to travel, to seek these blessings. Both had shared in Christ's Passion by the stigmata, like St. Francis, and both experienced a mystic marriage with Christ, their heavenly Spouse. They were examples to me.

Antonio and I visited Blessed Osanna Andreasi's tomb in Mantua around 1520, to pray there. Before her death in 1505, Blessed Osanna had belonged to the Third Order of the Dominicans, like the great Saint Catherine of Siena. Their way of life was something like my own, though in a different spiritual family. The holy Stefana shared her wisdom with me when I visited her in Soncino before her death. She had been in Brescia occasionally before that. She was Blessed Osanna's spiritual heir and the spiritual mother of Gian Francesco Gonzaga and other dukes, including Ludovico il Moro and my poor Francesco Sforza.

Following the footsteps of Jesus Christ in the Holy Land was the most blest pilgrimage, and by far the most difficult. We were not sure till the last moment that we could even go.

Q: Who were your companions?

Angela: Antonio and my cousin Bartolomeo Biancosi. Antonio wanted to go in 1524, and I jumped at the chance to accompany him. For a while we thought that year's voyage would be cancelled because of all the stormy, rainy weather. So instead Antonio went on to the May fair at Lanciano. But on the way he passed through Venice and found that the fleet would set sail after all. He rushed to make the final arrangements and sent for me. Bartolomeo and I had to hurry to get there in time. In our haste, we took chances. We were passing through Vicenza, near Montebello, where it had been raining very heavily for days. Crossing the swollen streams was really frightening.

When we arrived in Venice, I was excited to see the white flags with their red crosses fluttering from the masts of the pilgrim ships. Just a few days later was Corpus Christi, May 26 that year. According to the custom, we pilgrims—forty-some—walked in procession from San Marco Cathedral to the port, wearing our wide-brimmed hats and carrying our traveling sacks and water bottles and gripping our walking staffs. The bishop blessed us and the ship. The Doge and the Council members and ambassadors participated in the ceremonies too. The next day we launched out onto the sea. Never before had I seen anything so vast! The innumerable *drops* that make up those *waters*! And *the multitude of stars*! My spirit stretched out over the waters as though it were reaching for the face of God.

On the way, we put in at Canea on the northwest coast of Crete, where something strange happened. Suddenly, I was almost blind! When we landed at Jaffa, my companions kindly led me ashore and continued to guide me. Through all the holy places, the eyes of my soul showed me where our Lord and Savior lived and taught and healed. How I wept at Calvary and kissed the ground where *he poured out his blood for love of us*! All the way, my companions' care made God's love more visible than the places we visited. I had to depend on my walking staff and on them. I was reminded of the Prophet Isaiah's words, "I will lead the blind on their journey; by paths unknown I will guide them" (Isaiah 42:16). God surely fulfilled that promise!

The other women and I lodged at the monastery of the Tertiary Nuns of Mount Sion, who are Beguines. On our return to Jaffa, we had to stay eight days at Rama for safety, since armed assassins were lying in wait to kidnap us.

Q: Many dramatic events! But you can see now. What happened?

Angela: Amazingly, on our voyage home, God restored my sight as I prayed before a crucifix. I will never know how or why this strange blindness came upon me. The sailors said that some people suffer this way after gazing long hours at the shining waters. Or maybe it was a disease. Whatever the cause, God helped me to sharpen my inner sight and taught me to rely on my companions. Through this blindness came a way of seeing, not one I had planned. I had yearned to SEE the holy places, but I learned to EXPERIENCE them even without sight. We can never see God with our eyes, yet we can encounter the divine presence with our spirits and in the goodness of others. So a deep disappointment became a great gift.

Q: And soon you were safely home?

Angela: Oh no! A terrible storm separated us from the other two ships in our fleet and blew us off course as far as Tunisia. Meanwhile, since we flew the Venetian flag, Turkish pirates were menacing us. Near Durazzo, the Turkish captain came on board and we thought we might be attacked. We realized that the pirate fleet was lying in wait to attack us. How intensely we prayed! God must have guided the captain and sailors, because somehow we slipped by the ambush. We were saved.

We finally docked at Venice in early November, more than five months after we had first embarked.

Q: You must have been in a hurry to get home to Brescia.

Angela: Yes, but because the people of Venice do so much to assist pilgrims, it is customary to spend a while assisting the city's charities when pilgrims return. It is a way of making a thank-offering to God as well as of thanking the Venetians. So Antonio and Bartolomeo and I spent about three weeks there, helping out. I lodged with the nuns of the Holy Sepulchre, but so many visitors were coming, disrupting their household, that I moved to the Hospital for the Incurables. Ladies and gentlemen directing the charities visited, since they were looking for some help, especially with the Hospital.

Q: Did you see any of the great city?

Angela: We did some sight-seeing. So many great artists have beautified it! My artist friend Girolamo Romanino studied there when he was younger, at the feet of some great masters. One of my favorite art works was the series of paintings of Saint Ursula and her Companions. The painter, Carpaccio, shows them as though they were in Venice right now. These martyrs of the early Church seem to be heroines of our own day.

Q: Were you tempted to stay in such a grand place, where you could do so much good in the charities?

Angela: No. Even though I was not yet sure of how to complete my mission, it was clear to me that Brescia was where I had been led to do it. We hurried in a closed carriage, shivering in the November cold. At last, thank God! Safely home in Brescia! We arrived on the feast of Saint Catherine of Alexandria, November 25. For me, it has been a day of thanksgiving ever since.

Q: After that long trip, you must have given up travel for a while.

Angela: Not at all! The next year, 1525, was a Holy Year. A pilgrimage to Rome and especially to the four major basilicas, carried special blessings. I went as part of a group, with two priests from Brescia. Like Saint Ursula and her companions, we prayed at the sites sanctified by the martyrs' courage. The martyrs *shed their blood for love* of Christ! Their testimony of faith *opens up the blindness* of those who do not know him.

We saw Messer Piero Della Puglia, a papal chamberlain, whom I had met in the Holy Land, and he arranged for us to have an audience with Pope Clement VII. Messer Della Puglia had told the Holy Father about the charities in Brescia, and there were hints about the needs in Rome. The Holy Father asked that I stay in Rome in the charities. How could I refuse? Yet I knew that my mission was in Brescia, and I told the Pope that. The solution was shown to me in prayer. As soon as possible, we returned to Brescia.

Q: At that point, did you see what form your mission was to take, or only the location?

Angela: There was still a mist over my path. In fact, I made more pilgrimages, seeking guidance. Pilgrimage has been such an important part of my life that I hope to be buried with my pilgrim staff at my side. We walk on pilgrimage through life, too, seeking God.

Q: Where else did you go?

Angela: Twice to Varallo, in 1528 or '29 and again in 1532. Friar Bernardino had the idea of constructing small chapels there to replicate the holy sites in Jerusalem and Bethlehem. Since he died in 1499, the Franciscan friars have continued building shrines for the early and final events of Our Lord's life. In the Holy Land I had seen with my inner eye. Now I wanted to see, if I could, how these places looked. I hoped to renew the experience of the pilgrimage, to draw again upon its graces. In only a few shrines are the statues completed. But those are so real! I felt as though I were there again.

Q: Did you need to see with your outer eyes?

Angela: I value the grace of experiencing places and people directly, not just in memory or from a distance or through others' words. Somehow, that directness moves my heart more deeply.

Q: I'm surprised that you could travel in those years, with all the warfare in northern Italy.

Angela: It's true, there was great danger, and not only out on the roads. The worst threat was in September, 1529. Emperor Charles V and his army were marching to Piacenza, where Pope Clement VII was to crown him. Everyone feared that the Emperor's army would invade Brescia. The terrors and sufferings of 1512 were still quite fresh, painful memories. My friend Ippolita Gallo Dorosini, a young widow, was fleeing to Cremona with her brother Agostino Gallo and his wife Cecilia and their household. They invited me to join them there, near San Vittore. Girolamo Patengola was another of the many Brescian refugees in Cremona. We were all afraid.

Brescians in exile and others displaced from Milan and many of Cremona's inhabitants found their way to the Gallo house in Cremona. They were worried, uncertain of the future, afraid for their sons and daughters. They came seeking comfort and prayer. The crisis opened many hearts to grace. Agostino and Cecilia had given me a small room of my own, and it did tend to get crowded with visitors. So many crowded in when they thought I would die that they looked to me like the choirs of saints and angels.

Q: Die? Were you sick?

Angela: Yes, unto death, we all thought. My young friend Girolamo Patengola came to congratulate me on going to heaven. He had written a poem about heaven's joys and read it to me. It ended with the lines

And now, in heavenly bliss, with a crown of palms,
She lives in happiness among the Angels.

The very thought lifted my spirits so fully that I sat up. Agostino was there, and he tells me that I talked for half an hour about the joys of heaven. All of a sudden, I was better! When I realized that I had missed my chance to go to heaven, I burst into tears and scolded Girolamo for tricking me into recovering. Poor Girolamo! He didn't know what to say. He stammered that he was sure I was going to die within a day and hadn't wanted to displease me. But I didn't die, and I think that Girolamo was happier about that than anyone. He himself is in heaven now, before me. He didn't even reach forty years. Who would have thought it?

Q: Did the Emperor attack Brescia?

Angela: No. His army marched on in February 1530. Thank God, they ignored Brescia completely. So we went home in peace. Just about then, Antonio married Francesca, and I knew that they would soon have a family—they have three children by now. I thought it best to move from his home in Vicolo Santa Agata. Agostino and Cecilia were so loving! They invited me to make my home with them in the Vicolo San Clemente. When we were in Cremona they didn't have children yet. By now they have four daughters and a son. I'm glad that I still live close enough to go over and hold the new baby, little Angela Aurelia Ippolita. She was just born September 28 of this year.

Agostino thought about how crowded the little room in Cremona used to get. He insisted that I should have two rooms in their home in Brescia, one for myself and one for receiving visitors.

Q: Who were your visitors?

Angela: People with troubles, seeking consolation; people worried about decisions on family matters, like marriages, seeking counseling; people with ruptured relationships, wanting to make peace. Preachers and theologians wanting to talk over the Sacred Scriptures.

By then I was over fifty years old. It was helpful to be so close to the parish church for Mass each morning.

Q: So the Vicolo San Clemente is named for the church?

Angela: Yes. It is only a few steps across the little alleyway from the Gallo home to the small church of Saint Clement. About this time I got to know Agostino's good friend Alessandro Bonvicino, the painter people call Il Moretto because of his dark complexion. Seven or eight years ago he acquired a house around the corner from the Gallo family. Alessandro's spirit goes deep into his subjects. He prays before beginning each work. Over the years, he has been working on a series of paintings for Saint Clement Church. It's his parish. We often talk about what he is painting, about the saints and the mysteries of faith that he paints. He earnestly hopes to enkindle prayer in the faithful. Alessandro teases me and says he wants to paint my portrait, but I tease him in turn and say, "Over my dead body!"

Q: What are some of his paintings?

Angela: One of my favorites is *Saint Ursula and Her Companions*. I had always revered these martyrs, since Papa read to us about them from our book about the saints and martyrs.

Q: Some people say that the companion whose face is closest to Saint Ursula's in that painting by Moretto looks like you, a little younger.

Angela: Is that how I used to look? Maybe so. But focus on Saint Ursula. With what firmness she holds Christ's banner and shares it with her companions! She is not only royal. She is a leader, inspiring these women to steadfastness and to *celestial glory*.

Q: No wonder you chose her as the patron of your company of women!

Angela: Yes! The Company was beginning to gather, mostly servants and daughters of craftsmen. Over these years, many women and girls had confided to me the secrets of their hearts—their call to belong to *God alone*. Most of their families were planning marriages for them. Indeed, there seemed to be no other choice. Some might have welcomed life in a monastery, but if they were too poor to have a dowry that was not possible. Some families needed their care or support. Other women simply wanted to consecrate themselves to God while remaining in their homes or in their employment.

Q: But there was no place in society for single women, at least no place of dignity.

Angela: How true! Yet I had lived that way, cared for by God's providence, guided by the Holy Spirit, embraced by the love of the Son of God. I began to see that my vision so many years before had pointed to this, this way of life. I invited these women to pray together. They asked me to teach them the way of life that has brought me so much joy.

The fulfillment of my vision was ripening. Yet so many years had passed! I hesitated. I sought further guidance, again at Varallo. With fourteen other pilgrims, I traveled there in 1532. Agostino and Ippolita were part of our group, but not Cecilia. She had just given birth to Eugenia Isidora Josepha in July and couldn't travel.

Q: Did you receive the guidance you were hoping for?

Angela: O yes! God let me know that this was the moment, that I must *act, exert* myself!

Q: What did you do?

Angela: Gather the women who had heard a call to this life of the Company. Dear Isabetta Prato gave us the use of a large upstairs room in her house, on the Cathedral Piazza. It's our oratory. We had it frescoed in 1533 with scenes to inspire our prayer: in the center the Crucifixion with the Blessed Mother on the right and Saint John on the left, sharing the sufferings and the graces of Christ's Passion. There are scenes of the Annunciation, the Nativity, Jesus in the Temple, and the Assumption of Mary. On either side are figures of saints.

Q: Which saints? How did you choose them?

Angela: Saint Paula and her daughter Saint Eustochium are on board a ship bound for the Holy Land. They were a widow and a virgin, both dedicated to God and both involved in translating the Scriptures with Saint Jerome. Saint Elizabeth of Hungary is shown with the little girls she cared for. She reminds us that her namesake Isabetta Prato is devoted to the care of orphan girls. The martyrs Saints Faustinus, Jovita and Afra are our city's patrons. In the early Church they stood courageously faithful to Christ, the first two right here in Brescia and Saint Afra in Rome. Saint Ursula is on a ship carrying the banner of a victorious martyr. She and her companions were witnesses of faith, dedicated to Jesus Christ to the last *drop of their blood*.

Q: There are quite a few ships in your life and in your oratory. You do love to travel!

Angela: I've traveled much in my life, but not since the Company took shape. Now I am on a different road, a road of life that we travel *together.* The graces of a holy journey in companionship are more than just a multiplication of journeying alone. Companionship itself is like a basket, receiving and carrying the bread that sustains and nourishes us on the way. We are real "com-pan-ions," real "sharers-of-bread," of life, on our journey. The vision I had so many years ago at the Brudazzo seemed once more before my eyes, in the faces of these women, these flesh-and-blood women. I have not traveled since in search of guidance.

Q: What else did you do?

Angela: Move. I could not impose a further stream of visitors upon the Gallo family. First I took a room near St. Barnabas. But soon I moved here to this apartment by St. Afra Church, with Barbara Fontana. It's conveniently near the public fountain. My confessor, Father Serafino of Bologna, told me these rooms were available. He's one of the Lateran canons. After they came to St. Afra in 1519, they tore down the old church and built a new one. It's over the martyrs' relics, downstairs in the crypt. They keep adding on and adapting it. My bedroom is right out there, at the top of the stairs.

Q: Bedroom? Where? I didn't see a bed when I passed that little room.

Angela: Well, during the day I roll up my mat and put it away, out of sight.

This larger room that we're sitting in has been a good place for receiving my daughters who come to be instructed, and a good place for sharing a bowl of vegetable soup and a bit of bread. Matrons who help guide the Company gather here to consult and plan, along with the colonelle, the Ursulines who teach the others in their neighborhoods.

Some days are so full of visitors that I relish the night hours, when I can pray in deep silence downstairs in the crypt near the martyrs' relics.

Q: How did you really become a Company?

Angela: Along with our own prayer and regular gatherings, we had to work with the families, especially of the younger women and girls, whose parents were preparing for them to marry. The matrons and some of my gentlemen supporters would talk with their parents to secure permission, to assure that later the parents would not change their minds and force their Ursuline daughters to marry.

Q: Why would parents do that?

Angela: Some think that life as an unmarried woman is not respectable. They also worry that the future of a single woman is insecure. Our diocesan vicar, good Lorenzo Muzio, helped us to get approval for our Rule in 1536. When that happened, it was more clear that this way of life is one of integrity. Also, in an approved way of consecrated life, the members should be able to claim their dowries, which will help them to live with dignity. Otherwise they will always be dependent on their brothers or nephews or employers.

Q: When did you finally begin the Company?

Angela: On November 25, 1535. It was the feast of Saint Catherine of Alexandria and the anniversary of my return from the Holy Land. Saint Catherine's Day has always been holy to me, since she is my mother's patron saint. She was a woman of great wisdom. She also gave a shining example of the courage and faithfulness that the virgin martyrs of the early Church witnessed to their world. We too belong to Jesus Christ and hope to be faithful witnesses of his love in our world. That is our mission—to be his presence in our families and among our neighbors.

Q: What did you do on that day?

Angela: Twenty-eight *daughters and sisters* attended Mass together at St. Afra Church. Some of our friends and relatives joined us to pray for God's blessing. We began this way because in *the sacred Mass* we enter most closely into the love of Jesus, which draws us together. He is the center of our unity. After Mass we signed the Book of the Company. Each woman wrote her name in testimony of her promise to give herself to God as a member of this Company. Then we celebrated together. What rejoicing!

Q: Who are these twenty-eight?

Angela: I could talk on and on about *my very dear daughters and sisters*! But I notice that it's beginning to get dark outside, so I'll tell you about just a few of them. Let's see.... You've already met Barbara Fontana. She grew up in this very parish of St. Afra. Thank God for her *graciously assisting* me in my old age! She comes from a loving family. Her father Gian Pietro has been helping us. He was one of the witnesses at our first general meeting, in March 1537. I want to leave him *some little thing* when I die, my office book.

Maria dell'Olmo is one of our neighborhood leaders. She lives near here and guides the members around St. Afra. Maria, the daughter of Bertolino, gives good example and shares her enthusiasm about our life. Her two sisters are showing interest in the Company, too. I think she may have the qualities to be a leader in her neighborhood, near San Faustino Church.

We have two pairs of sisters, Catherine and Domenica, Dolza Drusilla's daughters, and Paola and Laura Peschiera. Paola shows signs of leadership. Their father is Doctor Gianpiero Peschiera.

Clara Gaffura is very young but deeply committed to God. Simona Borni is a maid-servant to Maria Avogadro, one of the widows we have elected for the Company's governance. Simona is fortunate to have a mistress who supports her vocation. It's not so easy for some others. Clara da Martinengo's family came here to Brescia from the Martinengo district outside the city. And my other *dear daughters*... Andriana di Zambelli, Peregrina Casali, Drusilla Zinelli and Laura and.... You can find all their names in the book of the Company, where we inscribed ourselves on November 25.

Q: Is November 25 the "birthday" of the Company, then?

Angela: It is indeed, and we celebrate by welcoming new members on that day each year. They too write their names in the Book of the Company. That is how they signify their gift of their hearts and lives to God. They also promise to *embrace the means and the ways* of making their gift authentic, the *means and ways* described in our Rule.

Q: What is in the Rule?

Angela: Please read it. Gabriele Cozzano has written it all down as I dictated it to him.

Q: Who is Gabriele Cozzano?

Angela: He is my firm friend and confidante. He's a teacher of literature and a notary. When I die, he will continue to encourage and protect the Company, which is so close to his heart.

Q: You are thinking ahead.

Angela: It took me four decades to realize how to bring about the vision God had sent me in the Brudazzo. But now it is alive. God and all creation have fostered this new life, and it has prospered. Yes, I am thinking about what will happen after my death.

To help the colonelle be good *teachers and guides* to my daughters, I have dictated to Gabriele my advice for them. To help the matrons guide the Company, Gabriele has written out my legacy to them—how to be the *mothers of so great a company*. The sisters elected me "Madre for life" in our election, which was held here in the kitchen on March 18, 1537. At my death, the Lady Lucrezia Lodrone will succeed me as the principal "mother." I have also recorded my bequests: my rosary, my hairshirt, my prayerbook.

In the past I humored my friends and those taking care of me by submitting to doctors' treatments, even though medicines usually affect me strangely. It seems as though I get more relief from eating onions and feel better after washing my hair. But this time my strength is truly failing. I'm grateful for Barbara's gracious and kindly assistance.

As a member of the Third Order of St. Francis, I had always expected to be buried in a Franciscan cemetery. But instead, in 1532 I petitioned Church authorities at the Sacred Apostolic Penitentiary and received permission to be buried in the Church of St. Afra, near the burial site of so many early Christian martyrs of Brescia. It's right downstairs from this apartment, in the martyrs' chapel, as I told you.

Yes, I look forward, but with a grateful look backward, too. *God has united us in doing good, and according to the divine plan we enjoy every prosperity.*

What we have done is turning out well, because we have God and every creature in our favor.

Realizing that I will soon be going to Heaven, people are visiting. My nephew Tracagno, who is a doctor in Salò, came recently, and another relative who is a canon of St. Nazaro. When Tomaso Gavardo and Giacomo Chizzola were here, I wasn't feeling strong enough to get up, so naturally our thoughts turned to life and death. We talked about Christian living. The topic itself made me feel better. Just as they were going—in fact, Giacomo was nearly out the door—Tomaso asked for a bequest from me, some spiritual teaching. I told him, "Do during this life what you would like to have done at the time of death."

Soon I will die, and *Jesus Christ, my kind and sweet spouse, will draw me* into the heavenly company of those who have lived for him alone. Our Marta is already in heaven, *crowned with that golden and brilliant virginal crown.* She was one of our earliest members, and she has been the first to walk our path all the way to its destination.

But I will always remain with *my dear daughters* still on earth, *along with Jesus, my Love and theirs, helping them with their prayers* and their *good works.* I don't know what the future will bring. They will have to make *changes if the times and circumstances require new rules* or a different way of doing things. If they *remain strongly united, and gather at the feet of Jesus Christ in fervent prayer together, he will enlighten them and teach them what to do.* Then this Company, which God has planted, will endure.

I long to guide and assist them, till we are all together in heaven. God will reunite us, too, with the matrons and men who have assisted our Company, and with our beloved families and friends, all sharing *the gladness and joy of eternal life.*

Part 2

A Letter from the Madre — Prologue

A Letter to My Beloved Daughters and Sisters

Angela Merici begins her Rule with a prologue *in the manner of letters* (Index of the *Chapters*). *She is addressing her beloved daughters and sisters* (Pr.:3). She speaks TO them out of her heart, not ABOUT them in a formal or distant tone. She often addresses them as sisters. She even inverts the usual Italian order (which would be *mie sorelle*), to the more emphatic and affectionate *sorelle mie*, "sisters mine," or "my very own sisters" (Pr.:7, 15, 22). The Prologue immediately sets the tone, a personal warmth which will color every topic. This warmth is intrinsic to the Rule, which presents the Company as a network of close relationships, suggesting a spiritual family. The word *company* (typical term for spiritual groups) suggests its Latin origin in *cum* and *panis*: with + bread, "bread-sharing," a group of people who share bread and thus life. Angela's intense, relational character stamped this companionship.

For its members, companionship constituted an entirely new reality. As unmarried women they were anonymous and invisible. The birth of a daughter was not usually celebrated, and daughters were often unnamed or even omitted entirely in the regular declarations made by heads of households. Single women had no connections with one another based upon their similar circumstances. The relationships within the Company would give them solidarity and transform them into a public presence in Brescia. That in itself was an historic phenomenon. They would continue to live in "the world" of family or employment but *apart from the darkness of this poor world* (Pr.:4), that is, enlightened by spiritual purpose and joy.[1] Angela drew creatively upon her experiences; her imagination catalyzed something new.[2]

Angela wants Ursulines to realize that the Rule is for them as individuals and as a community, since *God has granted you the grace of...joining you together* (Pr.:4). She stresses a unity that will persist from the moment of call to the moment when *all the others want to accompany her to the burial place, going two by two in charity* (Ch. XI:32). She speaks to each and to all.

This solemn letter opens *In the name of the blessed and undivided Trinity* (Pr.:1). The Trinity presides over the Rule: the Holy Spirit over the chapter on obedience; the Son, known in Jesus, over the chapter on virginity; and the provident Parent over the chapter on poverty.

In the first lines, the author addresses her overarching purpose, as dramatists do in their prologues and composers do in their overtures.

1 In the name of the blessed and undivided Trinity.

2 Prologue about the newly begun life of virgins who are called by the name Company of Saint Ursula.

3 To the beloved daughters and sisters of the Company of Saint Ursula.

4 Since, most beloved daughters and sisters, God has granted you the grace of separating you from the darkness of this poor world and joining you together to serve his divine Majesty,

5 you must give him infinite thanks for having granted such a singular gift especially to you,

6 for how many great persons, and others of every condition, do not have, nor will be able to have, such a grace!

The Prologue sketches a summary of Ursuline life, from beginning to end. Chapter I is "About the Manner of Receiving" members. The life unfolds until the last chapter looks beyond the grave to the members' heavenly destination. The Prologue strikes the tonalities and introduces the important themes elaborated throughout.

It also demonstrates her deft pedagogy, for example in her list of *snares and dangers...water, air, and earth, with all of hell, flesh and sensuality* (Pr.:19-21). As high as her spirit soars, she grounds her teaching firmly in concrete details. Lists are a part of this method. She often lists practical applications. For example, the chapter titled "How They Should Be Attired" is almost completely a list of items that a new member may need to put aside to be consistent with her calling. The series of clothing items also exemplifies Angela's method of ending a list, especially a list of "nots," with a positive summary that restates the major lesson. In the case of attire, the summation is *Finally, no styles or varieties...that could mar one's own conscience or that of others and may be contrary to virginal integrity* (Ch. II:8, 9). In "About Virginity" she emphasizes *honest and polite* behaviors and lists behaviors to avoid, ending with *not grumbling, not spreading gossip.... Indeed, let all our words, acts and conduct always be to teach and edify...having charity always burning in our hearts* (Ch. IX:18-22).

The Call – A Gift

The Prologue introduces the mainspring of the life described in the Rule. Ursuline scholars Luciana Mariani, Elisa

Tarroli and Marie Seynaeve describe the heart of Angela's message in these words: "Christ has taken the first step towards her by his initiative of love; he is the 'Lover.'"[3] The Rule's basic dynamic is God's loving initiative and our gratitude for *having been thus chosen* (Pr.:7). *[Y]ou must give him infinite thanks for having granted such a singular gift especially to you* (Pr.:5). Gratitude is the mainspring of Ursuline life.

[Y]ou have been called by God (Pr.:9). God's call is a gift. The whole Rule is about how to cherish the gift of invitation into intimacy with God. When we receive a precious gift, we treasure it. We take practical steps to care for it, use it well and preserve it. If the gift is an invitation to a life, the practical steps are the habits of that life. Angela calls them the *means and ways* (Pr.:10, 13).

The Prologue begins with the call. Every chapter is intended to support an Ursuline in her vocation, offering *means and ways* for answering her call. Chapters I to III teach the new member practices which, though relatively exterior, are grounded in spirit. They are ways of learning to live with integrity. Chapters IV to VII present spiritual practices, to draw her deeper into God. At the Rule's core are obedience, virginity and poverty (Chs. VIII to X), a Gospel-based commitment. Chapter XI sets up a network of relationships to support each and all in the vocation. The totality of the call is experienced through the person of Jesus Christ and is offered back to God through him.

The Rule, then, has little to do with rules. Through its pages, Angela talks to her daughters, members of the Company of Saint Ursula, about their new life. Her warmth is palpable. She dictated to her secretary, Gabriele Cozzano, no doubt speaking much as she did when the women sat, circled around her. Each chapter resembles such conversations, with the energy of personal presence, face to face with her *beloved...most beloved daughters and sisters...my very own sisters* (Pr.:3, 4, 7).

The Prologue makes it clear that the whole Rule is a personal statement, germinated in her own experience. Implicitly, she communicates how God has reached out to her, invited her to live deeply in Christ's love. Bit by bit, she worked out ways that helped her answer the invitation. That is what the Rule describes, a way of responding. It all starts with God. Always—God invites, we respond. When she dictated the Rule, Angela had been living her response for four decades.

Since the Prologue begins with the theme of vocation and response, let us reflect on Angela's experience of this dynamic. How

7 For this reason, my very own sisters, I call upon you, actually I beg and entreat you all: having been thus chosen to be true and virginal spouses of the Son of God,

8 first, be willing to recognize what such a thing means and what a new and wondrous dignity this is.

9 Then strive with all your might to keep yourselves as you have been called by God

10 and seek out, and desire all those means and ways that are necessary to persevere and prosper till the end.

11 Because merely beginning is not enough if not carried through. Therefore Truth says, "Qui perseveraverit usque in finem, hic salvus erit"; that is, "He who perseveres till the end will be saved."

12 And once again he says: "Beati qui audiunt verbum Dei et custodiunt illud"; that is, blessed are those into whose hearts God has infused the light of Truth, giving them the desire to long for their heavenly homeland, and then

had she worked out her highly unusual, almost unheard-of way? Perhaps her first intentional step took her to the Franciscans at Salò, who taught her the value of embracing certain spiritual practices. The Rule of their Third Order outlines a pattern that she followed from the time she was about twenty. Yet this was not her vocation. Secular (Third Order) Franciscans may follow vocations to marriage, priesthood or single life. Something else was drawing her.

Angela had a clear sense of God's call in her youth. It came powerfully in the Brudazzo field, when she saw angels and women on a ladder stretching between earth and heaven, heard their music and song. But she did not know then, or for many years, where the call would lead her.

Some people have dramatic illuminations like hers. A profound event can make one consider the meaning of her life. Or the death of a loved one may cast the light of eternity on her numbered days. God can speak to the depths of our hearts when we are in prayer, but also through music, in the golden sunlight poured on autumn leaves, or within a verse of the Bible. If the heart is ready, it takes only a single moment to recognize God's inviting, compelling voice. And one knows that she will never be whole unless she answers. She may resist or delay, or search for the path. But she knows that she is called.

Angela was quite young. Some are ready to hear such an invitation in that season of life. Others expect to marry, then do not, and find in their search an unexpected path. Does that make a celibate life their second choice? Second best? Or is it, for them, the truer choice of maturity? They reflect on their experience and see in it an opening that they had not originally anticipated. They find, perhaps, a place in themselves, deeper than they had ever known, and there hear an invitation to focus their lives on God, perhaps in the Company. Earlier they may not even have understood that they had this choice. Marriage was taken for granted. They wanted to center their lives on a relationship. Eventually they realize that Jesus Christ is attracting them into a divine love as that center. Prayer, the Gospels, and glimpses of Jesus through his followers gradually make that clear.

Called Together – The Company

These seekers may live faithfully,

they will try to preserve within themselves this voice of truth and noble yearning.

13 This sort of person will undoubtedly be able to take care of herself: one who will want to embrace the means and ways necessary to such an end,

14 since there is little or no difference between freely saying: "I no longer want to serve God" and not wanting the ways and the rules necessary to be able to keep one self in this.

prayerfully; yet they yearn for companionship. They sense that for them life would be fuller with the mutual support of other women who share the same call. Angela was sixty when she established this Company, this way of being *together*. It must have been growing in her for years. She had many close friends, women and men. There were kindred spirits among the Secular Franciscans. Yet she sought the sisterly company of other women whom God was drawing along the path of celibate, single life. At first glance, "single" and "company" may seem contradictory. Doesn't "single" mean "alone"? Angela challenges us to think in new ways. "Single" means "one by one"; it does not have to mean "alone." One of her favorite words, a theme struck early in the Prologue, is *insieme*, that is, *together. God has granted you the grace,* she says, *of…joining you together to serve his divine Majesty* (Pr.:4).

In sixteenth-century Italy, it was almost unheard of for anyone, especially a woman, to live alone. As a single woman in her hometown of Desenzano, Angela likely shared the family home and worked on the family farm, perhaps with her brother and his wife and children. Later, in Brescia, she spent nearly twenty years in large households where she was a respected guest but also contributed to the housework.[4]

Many of the first Ursulines lived in their own families, with parents or with married brothers or sisters. Others lived where they worked, often as maids or household servants. These were the typical situations of unmarried women.

The Company offers something more: a way of being *together* in a spiritual family of sisters. Like other adult siblings, these "sisters" do not necessarily live together; in fact, that is rare. Their ties are not of blood, nor of shared labor. Their connections are spiritual bonds, woven together through personal contact.

The Rule presents the main outlines for building this family (especially in Chapter XI), and the Counsels and Testament offer more details. Angela directs members to gather at least once a month for the sacraments and regularly for spiritual enrichment and, *talking over spiritual matters*, to *rejoice together and together encourage one another* (Ch. VII:12, 13; Eighth Legacy[5]). Twice a month the local leaders are to visit the members in their neighborhoods. They are to offer guidance and encouragement and, if a member has a problem, work out a way to help. If one of the women is in need because of poverty or illness or old age, others must care for her, in a sisterly spirit (Ch. XI:7-13). For Angela, companionship is part of the call, something necessary. Ursulines need each other. Their unity is a *mighty fortress* (Last Counsel:15). *Loving each other…in harmony together* is Angela's *sure sign* of *walking the path right and pleasing to God* (Tenth Legacy:12).

For an Ursuline, companionship is a factor in how the call is realized. *Each one embraces* the Rule, following its guidance in her own home and parish and work, singly. But not alone. The fact that others are faithful is a great strength and encouragement. United spirit and practice create an unseen circle of which we are, each and all, a part, even when we are apart.

The Company brought to fulfillment the call that Angela had experienced as a teenager. There is mystery in a call from God. Angela's vision in the Brudazzo had striking mystical elements. Angels and women on a ladder between heaven and earth—the sight and the music—put into image and sound a movement of spirit that must have been stirring in her already, and which she continued to unfold for years to come.

Each person has a call, a vocation. How can we hear it? Angela would tell us to go into *the secret recesses of the heart* and listen. God guides us through many voices, all around us (Ch. VIII, "About Obedience"). But to hear this call we must go deep inside. Each of us was created with particular capacities for living well and happily, for loving and being loved. We usually sense how we will do that best, along what path of life. In other words, God's call comes first through the divine breath that shaped us. It may take a while to hear this voice clearly. But the Holy Spirit continually teaches us our own truth.

From the awe-inspiring fact of God's call, the Prologue moves to stress the *new and wondrous dignity* of the Ursuline vocation (Pr.:8). *[F]or how many great persons...do not have...such a grace!* (Pr.:6) *...a life of such glory that we...will become queens in heaven* (Pr.:17). This assessment flies in the face of the sixteenth century's devaluation of an unmarried woman, with no standing, no security. Exploitation threatened her—all sorts of exploitation—and she had little recourse in society or the courts of law. Even today, for a woman to be alone can be fraught with danger. Yet the Ursuline is not alone, but single, and in a Company. Girls and single women may be the least-valued people in society. But the world's values do not measure one's worth. On the contrary, we know how God esteems and loves us—all of us! With that understanding, each member can lift her head and shape her life.

Enlightened and empowered by God's perspective, an Ursuline should share God's way of seeing, should see the dignity of all people whom society may disregard. Angela created in Chapter XI a counter-cultural, even revolutionary network of relationships. People with resources and social position were put at the service of their weakest neighbors. She envisioned a new familial structure bridging classes and clans. Angela's keen spiritual vision penetrated to the worth of each person. She drew others into new ways of seeing and relating. This dynamic has transcended the centuries, permeating all forms of Ursuline life. It continues its historic evolution, energizing us in a new millennium.

Spouse – The Mystery

The Prologue describes the character of the Ursuline vocation as being *spouses of the Son of God* (Pr.:7, 17). The authors of *Contribution towards a Biography* assert that "the specific note of Angela's spirituality would be the contemplation of this mystery of Christ-Spouse.... To make this mystery of Christ-Spouse present in the Church, to give witness to it in the world by one's life and by one's word, this would be the charism which Angela would bequeath to her daughters...."[6]

The cynic would assert that this terminology is just a psychic crutch, a way of making up for not having a husband. Yet "spouse" has a long and rich history that illuminates Angela's claim.

"Spouse" is the word that Scripture uses to show the covenant of deep love between God and Israel. In the biblical Covenant, God promised Israel a home in the Promised Land. Yet the Covenant is more about abiding in God's love than about geography. On Mt. Sinai, God and Israel forged a partnership of belonging to each other, a Covenant of love, honor, and faithfulness. The prophet Jeremiah put it like this, evoking God's voice, "This is the covenant which I will make with the house of Israel after those days.... I will place my law within them, and write it upon their hearts; I will be their God, and they shall be my people" (Jeremiah 31:33). Israel often strayed, worshipping false gods. Prophets such as Hosea cried out like a betrayed but forgiving spouse. In human terms, the prophets expressed God's enduring love. Hosea tried to understand God by drawing on his own willingness to forgive his wife's adultery and accept her back:

> So I will allure her;
> I will lead her into the desert
> and speak to her heart....
> I will heal their defection,
> I will love them freely.
> - Hosea 2:16; 14:5

The metaphor of "spouse" continues in the Church's life. We are the Church, and the Church is the daughter of Israel. Christians live the continuing Covenant, whatever their vocation may be.

Angela draws on this millennia-long tradition when she emphasizes that her daughters are *spouses of the Son of God* (Pr.:7). Jesus Christ is our human image of God. In him we see what God is like, how God deals with us. And what do we see? Jesus invites us, draws us, into a deep and intimate relationship with

15 My very own sisters, it is necessary that we be vigilant, and so much more so, as the undertaking is of such importance that there could be no greater,

16 in which lie our life and well-being,

17 and in which we are called to a life of such glory that we are spouses of the Son of God, and will become queens in heaven.

God. Angela uses the word "spouse" as a metaphor for the depth, the intimacy. Spousal language also shows how a life is shaped around one's relationship with Jesus Christ.

Unfortunately, patriarchal social structures create spousal relationships of domination and subordination, which we properly reject as models. Some spouses have oppressive or distant or merely functional relationships. In these situations, words like *spouses of the Son of God* become entangled in many negative issues. We cannot see ourselves as equals of a divine being. The reverse application—from God-human to human-human—seems to endorse inequality between human spouses. One is like God. The metaphor limps even more painfully if an assumption that the divine partner is male is used to devalue the female and this imbalance is applied to human relationships.

A scriptural reversal of this imbalance occurs in the Book of Wisdom, where King Solomon calls divine Wisdom his spouse. He says,

> I pleaded and the spirit of Wisdom came to me.
> I preferred her to scepter and throne,
> And deemed riches nothing in comparison with her,
>   nor did I liken any priceless gem to her;
> Because all gold, in view of her, is a little sand,
>   and before her, silver is to be accounted mire.
> Beyond health and comeliness I loved her....
> Indeed, she reaches from end to end mightily
>   and governs all things well.
> Her I loved and sought after from my youth;
>   I sought to take her for my bride
>   and was enamored of her beauty.
>   - Wisdom 7:7-10; 8:1, 2

Solomon's capacity to understand divinity in feminine terms expands the potential of the metaphor dramatically.

Let us acknowledge that no metaphor can express the whole of any reality. Perhaps new models of espousal can contribute to our understanding. Contemporary experience in many cultures offers new insight and further challenge. Some spouses live a real equality. One is not submerged in the sphere of the other. They collaborate. How might this newer idea of espousal illuminate our human situation *vis à vis* God? Mary Conroy, OSU, spoke of "a partnership of the whole of life."[7] A partnership with God! Partnership opens up wide horizons. To be

God's partner means that the relationship is bigger than any individual human being. It is not merely personal. It is not for its own sake. We become God's collaborators, make God's work our own! Jesus inaugurated his ministry with such a commitment "to bring glad tidings to the poor...to proclaim liberty to captives and recovery of sight to the blind, to let the oppressed go free..." (Luke 4:18). Jesus would do God's work.

Angela Merici lived such a partnership. Her deeply intimate prayer to Christ ripples outward to the circles *of family, relatives and friends* and to those *who do not know* [*him*]. It glows with her ardent zeal *to open up the blindness of their minds* (Ch. V:24, 31, 34). Her deeds lived out her words through service, witness and even liberation.

Words are always pale symbols of reality. For Angela, the word "spouse" symbolizes, in human terms, a mutually loving covenant of life. It is an idealized image, of course. Many human spouses do not live up to it. Israel and the Church do not live up to it. Many Ursulines do not live up to it. But God always does. No—God lives up to no description. God is the white-hot reality reflected in all our words and images and loves.

A more clinical era may find such mystic language excessively emotional, imaginary even. But Angela's earthy practicality balances it with common sense. The Rule is about habits and small daily actions, not about imagination. When she dictated the Rule, she was an old woman over sixty—no sentimental bride! She had learned the day-in-day-out, year-in-year-out *means and ways* of acting as Christ's in the midst of the world, not by a word, but by deeds. Again and again, in the Prologue and through the subsequent chapters, she insists on the need to *embrace* the Rule's sensible practices (Pr.:13, 29), *since there is little or no difference between freely saying: "I no longer want to serve God" and not wanting the ways and the rules necessary to be able to keep oneself in this* (Pr.:14).

Angela's Voice

In laying out the *means and ways*, i.e., the Rule, Angela is both urgent and invitational. Urgency derived from her knowledge that these *means are necessary to persevere and prosper till the end* (Pr.:10). With that realization, she utters a crescendo, *I call upon you, actually I beg and entreat you* (Pr.:7). The series of verbs allows us to overhear her process of oral composition in this dictated work, as she begins a thought and then reaches for a more and then a more intense way of communicating it. Her intensity permeates the Prologue and the Rule.

So does invitation. Throughout the Rule, her tone is invitational. Chapter after chapter opens with *Remember to...* (*se arricorda...*) or with *Let each one want to...* (*ogn'una voglie...*). The Italian verb for "want to" is also a polite way of making a request or of giving direction. Encouragement, never force, is Angela's method. This phrasing allows her to encourage each woman individually.[8] *Each one* must take responsibility for her own life. Angela's care to address herself to *each one* reflects her respect for individuals and her refusal to impose uniformity.

The life described in the Rule is both simple and challenging. Nothing is complex. Members integrate Ursuline practices into their very ordinary circumstances. Yet the Rule's ideals go counter to many accepted values. It offers the *means and ways* of treasuring this vocation, even when inner impulses and outer influences conspire against it. The Rule shows Ursulines how to act with integrity, true to their commitment: how to enter upon this life, how to dress and conduct themselves with integrity (Chs. I - III). The spiritual practices of fasting, the sacraments and private prayer are necessary means to fidelity (Chs. IV - VII).

Each component of the Rule has both an inward and an outward dynamic. Spiritual practices, for example, foster a contemplative spirit. Angela knew from her own experience and from the example of contemporaries that contemplation is not limited to cloisters. Cloisters shape the rhythms of the day to foster contemplation. But we can live contemplatively in the kitchen and on the street. We can pray contemplatively in the parish church or in our rooms. Contemplation is important for Ursulines because it nourishes deep intimacy with God. Moving outward, an authentic relationship with Christ flows to others as simple acts of love. Jesus said, "The Father and I are one" (John 10:30) and "I am in my Father and you are in me and I in you" (John 14:20). The more deeply we enter into his oneness with God, the more we learn to act as he did, making God's love present to everyone.

18 But one needs to be careful and prudent here, for greater labors and dangers may be involved when the undertaking is of greater value.

19 There is no type of evil which is not here to be resisted, considering that we are placed here in the midst of snares and dangers.

20 Indeed, armed against us are water, air, and earth with all of hell, because the flesh and our sensuality are not yet dead.

21 Our adversary, the devil, never even sleeps; he who never

rests, but always (as Saint Peter says), like a roaring lion looks and searches for how he can devour any of us with his cunning ways, so many that no one could count them.

22 However, my very own sisters, you must not be afraid of this:

23 because if you strive with all your might for a future of living as indeed is required of true spouses of the Most High,

24 and to observe this Rule which has been composed to be useful to you, indeed as the road for you to walk by,

25 I have this undaunted and firm faith and hope in the infinite divine goodness, that not only will we easily overcome all dangers and adversities, but we will conquer them, and with great glory and jubilation.

26 Actually, we will cross through this momentary life with consolation,

27 and our every pain and sadness will turn into joy and gladness, and thorny and rocky roads we will find flower-strewn for us, paved with finest gold,

Such a vocation is the project of a lifetime, not the dream of a day.

Angela's realism faces what she calls *dangers and adversities* (Pr.:19-25), both inner and outer. Interior shadows appear vividly in her prayer as *frightening beasts* (Ch. V:21). The Prologue alludes also to *the flesh and our sensuality* (Pr.:20). In her prayer she seeks to focus her *affections and senses* on goodness (Ch. V:18). Surrounding forces, *snares and dangers* (Pr.:19), seem so powerful and all-enveloping to her that she sums them up as *water, air, and earth with all of hell* (Pr.:20), evoking the four ancient elements of the cosmos.[9] To Brescians, who had recently suffered war's horror and demoralizing aftermath, followed by flood and earthquake, the language may have seemed not merely a standard rhetorical description but a very accurate assessment.[10] The power of evil, personified in [o]ur adversary, *the devil,...like a roaring lion* (Pr.:21; 1 Peter 5:8) had been prowling Brescia's streets and homes. The Company's members might expect to find this lion searching *for how he can devour any of us with his cunning ways, so many that no one could count them* (Pr.:21).

Angela is often praised for balance. Where is the balance in these dramatic descriptions? Angela achieves balance with point and counterpoint. That is, having painted causes for fear so vividly, she now does the same with causes for hope. *However, my very own sisters, you must not be afraid of this: because if you strive with all your might for a future of living as indeed is required of true spouses of the Most High and to observe this Rule which has been composed to be useful to you, indeed as the road for you to walk by, I have this undaunted and firm faith and hope in the infinite divine goodness, that not only will we easily overcome all dangers and adversities, but we will conquer them, and with great glory and jubilation* (Pr.:22-25). These and many other examples demonstrate her capacity to hold opposites in balance and to resolve their diverging energies. She could experience life holistically. She had no need to deny darkness in order to see the light. Nor did she forget joy when she tasted suffering.

Confronting frightening evils, each woman must courageously take responsibility for herself, her own well-being. But she is not alone. She walks in companionship and equipped with *this Rule which has been composed to be useful to you, indeed as the road for you to walk by* (Pr.:24).

This passage demonstrates one of Angela's teaching techniques, miniature stories. She uses vivid descriptive and narrative elements to bring her teaching to life in memorable language. Another tiny but

28 because the angels of eternal life will be with us insofar as we will partake of the angelic life.

29 Now to the task, with courage! Therefore let us all embrace this holy Rule that God through his grace has offered to us.

30 And, armed with his sacred precepts, let us conduct ourselves courageously, like holy Judith after she boldly lopped off the head of Holophernes, that is the devil, so that we may be able to return gloriously to our homeland,

31 where from all those in Heaven and on earth great glory and triumph will arise.

lively story comes later in the Prologue with allusions to Judith, a biblical heroine (Pr.:30, 31).[11]

Despite her awareness of temptations and evil, Angela was joyful and hopeful. People were attracted to her. The Prologue suggests the sources of that joy. When her road was *thorny and rocky*, she nonetheless recognized a heavenly presence. From experience she could encourage her daughters, in another counterpoint, that *our every pain and sadness will turn into joy and gladness, and thorny and rocky roads we will find flower-strewn for us, paved with finest gold* (Pr.:27). She could see flowers as well as thorns. The very rocks glowed as she realized that her way led to God (Pr.:26-28).

Joy had lighted her heart for forty years. In the field at the Brudazzo, she had seen a vision of angels and women on a ladder between heaven and the olive grove, her workplace. That moment started her along the path which she called *angelic life* (Pr.:28) because it faces heavenward. In times of uncertainty, she remembered that moment of vision and decision. She wanted to continue in the same direction. She recognized that *the angels of eternal life will be with us* (Pr.:28). Grounded in Scripture, she recognized angels as expressing God's presence, as did the three visitors who stopped at Abraham and Sarah's tent (Genesis 17). She recognized the staircase that Jacob saw in a dream, resting on the ground, with its top reaching to heaven, "and God's messengers [angels] were going up and down on it." God was present to Jacob, saying, "'Know that I am with you; I will protect you wherever you go, and bring you back to this land. I will never leave you until I have done what I promised you." Like Jacob, Angela could exclaim, "Truly, God is in this spot!" (Genesis 28:12-16).

Angela speaks with great confidence about her direction and about the Rule, sure that *God through his grace has offered [it] to us* (Pr.:29). The Rule distills a wisdom learned through trial and error. Spiritual guides had helped her to understand life's lessons. *The Holy Spirit* had *[taught her] every truth* (Ch. VIII:16). Her amazing assurance was based on the Holy Spirit. Confident energy permeates the Prologue: *Now to the task, with courage!* (Pr.:29).

Courage is the motif struck by the only specific person Angela holds up as a model in the Rule (other than Jesus): the widow Judith: *let us conduct ourselves courageously, like holy Judith after she boldly lopped off the head of Holofernes* (Pr.:30). Though the subject of a book of Scripture, Judith seems an unlikely model for simple Brescians. She had seduced and beheaded Holofernes, general of the Assyrian army besieging her hometown, Bethulia. Renaissance art and story portrayed her as something of a *femme fatale.* Yet Angela was not one to allow female experience to be interpreted from outside, i.e., by men. Judith was a heroine: brave, good, devoted to her people, willing to take a great risk for them, utterly devoted to God, utterly trusting of God, clever, creative, dignified, strong and strong-minded. Clearly, Angela admired that Judith *boldly lopped off the head of Holofernes* (Pr.:30).

Angela may also have drawn upon the medieval archetype of the "virile woman." She invites Ursulines to act *courageously.* The English *courageously* translates Angela's Italian word *virilmente.* Scholar Barbara Newman describes the "virile woman" in this medieval tradition as "fearless, outspoken, always ready for death, unmoved alike by family ties and tyrannical force." Newman compares this archetype with the tradition of the "bride of Christ—intimate, impassioned, always ready for love—and moved by every suffering creature's pain."[12]

Angela's knowledge of Scripture showed her several further reasons to admire Judith. Holofernes, whom Angela makes a figure of *the devil* (Pr.:30), was besieging Bethulia. Judith saw war from the point of view of women's experience. She understood that God hates the rape that accompanies it, when "foreigners...had immodestly loosened the maiden's girdle, shamefully exposed her thighs, and disgracefully violated her body" (Judith 9:2). Angela too had witnessed the suffering that results from rape, including rape in war, especially in the aftermath of the 1512 Sack of Brescia.

Judith had challenged Bethulia's leaders to act in defense of the people and of God's sanctuary. When they patronized her with condescending compliments, telling her to go home and pray, she replied, "Listen to me! I will do something..." (Judith 8:32). Judith acted, trusting God completely. She prayed to God in the knowledge that "Your strength is not in numbers, nor does your power depend upon horses, nor have the proud won your favor" (Judith 9:16 [Vulgate]). In that spirit, she and her maid faced and outwitted the enemy.

It makes an exciting story, and not just for Scripture scholars. Judith was such an icon of popular culture in the early sixteenth century that it was easy to buy inexpensive pictures of her, demonstrating strength and courage as well as beauty and sexual appeal.[13] The Book of Judith is an adventure, spiced with danger, violence, and sexuality. Most of all, Judith illustrates how God strengthens those who trust. Like Judith, we must use our *own attributes and knowledge* while trusting finally not in them, but in God (Ch. X:12).

Angela clearly wants her daughters to learn what they can be—like Judith! Yes, they will face dangers and problems. A woman who is determined to *carr[y] through* (Pr:11) can overcome these adversities. Within her are the strengths she needs. *This sort of person will undoubtedly be able to take care of herself* (Pr.:13). God will help her to use her inner resources. No matter how powerful evil may seem, even if we feel alone in the enemy's camp, God will accompany us.

We can be as confident as Judith was, trusting that we too will go home victorious. She returned to her hometown of Bethulia, where the whole people shared in her triumph. We too *will be able to return gloriously to our* heavenly *homeland, where from all those in Heaven and on earth great glory and triumph will arise* (Pr.:30, 31). Eternal communion of joy with *all those in Heaven and on earth* is the Company's final goal.

Prologue to a Life

The Prologue serves its artistic purpose: setting forth the structure and the themes to be developed in the work which follows. It begins with God's call to *the newly begun life...called by the name Company of Saint Ursula* (Pr.:2). That topic is developed in Chapter I, "About the Manner of Receiving." The Prologue emphasizes the *means and ways that are necessary to persevere and prosper till the end* (Pr.:10). The Rule teaches how to begin this life (Chs. I-III), the spiritual practices to nourish it (Chs. IV-VII) and the Gospel ways of *holy obedience, sacred virginity,* and *poverty* at its core (Ch. VIII-X). The Rule ends in Chapter XI with the relationships that support this vocation. Our loving relationships will continue in our heavenly life (Last Legacy:15-18). Both the Prologue and the Rule end with a promise of eternal joy. While still on earth (Pr.:27, 28), we can glimpse *celestial glory* (Ch. XI:36). We will enjoy it forever in Heaven.

It is a simple life, after all, not complex. Though challenging, it does not require special skills or lofty education. Just a heart open to truth, ready to love.

Experience had opened up for Angela the God-dimension of the here-and-now, every creature existing within the existence that God shares with us (Ch. X:6). God flows into us, through us, around us. God's providence sustains us in our needs, fills us with abundance and joy (Ch. X:14-18). God's Spirit speaks continually in our hearts (Ch. VIII:14). Ursuline life helps people open up to this reality in ourselves and others and the whole universe—through faith and focus, through prayer and contemplation.

The Rule is a guidebook along a certain path. It is not the way for everyone. But for those who are called to walk it, it is not the way to a far-off heaven. The road passes through the heavenly dimensions of our world, our here-and-now. God is not far off at the end of the road. Jesus himself accompanies us. He said, "I am the way." He shows us the way. He stretches himself out for us to walk in him.

Every authentic spiritual path leads to God. Why do some women choose to follow this one? A daughter of Angela might say, "In gratitude for God's invitation! Walking the Ursuline path is how I live my thanks. It is a way that fits how God made me. It is consistent with who I am. It keeps me open to hear and see and answer, or at least it keeps me trying."

32 So now, all of you kindly be attentive, with great and longing heart.

So now, all of you kindly be attentive, with great and longing heart (Pr.:32).

Reflection

❖ *The story of vocation is always a story of call and response. Find a line or phrase that speaks to you of your own call. You are invited to express your own gratitude.*

❖ *The God who captured Angela's heart captures us. How do you experience God's call as a gift?*

❖ *Who might be the invisible, anonymous person(s) whose value has never before occurred to you?*

[1] Part 5A of this book (on the Rule's Chapter III) discusses the negative concept attached to the Italian word *mondo* and the neutral implications of *secolo*, both translated into English as "world." In sum, Angela's use of *mondo* here does not indicate a negative attitude toward life's ordinary surroundings.

[2] Luigi Fossati, *L'Opera e la personalità di S. Angela* (Brescia: Tipografia Opera Pavoniana, 1992), p. 33.

[3] Luciana Mariani, Elisa Tarolli and Marie Seynaeve, *Angela Merici: Contribution towards a Biography*, trans. M. Ignatius Stone (Milan: Editrice Ancora Milano,1989), p. 286.

[4] Mariani, Tarolli, Seynaeve, p. 161.

[5] This and all subsequent quotations from the English translation of Angela Merici's Testament (Legacies) are quoted from *Writings: Rule, Counsels, Testament*, translation by a team of Ursulines of the Roman Union (Rome: Ursulines of the Roman Union, 1995).

[6] Mariani, Tarolli, Seynaeve, p. 286.

[7] Mary Conroy, "Veni Sponsa Christi … Today," address to an Inter-Ursuline meeting of superiors general (Rome, May 4, 1991), addendum.

[8] The phrase so characteristic of Angela, *each one* (in Italian *ogn'una*) appears in almost all the chapters.

[9] Fire, the fourth, is suggested by "hell."

[10] In addition to the Sack of 1512, Brescia had suffered an earthquake in 1527 and floods in 1527, 1531 and 1532. [M. Ignatius Stone, *Commentary on the Writings of Saint Angela Merici: Rule, Counsels, Legacies* (England, 1996), p. 9.]

[11] The same narrative technique appears, for example, in the Fourth Counsel (dealing with an urgent problem) and in the Fifth Legacy (dealing with a recalcitrant Ursuline).

[12] Barbara Newman, *From Virile Woman to WomanChrist: Studies in Medieval Religion and Literature* (Philadelphia: University of Pennsylvania Press, 1995), p. 247.

[13] Margarita Stocker, *Judith, Sexual Warrior: Women and Power in Western Culture* (New Haven, CT: Yale University Press, 1998), p. 50.

Part 3

At the Heart of the Rule

At the Heart of the Rule

The Rule spirals inward to its center in Chapters VIII to X: "About Obedience," "About Virginity" and "About Poverty."

Spiritual and artistic vision guided Angela's dictation. Her Trinitarian spirituality flowers in this heart of the Rule. "Light" and "truth," work of the Holy Spirit, are keywords to obedience. The keyword of virginity is "sacred"; Jesus Christ is its entry-point into God. "Hope" sets the tone of poverty, hope in a provident divine Parent.

Angela knew well the power of the final word. The Prologue ends with an eye upon heaven and a *great and longing heart*. The Rule itself ends with heaven's promise of a *golden and brilliant heavenly crown*. She uses the same effect to punctuate each of these three central chapters with a verbal exclamation point. She wraps up obedience with *one's own integrity*, virginity with *a sacred jewel*, and poverty with *your good and joy*. Each closing phrase leaves us on a spiritual pinnacle.

Part 3, "At the Heart of the Rule," incorporates elements from Chapters I to VII as they support the three central Gospel commitments. (Part 4 of this book focuses in detail on Chapters I to III, which integrate new members. Part 5 treats Chapters IV to VII, on spiritual practices.)

Blessed Mother Angela opens her Rule and founds the Company on St. Catherine's Day, 1535. Painting in the crypt of the Sanctuary of St. Angela Merici, Brescia—formerly St. Afra Church—by unknown artist. Courtesy of the Centro Mericiano, Brescia.

The Holy Spirit – Holy Obedience

Alight with the Spirit

Their faces glow. Their simple black and white clothing allows the painter to focus our attention on delicate skin tones that hold an inner light. Inward attentiveness marks their expressions. Young though they are, these women seem self-contained, serene. Each holds a book, the Rule of the Company of Saint Ursula. At their circle's center, Angela Merici teaches them the essence of Ursuline life, which the Rule describes. Her gesture indicates the Rule's source, the Holy Spirit symbolized by the dove overhead.

The unknown sixteenth-century artist may seek to suggest that Angela's Rule flowed from divine inspiration. The image illustrates her openness to the Spirit's guidance. The composition pictures her faith that the Spirit presides over the Company and continues to inspire a faithful living out of the Rule.

Throughout the Rule and her other works, the Counsels and the Testament, Angela's words demonstrate that her trust in the Holy Spirit's guidance is completely foundational to the Company, to Ursuline life. Nowhere is that more evident than in the Rule's Chapter VIII, "About Obedience." Here she expresses her confidence that the Holy Spirit is the primary guide, who sends a voice of counsel and inspiration *continually...into the heart.* Her trust both in the Spirit and in each woman's ability to hear that voice underlies the freedom that so characterizes Angela's way of life.

Angela discusses obedience in the context of guiding Ursulines toward living by the Spirit's counsel, according to God's will. She describes obedience as a process of listening, discernment and decision-making. Her words presuppose the material of two earlier chapters of her Rule, which will therefore be discussed in this section. "About Confession" explains the spiritual practices which cultivate interior freedom. Thus equipped, the woman is ready to listen well and discern authentic obedience to God. "On the Manner of Receiving" guarantees the personal freedom of each Ursuline in choosing this life. It also puts in place a support system to sustain her freedom of action.

The Context

Obedience was required of women in Renaissance Europe, prized second only to their chastity.

English-speakers may find in Shakespeare's *Romeo and Juliet* a familiar story that illustrates the strictures, especially on an unmarried woman in her parents' home. When Juliet balks at the marriage her father has arranged with Lord Paris, Lord Capulet scolds,

> Doth she not count her blest,
> Unworthy as she is, that we have wrought
> So worthy a gentleman...?

She acknowledges her father's love in arranging this marriage but refuses it. He threatens,

> Fettle your fine joints 'gainst Thursday next,
> To go with Paris to Saint Peter's Church,
> Or I will drag thee on a hurdle thither.
>
> - Act III, Scene V

Later, when Juliet has decided to evade his power by feigning death, she makes peace with her father, also deluding him with words that most fit his understanding of their relationship:

> I have learned me to repent the sin
> Of disobedient opposition
> To you and your behests...
> And beg your pardon.
> Henceforward I am ever rul'd by you.
>
> - Act IV, Scene IV

Yes, obedience was the norm for women in sixteenth-century Italy. If the Renaissance brought new freedoms to men, it had little meaning in the domestic sphere. Women, especially single women, were at the bottom of society's tiers. They had little power for self-determination, either from social position or from wealth.[1]

Some of the first Ursulines were household servants. Living outside their paternal homes, they may have had some slight independence, depending on their employers' dispositions. However, their future security depended almost completely on marriage, which would consolidate their position within a man's control. Middle-class women lived in the familial home, but in a very dependent position. Other people chose their path in life, usually the men in their families. The higher the class the greater the pressure to marry for position, and the earlier the arrangements were made. Engagements were often planned in childhood, either informally or by contract between the fathers. Few indeed were the Juliets who had the strength of will to determine their own futures. Sadly, their alternatives may have been obedience or death.

Philosophers of the period (male, of course) commonly taught that women are weak-minded and morally inferior, more physical and more lustful than men and more vulnerable to demonic influence, and that men are more spiritual. So men assumed that they had moral authority, from their vantage point of superior spirituality and wisdom. They were more like God and had closer access to the divine. Women were to be guided, to obey.

One of the worst injustices of any oppressive system is the self-hatred it so often induces in the oppressed. Indeed, this factor is both a tool and a result of the system. All the more amazing that Angela Merici could emerge within this historic milieu with a radical new understanding of obedience grounded in a woman's *own integrity*!

The Rule

Did Angela Merici really say this: *We call upon each one to observe holy obedience*? The Angela who, as a headstrong teenager, resisted her guardians' plans for her? The Angela who declined to follow the Pope's wishes? The Angela who helped other women to make life-choices outside the patriarchal family, even contrary to it? The Angela who created a support system for women to control their own lives?

What could she mean by *holy obedience*, when she seemed to show so little conformity to authorities and systems? Yet she devotes a full chapter (VIII) of the Rule to obedience. To understand her meaning, we can explore how Angela's insights and practice grew from her own experience. The *holy obedience* that she recommends so earnestly may offer us a new understanding of a word that often sparks negative reactions.

Angela's Path to Holy Obedience

The young woman we meet in her teens or early twenties had a strong sense of her integrity. The vision in the Brudazzo field, an inner experience of God's call, shaped her vision of her own future, even though she could not yet see its outlines clearly.

It was at Salò, after her parents' deaths, that she began to learn a way of listening and following God that would ripen into holy obedience. Her uncle and aunt Biancosi were very kind. They were sure they knew what was best for her: getting married. In her heart, though, the Holy Spirit was whispering. To obey God, to follow this call, she had to be free. She had to listen in her heart. That was not easy. Everyone around her seemed so sure! Her own feelings clamored, too...the happiness of family life...being attracted to sons of her aunt's and uncle's friends, when she was introduced at weddings and dances...the flattery of compliments, especially about her blond hair—quite the fashion then![2]

But, in the quiet of her own room, she faced honestly the truth that these attractions did not resonate with the experience of her vision at the Brudazzo, with her own inner call from God. It would surely be possible to allow others' words and her own feelings to drown out the divine whisper. Truth told her that the Holy Spirit was inviting her to belong to God alone. It was truth that she chose to obey.

It was hard to stand up to the authority figures in her family. Amid stress and arguments she remained firm and loving. However, given to dramatic adolescent gestures, Angela was not always wise. To make her point about not seeking to attract a husband, she rubbed ashes into that blond hair. But she and her relatives kept communication open.

Furthermore, she developed relationships with the Franciscan friars and members of the Franciscan Third Order. Their understanding, and perhaps direct support, helped her carve out a freedom of action to follow her calling. Eventually, the family agreed.[3]

Listening clearly. Acting freely. This is Angela's holy obedience.

Angela wanted her daughters to *observe holy obedience* mostly because she had learned how it unites us with God. It is a way of listening to the Holy Spirit and then acting. It is not "doing-as-you're-told." That sort of compliance can be very unwholesome, even unholy. What she calls *holy obedience* is very different. It is first and foremost about obeying God. Only a very free person can practice holy obedience. Freedom is its foundation stone.

Freedom must have seemed remote for women whose lives were largely under the control of patriarchs in their families, in society, in the

Church. But Angela trusted that women can hear God's Spirit speaking in all the circumstances of life. She trusts that we can sort out God's voice from all the rest.

Angela's discerning heart did just that when she met the Pope.

When she and some Brescian companions made the Holy Year pilgrimage to Rome in 1525, they had the unusual honor of a private audience with Pope Clement VII. A papal chamberlain, Piero Della Puglia, arranged it, a man whom she had met in the Holy Land the year before. Angela respected the Pope, yet she did not do as he wished. The situation was intricate. Apparently Messer Della Puglia had told the Pope about the charitable works of zealous women and men in Brescia. A group of men, some of them Angela's friends, had begun a Hospital for Incurables. Women in Angela's circle provided a home, called the *Carità*, for orphaned girls. Messer Della Puglia may have mentioned Angela's role of encouragement and spiritual support. The Pope began to talk in that vein, referring to the needs among the charitable works in Rome. He asked Angela to remain there.

She must have taken his words very seriously. No doubt she prayerfully considered them. She also reflected on her growing understanding of her mission in Brescia. More and more clearly, her work among Brescia's women was taking shape as the meaning of her youthful vision in the Brudazzo field. When Angela weighed this inspiration against the needs in Rome, the answer in her heart was sure. No matter what other good was to be done in the world, her call was to Brescia. And there she returned.

Angela lived freely her obedience to God. She listened. She acted. In her Rule she shows us how.

Freedom and Obedience

Freedom and obedience may not seem to go together. But freedom and *holy obedience* do. God is always speaking to us, always leading us. Are we able to listen? Are we free to follow? Inner freedom grows in a continuing process of liberation from compulsions, from false values, from feelings of guilt and from the lingering wounds of trauma and abuse. For example, shaming words uttered decades ago can hold us back from success. Or we may work as drudges—to buy gadgets that advertisers convince us to "need." Or we may dedicate ourselves to competition, trying desperately to fill the bottomless pit of damaged self-esteem. How many people live in this bondage! Perhaps all of us, in different ways. Saint Paul complained that "I do not do what I want, but I do what I hate" (Romans 7:15) and called his plight "slavery."

Powerful forces may drive our decisions and actions, forces that enslave us to old wounds. They can speak so loudly inside us that we cannot hear more true and life-giving voices. We may turn a deaf ear to affirmation with "Yes, but...." We may shut our ears to Christ's challenging, inviting words. We may automatically reject the wisdom of a supervisor's instructions. A co-worker's need cries out, but we may hear only our own pain. Holy obedience requires freedom from such inner compulsions as these. Inner freedom opens us up. It helps us to hear authentic and healthy voices, to listen to God's guidance.

Freedom from outer constraints is also essential. Without it we may not be able to act as God directs. Outer forces often operate through cultural expectations. How many women have accepted a passive definition of a "nice girl"! Society limits our field of action, and closes doors we feel called to pass through. Many churches—certainly the Catholic Church—shut women out from full ministry. Social pressures force us into situations repugnant to our spirits. Economic pressures chain us in destructive relationships. A person who is limited in these ways may see what God asks of her. But she may be prevented from acting on what she sees. Society, family, church, work, relationships...any of these can confine us. Freedom in these spheres allows us to act, to take the steps that God's Spirit points out.

Angela's emphasis on obedience could be misused to reinforce a subservient position. However, it is important to recognize her audience. The women to whom Angela addressed the Rule already had a high degree of inner freedom. They had made an extraordinary choice about their lives. In the midst of many influences they had listened deeply. Most joined the Company in the face of opposition. Like Angela's aunt and uncle Biancosi, the more well-intentioned and concerned their relatives, employers and friends were, the more they tried to dissuade these women. We can almost hear Mama's words, "Now Lucia, be reasonable! You'll be an old maid. Who will take care of you?" And Papa's words, "Alfonso comes from a fine family. You'll marry him, and that's that!"

The alternative might be, "Your cousin Maria is in the monastery. We've decided that's just the life for you." However, since the monasteries required dowers to sustain themselves, religious life was not even an alternative for women of the lower classes.

Women's dependent position reinforced society's structures and economics. Without social or economic support for alternative choices, most women did as they were told, in taking a path in life and in the daily round of activity.

Supporting Freedom: Chapter I on Receiving

The Company turned that dependency upside down. The Rule's Chapter I, "On the Manner of Receiving," tells how the Company supported women in freely choosing a way of life. That was truly a revolutionary concept. Angela requires that the candidate have *the firm intention of serving God in this sort of life. Then, she should enter it happily and of her own will* (Ch. I:2-4). *Her own will!* Happiness indicates that her choice is free. The personal commitment required in this vocation comes from the woman's own heart and will. Only free and happy Ursulines will be able to observe this way of life. The Company has no means of compelling obedience, no interest in doing so. Each one practices it in her own home, in her own neighborhood, in her own heart.

Angela created an inventive process for receiving members into the Company. It is an amazing combination of vision and pragmatism. The Company reversed the usual social processes, in which a woman had little or no initiative. Instead, this process began when a woman wished to join the Company *of her own will.* Angela encourages her to discuss her decision with her parents or guardians, seeking their agreement, or at least their agreement to discuss the matter. Recognizing the situation of a single woman, her position in the family or household employment, Angela says that *she should first ask...permission* (Ch. I: 6). This was as much a given in the sixteenth century as it seems anathema in ours. This line is remarkable for what it does not say. Angela presumes that this Ursuline-to-be has chosen a life that has not already been determined for her—a situation totally outside the prevailing norms.

She continues with the strategy: *...so that the governors [women and men] of the Company may talk with [the parents or other superiors] so that [they may verify that] they do not have any legitimate cause if by chance they should afterwards want* *to prevent her from entering* (Ch. VIII: 7). Some of the Company's friends, widows and gentlemen, paid a visit. These older persons were on a more equal footing with the parents or employer. They asked about the woman's freedom to join the Company. It was important that she be really free of any contrary commitments. She must be unmarried and not engaged to be married. Nor could she have promised herself to a religious community. The interview would clarify the situation.

Once the friends—matrons and gentlemen[4]—had verified that there was no *legitimate* obstacle, the parents could not later allege something to prevent her from following her vocation (Ch. I:7). Some tried to. The "governors" guaranteed the new member's freedom. They would support her, even in the face of her parents' efforts to prevent their daughter from freely following her vocation. What a countercultural provision! Ursuline life was so much outside the norm that the practical measure of this support system proved necessary.

The Company enlisted power to serve the powerless. People with social position provided credibility. Their network made resources available and defended the economic and legal rights of the Ursulines. In the last part of the Rule, called "On Governance," and in her Testament, Angela explains more about how these people used their influence on behalf of the members.

As Angela describes the process in "On the Manner of Receiving," the Company's dynamics supported an unusual degree of personal autonomy for women. Making one's own choice of a way of life, and a highly unusual one at that! Enlisting people of social standing to support a dependent young woman in making such a choice! This process makes clear an important assumption about *holy obedience*. In a world where women's subordination and compliance were taken for granted, such is not the obedience which Angela counsels.

From "Mine" to "Thine"

Let us now look at how the Rule outlines Angela's strategies for *holy obedience*.

The women for whom Angela urged holy obedience had already demonstrated that they could choose freely. They were unlikely to confuse holy obedience with being passive or subservient. Their capacity for self-direction appears at the very beginning of the Rule and is intrinsic to the very first steps of Ursuline life. As we have seen, the Company (in the person of the "governors") acted on behalf of the future members' choice, their *own will* (Ch. I:4).

Angela confuses us at first when she uses the same phrase, one's "*own will*," at the beginning of Chapter VIII. Here she calls *holy obedience the only true self-denial of one's own will which is within us like murky hell* (Ch. VIII:1, 2). How negative! If we hope to follow her line of thought, we have to be patient and pay attention to that phrase, "*one's own*," in Italian *propria*. We must keep that expression in mind. It will reoccur at the end of the chapter.

Here, at the beginning of Chapter VIII, Angela is referring to what happens when we wrap ourselves in *murky* darkness, when our self is so narrow as to wrap us 'round, tightly closed off from others, from other voices. That's when "my own" is small and shuts out light. We are acting like the little child who hugs a toy tightly, repeating, "Mine! Mine!" It is a long road from "Mine! Mine!" to "Not my will but thine be done!"

In the course of Chapter VIII, we will find that *holy obedience* expands the notion of "*one's own*." It will grow to mean the self open to others, flooded with light, united with God. By the chapter's end, we will read Angela's amazing declaration of one's ability to find truth within *one's own* self when that self is opened to God's voice, God's messages spoken everywhere.

Every human being must go through a growing process into a larger, fuller self. Yes, even Jesus had to grow through his human limitations in this way. Even he had to stretch to embrace God's way fully. He struggled, agonized, saying, "Abba, Father, all things are possible to you. Take this cup away from me, but not what I will but what you will" (Mark 14:36). As the Letter to the Hebrews says, "Son though he was, he learned obedience from what he suffered; and when he was made perfect, he became the source of eternal salvation for all who obey him" (Hebrews 5:8, 9). We shouldn't be surprised if obedience is a struggle for us, too.

As always, Angela looks to Jesus as a model of life. He shows in human terms how to live God's way. Early in Chapter VIII, "About Obedience," she quotes his words, "I have not come to do my will, but that of the Father who has sent me" (cf. John 6:38; Ch. VIII: 3).

When she presents Jesus as the model of Ursuline obedience, she focuses on the essence of Jesus' *holy obedience*. That means doing God's

1 Again, we call upon each one to observe holy obedience,

2 the only true self-denial of one's own will, which is within us like murky hell.

3 But Jesus Christ says: "Non veni facere voluntatem meam, sed eius qui misit me Pater"; that is, I have not come to do my will, but that of the Father who has sent me.

4 Because obedience is in man like a great light which makes every work good and acceptable,

5 and so one reads: "Melius est obedire, quam sacrificare"; that is, obedience is better than sacrifice.

6 And the sacred canons say: "Nullum bonum est extra obedientiam"; that is, it is necessary for every thing of ours, if it is supposed to be good, to be done in obedience.

will. Let us look at this Gospel passage. (Angela, we must remember, was sought out even by scholars and preachers for her rich understanding of Scripture. They went away, Gallo says, "amazed."[5] When she makes a scriptural reference, we must assume that it has a wealth of meaning for her, and therefore for us.)

The sixth chapter of John's Gospel begins with Jesus multiplying loaves and fishes to feed a multitude. Enthusiastic followers wish to make him king, no doubt anticipating unending abundance. He eludes them on the mountainside. Meanwhile, the apostles set out by boat on waters that soon become dangerous, as heavy winds rise up. Inexplicably, Jesus is with them, settling the storm. Suddenly they find themselves safely at shore.

The next day, the crowds clamor for miracles and for more bread from heaven. Jesus responds that he is the bread from heaven, come "to give life to the world." This is where we find the verse that Angela quotes, *"I came down from heaven not to do my own will but the will of the one who sent me. And this is the will of the one who sent me, that I should not lose anything of what he gave me, but that I should raise it [on] the last day. For this is the will of my Father, that everyone who sees the Son and believes in him may have eternal life"* (John 6:38-40). Jesus' obedience meant uniting himself with God's will. And God's will is our eternal life. In that one-ness, Jesus lived out his mission. He nourished, healed, forgave. He drew people to God by showing them this face of divine love.

This is the divine/human example of obedience that Angela finds in the Gospel. It is God-focused. It is a way of sharing in God's life-giving love for the world. This obedience is not a matter of breaking one's will but of uniting it with God's will. It is progressive, a continual shaping of one's life by the Spirit's guidance. In that sense, God rather than self becomes more and more our point of reference, as God was Jesus' point of reference.

Everyone who sees Jesus with eyes of faith is led toward life. His humanity sheds light on who God is. He is the divine light shining in the world. Faithful obedience to God is *like a great light* (Ch. VIII: 4), Angela says—like the lighthouse at Desenzano on Lake Garda's shore, which shows the way into the harbor. Without it we are lost in dark and pathless waters, vulnerable to wind and wave. Jesus comes to save us from drowning. His light shows us the way to shore, the way home.

This light shines inside us. Holy obedience is not imposed from the outside. It radiates from our inner desire to be one with God. That desire and union naturally shine outward into our actions. *Holy obedience* lights our way to God by guiding our choices. It also shines through our deeds to illumine for others the way to God.

Union with God! That is the most important reality about holy obedience. Once again we meet this woman of passionate intensity. Angela is fervent in extolling obedience, saying that it makes things good, that (again quoting Scripture) it is *better than sacrifice* (1 Samuel 15:22; Ch. VIII:5). She even states that, *to be good,* all our deeds must *be done in obedience* (Ch. VIII:6). Even good deeds, even religious acts, can be done for the wrong reasons. We can do them for some personal benefit. Or we can do them by rote, without thought, without passion. Angela challenges us to keep alight our desire to live God's way. That is *holy obedience*.

Listening – The Voices and the Spirit

But how can we know God's will for us? All alone, the self may have trouble discovering it. Angela tells us: by listening. Listen to God present in all of creation. Then listen again, as God's Spirit whispers in our hearts.

She had felt God's presence. She had heard that whisper. She knew that God is the very Be-ing of our being. Everything that exists is in God, and God is in everything that exists. The God whose presence permeates creation is always reaching out to us from within the world. It is easy to find God's fingerprint in the natural world—in magnificent sunsets, powerful waves, gentle flowers, innocent babies. It can be harder to see the divine image in other women and men, even harder to listen for God's voice through them.

Competing messages swirl around us constantly. To know which voices carry God's guidance, we must always be alert. Everyone on our path can bear a message, even very surprising people and situations. Each of us is responsible for our own inner listening that clarifies what is of God, what is merely human and what is distorted.

The wisdom and counter-cultural perspective that the Rule embodies grew out of Angela's personal experience. She had learned to hear God's Spirit speaking in everyone and everything, above all in her own heart. She was an acute listener. Her honesty sifted the competing noises and heard the Spirit's voice. She had also learned to act from her own integrity instead of from outside pressures. She used freedom to serve God and others. The Rule includes her strategies for this *holy obedience*.

The Many Voices

Each of us has a God-given environment made up of people and resources. Angela uses her favorite pedagogical device, a list, to make her spiritual teaching specific and concrete. She enumerates voices. Consistently paying attention to them is important and rewarding. It is a way of finding God in the people and world around us, God in the circumstances of our lives. Angela speaks in the Rule about obeying them. Although *holy obedience* is always to God's will, it begins with open-hearted listening, a willingness to learn from everyone and everything. Then in the heart we sift what we have heard, seeking to discern what elements of it may suggest God's guidance. From listening and discernment we move to action, that is, to obeying.

This is how obeying God sometimes takes the form of obeying other people or government. Human and limited though they may be, they can signal God's guidance to us. Angela catalogues many forms of human authority. She then situates the capacity for and the responsibility of discernment squarely in the individual human heart.

Her list emerges from the circumstances of women in her time and place. First among these guideposts are God's commandments (Ch. VIII:7), not only the Ten, but other scriptural teachings. She was familiar with both Testaments. We notice throughout her writings how often Angela herself looks for guidance to the Bible and to Jesus' life. She quotes Scripture constantly. Usually these lines are in Latin from the Vulgate edition of the Bible current in her day. Often she then translates the biblical verse into Italian or paraphrases it. Her applications of these teachings show her openness to God's word. She lived the Psalmist's prayer,

> Your word is a lamp for my feet,
> a light for my path.
> - Psalm 119:105

Next, the Church's teachings are also very important (Ch. VIII:8). Truth—one of her favorite names for Jesus—has given us his Spirit in the Church to guide us. He has told us to listen very closely and respectfully to the Church's voice. Angela quotes Jesus' saying, *"who listens to you, listens to me; who scorns you, scorns me"* (cf. Luke 10:16, Ch. VIII:8). What constitutes the Church's voice? Who can claim it?

Angela tells us to pray *that God not abandon [the] Church, but reform it as he pleases* (Seventh Counsel:24). Clearly she does not think that all churchmen speak with the voice of Christ! In fact, in the Seventh Counsel she also warns us against that mistake, citing the possibility that *a confessor, or some other religious, [may] turn them away from some good inspiration* (Seventh Counsel:6). In Chapter VIII, she lists the Church and then, separately, *one's own bishop and pastor*. They are a very important part of the Church, of course. But we must not equate them with the Church. Brescia's unfortunate situation made that clear. Its absentee bishops did not serve their diocese. Brescia heard very little about them other than the collection of the taxes paid to them. Angela was grateful, though, for the service of Cardinal Cornaro's vicar, Lorenzo Muzio, who helped her obtain diocesan approval for the Rule in August 1536.

7 For this reason let each one want to obey: first, the commandments of God, since Scripture says: "Maledictus qui declinat a mandatis tuis"; that is, accursed is he who does not observe your commandments;

8 then, that which Holy Mother Church commands, because Truth says: "Qui vos audit me audit, et qui vos spernit me spernit"; that is, "who listens to you, listens to me; who scorns you, scorns me."

9 Third, to obey one's own bishop and pastor, and one's own spiritual father,...

Yet Angela did not consider that every word, even from the Pope, must be heard as the voice of the Church, or the voice of Christ, as we have seen. Out of respect, she would not have relished refusing him directly. She had listened respectfully to the Pope, and she had discerned the Holy Spirit's direction in her heart. The result of that process was clear to her. Her solution was to explain her sense of mission in Brescia and then to return home.[6] Angela had to pursue the integrity of her own mission.

Her *own*! *Propria*! That word again! Not the dark "own" that is *like murky hell*? She hoped not. She trusted not. By 1525, the fifty-year-old Angela had long been listening to others, to the Spirit's leading, and to the gradual unfolding of events in her life. She trusted the Holy Spirit's guidance through all these channels, over many years.

So churchmen are not necessarily the same as the Church. In Chapter VIII Angela distinguishes between the Church and churchmen, or churchwomen, for that matter. The Church is made up of the saints and sinners of all the ages. We may have to listen very carefully, very prayerfully, to hear how Christ speaks to us through the Church, especially in turbulent times.

Besides bishops and pastors, this list in Chapter VIII mentions a *spiritual father* (Ch. VIII:9), someone wise and experienced in the spiritual life; someone we can consult regularly in these matters. Angela's own early experience of spiritual direction came when she lived in Salò. The Franciscan friaries at San Bernardino and on the Isola dei Fratri, a nearby island in Lake Garda, drew many lay people in search of good advice and spiritual guidance.

Angela Merici had been an impetuous girl, eager to serve God. The Franciscans showed her how to pray. They taught her spiritual practices that developed stability and consistency. They must have challenged and cautioned this teenager as she needed. They invited her to serve God in others. They counseled her in observing the Rule of the Third Order of St. Francis, which framed her life of prayer and action. In the approximately twenty years after she had returned home to Desenzano, she periodically returned to Salò to visit her Biancosi relatives and to seek spiritual guidance from the Franciscans there.[7] When the friars asked her to travel to Brescia in 1516 to console the bereaved Caterina Patengola, she was a little over forty. In Brescia, Angela sought a *spiritual father*. Toward the end of her life it was Father Serafino of Bologna, one of the Lateran canons at St. Afra Church.

Unless we listen regularly to a wise guide, we tend to hear only the voice of that small self that needs to grow and grow. How do we identify such a person? There is no foolproof way to recognize wisdom. But a wise guide in the spiritual life should be prayerful, true to Holy Scripture in word and in integrity of life. S/he should be listening, perceptive, respectful. The person should have common sense and know human nature and the ways of God's Spirit. One touchstone might be, "Does this person lead me to my own deeper truth, invite me closer to God and encourage me to generous service?" Angela warns her daughters to avoid those who try to steer them away from the practices of Ursuline life or who begin to cross the boundary to inappropriate *familiarity* (Seventh Counsel:3, 6-11).

Angela also sought guidance from holy women. She visited Stefana Quinzani in Soncino and probably also when Stefana occasionally came to Brescia. As a Third Order Franciscan, she must have revered the Franciscan Saint Clare and Saint Catherine of Siena (a member of the Dominican Third Order). The frescoes in Isabetta Prato's oratory picture Saints Paula and Eustochium, holy women of antiquity. The simplest people and popes and queens had called these women "*madre.*" Many Brescians came to Angela for spiritual counseling. Even Francesco Sforza, Duke of Milan, asked her to be his spiritual mother. He visited her in Cremona and in Brescia, and she visited him on her way home from Varallo. Like Francesco Sforza, many called Angela "*Madre.*"

So why does Chapter VIII speak of a spiritual FATHER? Why not a spiritual MOTHER, a reality that was very much within Angela's experience? Clearly, we should listen to God's leading, even seek it, through spiritual mothers, too. But in her day men most often filled this role. Besides the force of custom, many people sought spiritual guidance when they went to sacramental confession, thus to a priest. Furthermore, in sixteenth-century Italy priests were usually the persons best trained in spirituality.

Responsibility, Relationships: Chapter XI on Governance

Angela lists other sources of wise guidance, for example, the people responsible for guiding the Company, which Angela saw as a spiritual family. We know little of Angela's early family life, where her attitudes related to obedience and to family may have been formed. The Counsels and Testament may hold clues. There she consistently uses familial imagery in speaking of the Company: sisters, mothers, even fathers.

The familial model that emerges, especially in the Rule's chapter "About Governance," is marked by the principle of subsidiarity. That is, matters should be handled as much as possible by those directly involved, not passed up and down a chain of command. Those closest to a situation have responsibility for it. Others assist according to their special competence.

(The following description of the Company's governance model refers to Angela's original conception, as outlined in the Rule. With time, many changes took place.)

First and foremost, each member of the Company is responsible for her own life. She makes her own decisions. Special roles of leadership emerge to handle special needs, but not to control the women's activities. For example, the members elect neighborhood leaders, the *colonelle*, to be *teachers and guides in the spiritual life* (Ch. XI:4). Colonelle have no power over the members entrusted to their guidance but assist those who face difficulties.

Another group, the *widowed matrons*, also consists of elected leaders (Ch. XI:2). Their function is to manage the affairs of the Company as a whole—shared activities, administering any income the Company may receive. They support Ursulines who need help in conflicts with family members or employers. They guide members in practical matters, providing instruction and correction when necessary. They make decisions about matters affecting the whole Company. Their decisions have the authority of loving concern, which Angela describes as motherly. But, she says, *not...anything done by force, because God has given free will to everyone, and wants to force no one, but only proposes, invites and counsels...* (Third Legacy:8-11).

10 and the governors [men and women] of the Company.

11 Furthermore, to obey their fathers and mothers, and other household superiors,

12 of whom we advise them to ask pardon once a week as a sign of deference and of preserving charity;

13 again, to obey the laws and statutes of the Lords and the governors of the republics.

All is invitational. The dynamic is anything but hierarchical. *Colonelle* and *matrons* work together to resolve difficulties which are beyond the resources of either group alone.

Even less is the Company patriarchal. Angela provides that *four mature men* function as *agents* on behalf of the Company, with the loving concern of *fathers* (Ch. XI:3, 6). When problems require legal or business expertise, the *matrons* enlist the assistance of the *four mature men*, also elected by the members. The men are to represent the Ursulines in spheres of law and business to which women did not have access. The distinctive "fatherly" quality is loving concern, not control. This perspective was quite unusual in the culture.

Does the Company's dynamic indicate that Angela grew up in a family that functioned with mutual respect and cooperation? Perhaps that is how she learned so early to trust herself. Trust became her hallmark. She trusted her own—and other women's—capacity to make sound decisions. She created a Company based on mutual trust and collaboration.

Listening to the *governors of the Company* is an important avenue of the Spirit's guidance on issues related to the Company and to one's living of the Rule. Respecting and cooperating with their authority shows that *one's own will* has expanded to include the common good.

Clearly, Angela is talking about relationships. *Holy obedience* may ultimately focus on God, but we live it in the web of life, a web woven of relationships. Authentic openness to God leads us to be open to others.

How true this is in the home, especially! Chapter VIII counsels obedience to *fathers and mothers, and other household superiors,* who might be relatives or employers or supervisors at work (Ch. VIII:11). Many early Ursulines lived in their family homes. If the father had died, the brother might be the head of the household, as may have been the case when Angela lived in Desenzano at the family farm through her twenties and thirties. A few older members of the Company may have rented rooms, but many members lived where they worked. Most employed women were household servants: maids, cooks, seamstresses, ladies' companions. Regardless of one's residence or job, respect and cooperation can light up the home or workplace.

In these relational settings, Angela encourages a regular practice of saying, "I'm sorry," being willing to acknowledge faults and offenses and to *ask pardon* (Ch. VIII:12). Being "right" is not so important as being in right relationship. The person who is always in the right is indeed blind and deaf to her own truth. That is the person who cannot see the bright light of *holy obedience*. She cannot hear the Spirit's voice.

So often, though, human authorities are domineering, unjust or abusive! What can we do in oppressive situations? If holy obedience is not about doing-as-you're-told, what alternatives are there?

Complying with injustice or abuse is definitely not *holy obedience*! This is where the Rule directs the Company to step in, just as when a woman seeks to join. Chapters I, III and XI identify situations where community leaders might be needed to support an Ursuline whose family or employer was bringing pressures contrary to her vocation, her safety, or justice in her economic interests.

In Chapter XI, "About Governance," Angela directs the *colonelle* to visit the Ursulines of their neighborhoods twice a month. One reason for these visits is *to check whether [her] household superiors may be abusive in any way or may want to hinder [her] from some sort of good or pressure [her] into some danger of evil* (Ch. XI:9-12). The *colonella* tried to help the member work out a way of handling the problem. If that was not successful, the *colonella* presented it to the council composed of *colonelle* and matrons. Often a matron could help work it out. She brought a certain influence to bear with a parent or employer, influence that unmarried and poor women did not have. If the situation required confronting a powerful person or involved business or legal transactions, the matrons or men were called in, depending on the problem (Ch. XI:13, 14).

So obeying *household superiors*, or any other human beings, is not absolute. Listening, respecting, cooperating, and—yes—obeying the just exercise of authority and responsibility: these serve the relationships and the common good. These habits may well be ways to obey God's will.

That is true for civil government, too, *the laws and statutes of the Lords and the governors of the republics* (Ch. VIII:13). Respect, cooperation, the common good. And the light of discernment to direct our actions.

Discerning the Voice of the Holy Spirit

Discerning freedom of choice, situated realistically in a family and society, was a prerequisite of Ursuline membership. The very process of choosing this life requires the ability to claim one's inner authority and be responsible for one's decisions. Angela tells women, even young women, so accustomed to conforming their whole lives to the instructions of outer authorities, that they can *continually* hear *the counsels and inspirations* of the Holy Spirit within their hearts (Ch. VIII:14).[8] Obedience requires that they continue to listen for God's voice.

Discernment again! The Holy Spirit is always inspiring our hearts, always counseling us, Angela insists. It could be easy, then, to jump to the conclusion that "Whatever I decide to do is right!" But it is not so simple. So far, Angela has explained the importance of outward listening to the voices in our world. Now she discusses inner listening to the Spirit. Just because a thought comes to mind, that fact does not necessarily mean that it is the Spirit's voice. There are other voices inside us, too.

Voices from our past life ring in our ears. Family members have crafted the lens through which we see ourselves and others. Their words of love or esteem or scorn or brutality or suspicion or generosity still echo in us. Since some parents think little of their daughters, many women have little sense of their dignity. Perhaps as a corrective, Angela emphasizes *what a new and wondrous dignity this [vocation] is* (Pr.:8). "*[S]o noble a flock,*" she tells the matrons (Prologue to the Testament:19), and "*[Y]ou must esteem them,*" she instructs the *colonelle* (Prologue to the Counsels:9).

Society's values are also inside us. Some may strengthen our spirits, but others are far from God. In Brescia, for example, vengeance was a powerful motive, often disguised as honor. We know how Angela influenced Filippo Sala and Francesco Martinengo, who were prepared to duel to the death under the influence of that false value. If we are honest, we recognize that our own nature is infected with sinful tendencies. Selfishness of all sorts speaks loudly. We often act out of pride or fear or acquisitiveness or self-indulgence or anger. That is a false obedience.

Be clear on this. In any situation, we will choose to act or not to act. We will obey. The question is whether we will obey God or something else. Will we obey our conscience or our compulsions? Discerning the

14 And above all, to obey the counsels and inspirations which the Holy Spirit continually sends into the heart,

15 whose voice we will hear all the more clearly the more purified and clean our conscience,

16 since the Holy Spirit is he who (as Jesus Christ says): "docet nos omnem veritatem"; that is, teaches us every truth.

difference is a lifelong process. We have to work at it. How are we to hear what God is saying through multiple, fallible voices?

A person who listens is no longer wrapped tightly in the narrow limits of the self which, all alone, is *like a murky hell.* She has opened herself, and in her heart has shone that *great light.* Wise guidance helps us to sort out conflicting voices. Experienced people shed light on our situation.

Honesty and Healing: Chapter VII on Confession

The issue is discernment, and Confession can be a tool of discernment. That is one reason why Angela includes Chapter VII, "About Confession," in the Rule, since the sacrament offers a source of spiritual guidance and inner honesty.

Confession involves much more, though. More deeply, Angela sees Confession as *a necessary medicine for the wounds of our souls* (Ch. VII:1). The wounds are our own sinfulness and others' offenses that have damaged or infected us. *In truth of conscience* we face and name our sins (Ch. VII:9). Let us be *totally sincere* (Ch. VII:9)! Let us take responsibility for our actions—exterior and interior. We face the confessor with our truth. Let us *ask forgiveness* in complete trust (Ch. VII:10). God's love for us was poured out on the cross. God's forgiveness is ours before we ask. Asking is our human act of reaching out for it, opening our hands and hearts to receive.

This *medicine* of Confession heals in a lifelong process. Our sinfulness and weaknesses persist in us, like the weeds among the wheat in the Gospel parable. The divine Farmer lets both exist side by side till the harvest. Tearing out the weeds could damage the wheat.

Confession contributes to discernment and obedience because within its process our own inner work and God's grace combine to *purif[y] and clean our conscience.* In direct proportion to that cleansing process, Angela explains, we are able to hear the Holy Spirit, *whose voice we will hear all the more clearly the more purified and clean our conscience* (Ch. VIII:15). This is the crucial requirement for holy obedience: honest effort and openness to grace, that our hearing may be clear of distortion.

Spirit-based Obedience

The Holy Spirit *teaches us every truth* (cf. John 16:13; Ch. VIII:16). We gradually learn to live by the truth. For Angela, truth is not an abstraction. She often uses *Truth* as her name for Jesus (e.g., Ch. VIII:8). His example, his Gospel—that is what the Spirit teaches us. If we act by the Gospel, we will be doing God's will. We learn to distinguish this voice of truth from false voices. It lights up our shadows. We grow from false obedience into *holy obedience.*

The Holy Spirit is the central principle in our obedience, guiding our response to God's call, guiding our prayer and actions, guiding the plans and decisions of the whole Company and of its leaders. The Spirit is the foundation of the mutual trust on which Angela constructed her Company. She provides in the Rule no mechanism of enforcement, no way to control the members. The Company depends completely on each individual's conscientious commitment. It exemplifies the charismatic moment of pre-Reformation Church renewal, in which lay Catholics turned to the Holy Spirit to restore and guarantee religious authenticity.

The Testament, probably composed a little later than the Rule, demonstrates an evolution based on practical experience. In her final words to the matrons leading the Company, Angela suggests ways of coping with the fact that some early Ursulines were not being consistent in their observance. Faced with inconstancies, Angela reminds the leaders, as we noted above, *not to want to get anything done by force, because God has given free will to everyone, and wants to force no one* (Third Legacy:8-10). She considers the possibility that *reproaches and severity* may *occasionally* be *necessary* (Third Legacy:13). Even *reproaches* can exist in the dynamics of a respectful and trusting relationship, when one is willing to use painful honesty, but not force.

It was risky for Angela to leave so much to individuals. Not everyone is at the same point of spiritual maturity or understands things the same way. That risk is the price of our freedom of conscience. She may have realized that the day would come when her daughters would take different views on the decisions before them. She prayed that such differences might not rupture their unity. Yet it did.[9]

If we weighed in Angela's scales the outer voices and the voice of conscience, conscience would be the weightier. A priority is established. The inner *counsels* of *the Holy Spirit* are *above all* (Ch. VIII:14). In *the heart* the sorting and sifting of discernment takes place. Each person must be responsible before God for her own deeds. Yet our conscience is not infallible. It depends on our open-hearted listening and on God's grace. At times we may even recognize that our confusion requires us to trust another person's judgment. A constant challenge!

Angela's prayer expressed in Chapter V acknowledges sinfulness in her own dark places, what today would be called her "shadow." This truth kept her humble. Humility may be the surest "hearing aid" for receiving the Holy Spirit's guidance.

Angela's way of obedience was far indeed from the norms of her world, where fathers and husbands and clerics usually made decisions for women—presumably weak-minded and morally inferior. Experience had shown Angela that the Holy Spirit speaks in a woman's heart as clearly as in a man's. The Company reflected that fact. No men held authority in the Company, and none held authority over it. The male *governors* acted on behalf of members and guided them in business negotiations and represented them in law courts, where women could not go. But they did not govern the members' lives. Nor were clerics involved.

Obeying God

Chapter VIII concludes with a sweeping statement: *obey God and each creature for love of God, as the Apostle says* (Ch. VIII:17). She paraphrases the *Apostle* Peter, teaching his community of disciples to "Be subject to every human institution for the Lord's sake..." (1 Peter 2:13). Peter continues, "Be free, yet without using freedom as a pretext for evil.... Give honor to all, love the community, fear God, honor the king" (1 Peter 2:16, 17). In other words, combine spiritual freedom with communal responsibility and relationships.

How can we obey *each creature*? Angela experienced God as the innermost reality of every being, reaching out to us and speaking to us from within all of creation. That is true for the natural world as well as for human beings (who are really an organic part of nature). Loving

17 Now, in conclusion, obey God and each creature for love of God, as the Apostle says,

18 as long as nothing is commanded against the honor of God and of one's own integrity.

God means respecting how God works in everything and treating it accordingly—the land, the animals, everything, everyone. Angela expresses the need to listen to and obey human beings. We also obey God when we listen to other creatures and allow what we hear to guide our actions. God is in them, too.

It is all about God. The challenge of this chapter is to be so adept at listening that we can hear God's word in anything and anyone, so honest that the self is freed of self-deceit, narrow limits and compulsions, and so discerning that we hear the Holy Spirit's voice clearly in our hearts.

The last line in Chapter VIII states Angela's final criterion for discernment. She says to obey...*as long as nothing is commanded against the honor* (Italian: *l'honor*) *of God and of one's own integrity* (Italian: *propria honestate*, var. *honestade*) (Ch. VIII:18). One's *honestate* is one's truth. The Italian words show that *honestate* is linked with *honor*. Truth. Dignity. God's. Ours.

One's Own...God's

Finally the question raised at the beginning of this chapter is answered. Finally indeed! The last words of Chapter VIII express the last criterion for discerning *holy obedience: one's own integrity: propria honestate.* "Own": that word from line 2, the word to watch for. At the beginning of Chapter VIII, Angela says that *one's own will...is within us like murky hell* (Ch. VIII:2). At the chapter's end, *one's own* is a blessing. Throughout Chapter VIII, she has been expanding the word, opening it up to fuller meaning. If we open our ears to listen and our hearts to act with love, our *own* expands. It is no longer so small as the self. We no longer think and act only in terms of our narrow self. We locate ourselves in community. We grow into God. The self is filled with God.

Filled with God! As we enter more and more deeply into God and into the truth of our own being, we find the point of union. God's Being, filling each of us and all creation, loves us into existence in our uniqueness. Yes, even with our flaws. When we experience ourselves and God this way, we eagerly search out how to live this union in the concrete actions of our daily lives. This is our deepest, truest integrity.

Despite all that has been said about listening, it is not enough. We must act. *Obey.* Listen for the truth of God that each creature reveals, listen to the voice of the Spirit, and act on what you hear. Angela locates the Spirit's counsels in the heart. A person as passionate as she knows the energy for action that emerges from the heart.

We listen. We follow the example of Jesus. Angela repeatedly stresses the importance of acting in response to God's gracious self-revelation,

God's invitation to *a new and wondrous dignity* (Pr.:8). The Prologue frames our actions in loving gratitude. This is *holy obedience*.

Reflection

❖ Have you ever found a conflict between external and internal voices?

❖ How does the situation of women around you compare with that of Brescia's women in Angela's day?

❖ For Angela, freedom is foundational to obedience. What aids your growth in authentic freedom?

❖ Does Angela's idea of *holy obedience* challenge you to listen more earnestly?

❖ Does Angela challenge you to move away from compliance in any particular situation?

❖ Consider the environmental implications of Angela's summary, "obey God and each creature for love of God."

[1] Germanic influence in parts of Northern Italy degraded the greater equality of the sexes which existed under Roman law and led to a kind of permanent dependent state of guardianship for a woman, "without a penny at her own disposal." [Fossati, p. 22.]

[2] Cesare Vecellio's engravings of Renaissance-era clothing includes one (#112) of a "Venetian woman bleaching her hair in the sun on a rooftop gallery." She has drawn her locks through the open crown of a wide-brimmed hat that presumably protects her fair complexion. [Cesare Vecellio, *Vecellio's Renaissance Costume Book: All 500 Woodcut Illustrations from the Famous Sixteenth-Century Compendium of World Costume* (New York: Dover Publications, Inc., 1977), p. 33.] See p. 22.

[3] Unmarried women were not usually accepted into the Third Order before the fifteenth century; their lives were usually more confined because of concerns about their chastity. [Gabriella Zarri, "From Prophesy to Discipline: 1450-1650," trans. Keith Botsford, *Women and Faith: Catholic Religious Life in Italy from Late Antiquity to the Present*, eds. Lucetta Scaraffia and Gabriella Zarri (Cambridge, Massachusetts: Harvard University Press, 1999), p. 89.]

[4] "Governors" in feminine and masculine forms in Italian: *governatrici et governatori*.

[5] Gallo in the *Processo Nazari*, Appendix 16 of Mariani, Tarolli, Seynaeve, p. 601.

[6] Mariani, Tarolli, Seynaeve, p. 204.

[7] Two discussions of Franciscan influence on Angela's spirituality appear in Gianpietro Belotti's "Influssi francescani sulla spiritualità di sant'Angela" in Gianpietro Belotti, *Angela Merici: La società, la vita, le opere, il carisma*, ed. Gianpietro Belotti (Brescia: Centro Mericiano, 2004), pp. 62-71, and in "The Christology of St. Angela Merici" by Mary Germaine Thorburn, OSU (Unpublished paper, 1975).

[8] Angela understood this listening to the Holy Spirit to be direct, unmediated. Several decades later, the Borromean alterations to the Rule interposed a clerical interpreter for the women.

[9] The schism that followed her death and lasted from 1545 to about 1558/59 is not within the scope of this work.

The Mystic Marriage of St. Catherine by Girolamo Romanino (1484/87 - after 1559). Memphis Brooks Museum of Art, Memphis, TN; Gift of the Samuel H. Kress Foundation 61.202.

Christ at the Center – Sacred Virginity

The Mystic Marriage

At the center: Christ. This focal point of Girolamo Romanino's painting says visually what Angela Merici explains in her Rule's Chapter IX, "On Virginity." Christ is at the center of the Ursuline heart. Romanino painted this *Mystic Marriage of St. Catherine* to commemorate the foundation of the Company of Saint Ursula on Saint Catherine's feast day in 1535. It serves as an aesthetic expression of the Company's life and meaning (a reality to be developed more fully in the last section of this book).

The Christ figure is not only the technical center of the painting. He is the focal point of all eyes, even those of Ursula, who faces forward. Angela's folded hands point to him. The painting's major diagonal, moving up from the lower left of Catherine's skirt, through the Virgin's shoulder, to Ursula's banner in the upper right, passes through the outstretched hands that are the point of mystic contact, as Christ places a ring on Catherine's finger.

Romanino sets the sacred scene overlooking Brescia in his day. The mystic moment occurs in the here-and-now. Here is its message. Our world shimmers with the presence of God. God reaches out to us from within our world. We touch Christ in daily life. The Company of Saint Ursula is based on this truth, this experience. Magnetized to Christ, through consecrated celibacy we are invited to focus our total selfhood, to shape our lives around that relationship. The world is not apart from God. It is the sacred context for living deeply in God.

The Context

The approach to Chapter IX "On Virginity" requires dealing with historic, cultural and linguistic issues even in the very title. We must explore the word *virginity* to know, "What did this mean for Angela? What did it mean for her world? For ours? What does it mean for us?" (The following pages summarize developments in western European and Euro-American cultural and religious attitudes. This was Angela's context. Her daughters in other cultural streams enrich the discussion with their distinct perspectives.)

To begin at the beginning, what is "virginity"?

The Many Meanings of Virginity

The common answer, common to both eras, is that virginity is a PHYSICAL CONDITION of a person who has not experienced sexual intercourse. Because marriage is a general expectation, *virginity* often carries the message of "not yet" or "until." In other words, VIRGINITY IS AN INTERIM STATE, AWAITING FULFILLMENT. A culture which expects sexual relationships before or alternative to marriage sees the virgin as inexperienced, naive, even afraid. In this context, virginity is a negative and a virgin is described by negation, by what is not.

A patriarchal society, such as sixteenth-century Italy, defines women by their relationship to men. So a woman is daughter, wife, mother, perhaps sister. Before her marriage, a daughter is defined as a "virgin," a word often equivalent merely to "girl" or, in English, "maiden" (thus, "old maid").[1] A woman related to men outside the family is defined as a prostitute or whore. An unmarried daughter is a commodity whose marriageability serves the purposes of the family. She is exchanged to create familial alliances, preferably to the social or economic advantage of her birth family. For the family into which she marries, her function is to provide a male heir. She must come into the marriage as a physical virgin to assure her husband's family that their property will truly pass to one of their own blood.[2] Not only is the woman a marketable quantity. So is her virginity. Without it, her value plunges. In this scheme, virginity is not merely negation. It is a thing, SOMETHING PHYSICAL, AN INTACT HYMEN, SOMETHING ECONOMICALLY VALUABLE.

In early Christianity, some women chose a celibate life because of the powerful attraction that God exerted on their hearts. Jesus had demonstrated God's presence to women directly, not mediated through fathers or husbands. He counted women among his disciples. This "discipleship of equals" survived into the first Christian communities before being squelched by patriarchy. Some women committed themselves to celibacy as a way to live their relationship with God, through Jesus, in semi-autonomy. Barbara Newman says that they "invented new ways of being women precisely because they tried to be Christians first."[3] In this spirit, VIRGINITY IS RELATIONSHIP. The nature of the relationship came to be expressed as espousal, an intimate, life-long partnership of love, heart and body reserved exclusively to the divine Lover. Since Jesus was the clearest human expression of God, the phrase "spouse of Christ" developed as a term for this shaping of one's life in the love of God.

These early Christian women took charge of their lives; some connected loosely in female-directed communities.[4] Especially in the ancient world, patriarchy reacted to this alternative as to a challenge or threat. Such a life-choice took tremendous courage and often resulted in martyrdom, as families and the state tried to bend these women to their predefined role in the world. This is the real meaning of the stories of Agatha, Cecilia, Barbara, and so many others.

Shortly after the age of the martyrs, and for another thousand years, European thought was influenced by neo-Platonic dualism. This philosophical system separated spirit and body and placed the former above the latter. It affected theology and spirituality in many ways. Men were identified (by men) with spirit, women with body. Supposedly more corrupted by the Fall, women needed to rise above their bodies, above their entire female nature.[5] Virginity seemed to fulfill this imperative. For example, the virgin martyrs of the early Church were reinterpreted by male writers and preachers. The ancient understanding of their bold witness of faith was lost. Instead, they came to be venerated primarily as refusing sexual contact. Names like Agnes and Agatha stand for a myriad. Their lives were retold to support this misunderstanding, as women seldom controlled the processes of writing, preaching and art, through which their actions were interpreted.[6] In this frame of reference, VIRGINITY IS SPIRITUAL SUPERIORITY.

Elaborate social subsystems developed to safeguard a young woman's (but not a young man's) virginity. In some cultures this has involved actual confinement of girls. In many places their movements have been restricted and chaperoned.[7] A mystique developed around virginity, supporting the cultural norms. Religious ideas were among the strongest pillars. Virginity was equated with innocence, even holiness, as though sexual experience were rooted in sin. Mary of Nazareth, often called simply "the Virgin," inhabited a marble pedestal far above the things of the flesh.

Women who did not marry remained perpetual daughters and sisters. Presumably and by definition physical virgins, they were restricted and dependent. Actually, women of the working classes were often less restricted than those of higher classes. The more wealth rested on one's virginity, the more closely it was guarded. Working women's dependence on fathers and brothers was often replaced by dependence on employers. For these unmarried women of either class, VIRGINITY WAS A SOCIAL POSITION.

Meanwhile, the Church had a long tradition of religious life. Women (again, not men) were presumed to enter this life-long celibate state as physical virgins. Monastic life had emerged in the early Middle Ages as a communal way to live consecration to God. Within the tradition, Benedictine and Cistercian mysticism saw the loving soul as one who stands for the real Bride of Christ, the Church.[8] For those embracing the life with authenticity, a community of women can be an energizing matrix of spirituality, intellectual pursuits, even the arts. Hildegard of Bingen was a multi-talented genius who flourished in monastic life.

Sadly, many a woman found herself in a monastery because of familial decisions. Maybe the family could not afford a large dowry to attract a "suitable" husband. Or perhaps she was sent to a monastery so that a larger dowry could be settled on her prettier, more marriageable sister. In some instances, families sought control of a monastery's resources by settling a cohort of sisters or cousins there.[9] Very uneven motivations led to life-long celibacy. But it was supported by the mystique of virginity, supposedly far superior to all the physical dimensions of married life: sexual intercourse, child-bearing, parenting and household labors.[10]

Much medieval literature for nuns emphasized chastity as the essence of women's consecration. This perspective fostered a piety that was self-contained and static rather than social and dynamic.[11] The relationship with God through Christ was often portrayed in sentimental and even eroticized ways. This approach reduced the strong spousal image to a trivialized picture of a Bride of Christ, wherein VIRGINITY IS A SPIRITUALIZED SUBLIMATION. It can disguise one's flight from sexuality. Though most women who embrace this image eventually grow through it to a fully adult spiritual life, the stereotype remains: forever a bride, forever naive and innocent, forever a girl, a spiritually romantic girl.

In the monastic setting, women's days involved a full round of prayer and work, humor and conflict and friendship, art and organization. Nuns could—and still can—develop their personhood at some distance from attitudes that demean women. Self-governance called upon a range of skills and roles not open to women in the wider society.

Women were socialized by other women into positive self-under-standing.[12] Yet the focal point, the center around which the life together turned and still turns, is the common commitment of celibate consecration. Here VIRGINITY BECOMES A WAY OF LIFE.

As religious life developed in the eighteenth century into apostolic ministries outside the monastery, many women and men adopted the rationale of "celibacy for the sake of the Kingdom." Their ideal is to give themselves so completely to the service of others that they forgo marriage, family life and all couple relationships. Celibate, same-sex communities powerfully support their dedication and work. Celibacy opens up their hearts in LOVING SERVICE TO GOD'S PEOPLE. Examples are legion; the most famous recent name may be Mother Teresa of Calcutta.

Our era's psychological perspective offers other definitions of virginity. For both men and women it may be seen primarily as a state of inexperience. When so much emphasis is placed on self-realization, the virgin is one who has not developed certain physical and affective dimensions of her/himself, important ways of love and commitment. Insofar as the human person is complete only in relationship, the virgin seems to lack an essential element of personhood. Thus VIRGINITY IS SEEN AS INCOMPLETENESS.

More positive light shines upon another approach. Neither spouse nor parent, the virgin belongs to herself. Her potential is hers to unfold. Her life-force is hers to direct. A figure representing such self-contained strength is Joan of Arc, a powerful woman in fifteenth-century France and an icon for some feminists today. In her, VIRGINITY IS PERSONAL POWER.

Some women and men find themselves irresistibly drawn to give that full self to God. They encounter a Person who loves them, and their own love surges in return. Nothing will satisfy them but a life shaped around this love, be it exchanged in contemplation or in service or both. For them, VIRGINITY IS A RESPONSE TO LOVE.

This is Angela.

We find many definitions of virginity:

a physical condition

a negative

an economic quantity

relationship

spiritual superiority
a way of life
sublimation
focus for service
incompleteness
personal power
response to love.

Contemporary Issues

The twenty-first century raises some new issues around "virginity." For example, the phrase "secondary virginity" has been coined recently for or by young people. Some who have been sexually active decide to be chaste, to be celibate until they marry or otherwise commit themselves. They choose to link sexual relationships with serious life-commitment. Young people invoke "secondary virginity" to reclaim this sort of integrity. The term reinforces their choice as a self-definition. Their moral considerations and esteem for chastity reinforce a value to be found in virginity.

In another development, not new but receiving new attention, people choose temporary or life-long celibacy for reasons of mental, emotional, and spiritual focus.[13] Renewed interest in spirituality and in the spiritual dimension of all creation validates this choice. These contemporary attitudes show that virginity, in some form, continues to be meaningful to many people.

It is difficult to shake loose from our focus on the physical definition of virginity alone, difficult to allow other elements to define virginity in some other way. However, we have let go of some of the other definitions as outdated. For example, in most of Western society, physical virginity no longer has economic value as a requirement for marriage. Also, we have rightly set aside ideas of spiritual superiority; we value sexual intimacy as potentially holy. Though the spousal image remains a rich scriptural vein for us to mine, saccharine images of the Bride of Christ belong to a bygone day.

A chapter with the title "About Virginity" risks being dismissed with one of the definitions we find meaningless. But, recognizing how many possible definitions it may have, let us ask Angela for hers. Two seemingly contradictory clues may help us discover it.

A Newly Begun Life

First, the opening lines of Chapter I "About the Manner of Receiving" say, *[R]emember how each one who will be entering or be admitted into this Company ought to be a virgin and should have the firm intention of serving God in this sort of life* (Ch. I:1, 2). What sort of life? The life of the Company? Or is virginity understood here as a way of life? Or are both true, that is, the Company is a *newly begun life of virgins* (Pr.:2)? The Prologue makes it abundantly clear that Angela means a way of living in response to God's invitation.

Our second possible clue is the fact that, within Angela's lifetime, the Company admitted a member, Marta, who was the daughter of a *colonella* called La Pizza. Was this *colonella*, then, a member, as the Rule requires? If so, Angela must not have considered a physical state as the summation of virginity. La Pizza must have had *the firm intention of serving God in this sort of life*. To be honest, however, we must admit the possibility that a widow was selected to fill the position of *colonella* for some reason. That situation did occur after Angela's death.

In any case, Angela's topic in Chapter IX is a way of life, a way of love received, responded to and shared.

Before we explore that with her, we might reflect again on the word *virginity*. A translator faces a challenge whenever the usage of a word in the original work has shifted in the receiving language. For example, both the words *homo* (Latin) and *man* (English) were once considered as equivalents for all human beings. We might argue about whether they ever really affirmed the full humanity of anyone but men. Regardless, English usage has shifted in such a way that *man* is no longer an accepted term for all human beings. Therefore, the word *man* is not a correct translation of *homo* in many texts.

When we look at all the overtones of the word *virginity*, both positive and negative, we see that it no longer carries the sense of a way of life that Angela meant to convey. Today a more useful term might be "consecrated celibacy." This expresses a way of life which does not depend on a physical condition or any previous sexual experience or lack thereof. Rather, it speaks of commitment and implies the One to whom consecration is made, a gift of body, heart and spirit, of our power to love and to give life.

Sacred

Angela calls this life *sacred virginity*. She speaks of one *voluntarily making a sacrifice to God of her own heart* (Ch. I:2). We may need to look at the word *sacred* and the related word *sacrifice* nearly as closely as we looked at *virginity*. Again, we leap to the assumption that we know what *sacred* means: holy. No! It really means "set aside," "devoted to God," "con<u>sec</u>rated" (derived from the same root word as *sacred*). A cup or a dish set aside for use in the Mass is not holy. It has no virtue, no sanctity. Yet it belongs to God. Any vessel could be used, then returned to the kitchen cupboard. A cup intentionally set aside only for God's service has been consecrated. Just so, virginity is not in itself more or less holy than any other state. The virginity that Angela is preparing to discuss is something that has been given to God.

What is *sacrifice*? Ancient Israel, like many societies, regularly presented gifts to God in sacrifices, rituals of offering. Such gifts became sacred. The people took fruit, grain or an animal and made it sacred (in Latin *sacrum facere, sacrificere*, "sacrifice") by giving it to God. Most sacrifices were offered, then distributed back to the offerers to be shared in a meal. In this sacred meal the participants came closer to God, who had first given them this gift. They had made a grateful return of it, and God had now given it back to them. The meal sealed the mutual exchange of life. Both sacrifice and meal directed the worshippers' and diners' awareness to the divine Giver.

The Jewish Passover meal is the sacrifice most familiar to Christians, because this was Jesus' "Last Supper." He and his disciples shared a meal, gave thanks and ate the lamb which had been sacrificed in remembrance of the Passover. Jesus instructed his disciples to remember him in the same way. We identify him with the lamb, slain as he was on Calvary. At his Last Supper, he looked ahead to this moment when he shared bread and wine with those around the table, saying, "This is my body, which shall be given up for you...my blood, which will be poured out for you." The preëminent sacrifice was Christ's self-gift, his life lived and poured out to the last drop for his brothers and sisters.

All these rich events shaped Angela's understanding. For her, a sacrifice is the gift given to God and shared with the community. It is sacred in the giving and sacred in the sharing. It nourishes those around the table. We shall see in the chapter "About Virginity" that Angela understands her way of life as a way of love shared with others in daily life.

Finally, we must put the two words together: "sacred virginity," a more amazing combination than at first appears. Some will find it incongruous. It challenges a point of view that virginity (consecrated celibacy) is meaningless or, at best, relevant only to girlhood or to a seemingly remote religious life. The phrase also challenges the world-view that would separate the sacred from the secular. It had been assumed that one went to the monastery to find the sacred. Yet the Company of Saint Ursula incarnates consecration to God in the midst of the world, in the so-called secular sphere.

Angela could combine these two words because she lived them both authentically. Angela Merici's genius was to find God fully present in her surroundings. So complete was her experience of God that she could call this way of life, in the world, *sacred*.

Having probed the words, let us now look to Angela, who offers her own description of *sacred virginity*. She teaches it in her Rule's Chapter IX.

The Rule

A Freely Chosen Life

When Angela begins this chapter with the exhortation *Let each one want to preserve sacred virginity* (Ch. I:1), she is speaking to women who have already heard God asking for their hearts. She offers them inspiration and practical guidelines on how to be consistent with the commitment at the center of their lives.

Opening Chapter IX with the exhortation to preserve *sacred virginity*, Angela implies a contrast. Her focus is not on physical virginity, a valuable economic quantity in the marriage mart. A sixteenth-century bride's family had tried to assure

1 Again, let each one want to preserve sacred virginity

2 not on account of making a vow through any human urging, but voluntarily making a sacrifice to God of her own heart,

3 since virginity (as, again, the canonists say) is the sister of all the angels,

4 victory over the appetites, queen of the virtues,

5 possessing all good things.

that she was a virgin. That was about her body, and also about her chastity as a virtue. But it was not sacred. Angela's *sacred virginity* is a freely chosen way of life.

Sacred virginity can certainly be a reality in monasteries. Myriads of nuns have heard the heart-call and have answered it in religious life. Unfortunately, many nuns of Angela's time had not made a free choice. They were sent into monasteries by their families. The market for dowries was so high in Italy that families often could not save enough money to negotiate a socially advantageous marriage for more than one daughter. Then parents chose which daughter would marry and which one would be sent to a monastery, where a lower dowry would be accepted. Furthermore, wars and ventures of exploration had so decimated the young male population that marriageable women out-numbered men. Parents who gave up on finding a husband might set-tle on religious life as the only possible future for their daughters. Such young women did not choose religious life as their vocation, though some found their vocation there. Of course, daughters had almost no choices about marriage, either. They made the vows their parents had chosen for them.

Brescian parents never chose the Company of Saint Ursula for their daughters. It offered no social advantage or security. No wonder we hear Angela so often repeat the motif *Voluntarily!* (Ch. IX:2) *She should enter it happily and of her own will* (Ch. III:3, 4). That is how women came to the Company, then and now. That is how we give ourselves to God. Heart, will, body. The whole. As Angela prays, *everything of mine, interior as well as exterior* (Ch. V:41).

Women in the Company of Saint Ursula have felt God's call course through our hearts, bodies and spirits like a magnetic power, stronger than all other attractions. What we feel called to is not primarily some-thing physical (or non-physical), but a way of life. Saint Paul talked about unmarried people who concentrate on "the things of God" (I Corinthians 7:32-34). He was not talking about their bodies, but about how they focus their energy, attention and time. The women of the Company follow a way of life that focuses "on the things of God" in the midst of the world.

This is the spirit in which Angela calls virginity *the sister of all the angels* (Ch. IX:3). We are reminded of the angels who appeared with her sister in the vision of the Machet and of the angelic ladder in the Brudazzo field, linking earth and heaven. There are echoes of Jesus' teaching that in the resurrection people will not be married, but will be "like the angels" (Matthew 22:30, Mark 12:25, Luke 20:36). Similarly, in the Prologue, Angela promises that *the angels of eternal life will be with us insofar as we will partake of the angelic life* (Pr.:28). To focus on God may be to anticipate and image heaven, a perspective that theologians call "eschatology." Angela finds a path to the heavenly through life's dailyness. Her eschatology runs through the world, not away from it.

In what sense can she call virginity *queen of the virtues, possessing all good things* (Ch. IX:4,5)? Virtues are generally lived in one or another aspect of life. We may exercise patience when strained or frustrated. We may be courageous in danger, compassionate toward the suffering, generous to the needy. Virginity, however, as Angela envisions it, refers to a whole life given to God. The totality incorporates all virtues, each practiced when appropriate. The benefits that enrich such a life make it royal—a *queen*—and wealthy—*possessing all. Sacrific[ing one's] heart* and *possessing all!* Once again we see Angela's intriguing polarities.

Angela speaks often about the heart. It stands for emotions, shifting though they are. Her sense of the heart is much deeper and fuller: the vessel of love. The love she talks of is her own experience, and ours, of Jesus as the One who reaches into the heart's core. He sees our truth. He touches it lovingly with the touch of God, and we become more alive. The heart rushes out in response, wanting to be grappled to him, him alone.

This was how God called Angela in her teens, with a call that deepened as she matured. The heart God gave her she gave back. She found that God shared love with her, multiplied in return. This is Ursuline life, this relationship, this exchange. This is *sacred virginity.*

Angela, and all of us, spend a lifetime growing into it. Virginity may sound like something to be kept intact, or even outgrown, not grown into. Yet growing into a relationship takes time. As a girl, Angela heard God's invitation, there in the field, among the angels. (After forty years, she could still hear their song.) Its melody rang in her heart and lifted it toward heaven. At that moment she had given herself to God.

Then she went back to work in the olive harvest. Then she began to live the gift. It is a long process. But its energy is love. The process involves bringing every part of ourselves into harmony. We hear Angela pray, *Keep my affections and my senses safe so that they may not lead me astray, neither to the right nor to the left, nor turn me away from your brilliant face which soothes every afflicted heart* (Ch.V:18, 19). When our appetites hunger for anything that turns us away from Christ, we ask his help to focus them on the All-good. When our habits lead us to sin, we seek forgiveness and God's grace to rein them in and help us develop healthy virtues instead.

Integrity: Chapter III on Interacting

Nurturing such harmony is the focus of the first few chapters in Angela's Rule. For example, Chapter III, "About the Manner of Interacting in the World," guides a new Ursuline's first steps in conducting herself as a *spouse of the Most High*. She practices ways of interacting and speaking that harmonize with her vocation. Our life is in the world. How we live it flows from inside. Far from holding herself apart, Angela hoped to teach and build up the people around her, simply by living in faith and love, interacting with them as Jesus would. This is the interaction that she calls her daughters to.

Chapter III lays out things NOT to do. The list has two functions. First, in learning ways of behaving that are consistent with her new life, a new Ursuline may have to make changes in what she has been accustomed to doing. Even if her actions before were not wrong, they may have been suitable for a different life, an uncommitted life. Secondly, there are some influences that we should try to avoid, and it makes sense to be honest about that. Even though she is continuing her regular activities at home or at her job, she does so now from a different point of reference.

Angela is instructing her daughters, as though she were to say, "The path of sacred virginity is not the path to marriage. For example, the flirtations that take place on balconies, the serenades, ARE the path to marriage. Parents want their daughters to be seen this way. Or they present their daughters at social occasions like weddings and dances and jousts. Aunt and Uncle Biancosi took me to these events so that young men and their families would see me as marriageable. My aunt paid special attention to my blond hair, so that I would make an impression. *Standing on the balconies* (Ch. III:4) is common in Salò, just as here in Brescia. With a chaperone present, it's quite respectable. People see that a woman is available. Because my heart already belonged to

Christ, I was very uncooperative with my poor aunt, until our family worked out an understanding that allowed me to follow his call."

Angela mentions other habits to avoid. Lingering in open doorways or standing around on the street (Ch. III:4) made a young woman seem even more available. Sometimes flirtations led to bad reputations, whether or not they were deserved. Some women got into the habit of receiving private messages from men, maybe passed to them by a servant or a relative. There is nothing wicked about these activities, of course. The issue is not about avoiding sins, but about making choices among good things, and then living out the choices with consistency and integrity.

Perhaps Angela could have just humored her aunt, but that would not have been honest. Her aunt and uncle would have kept working toward a marriage for her. It would not have been fair to them. And acting as though she were open to marriage would not have honored the One to whom she had given herself. Authenticity, one of Angela's major themes, resounds through Chapter III: inner spirit guiding outer actions!

Who knows? Maybe her own purpose and integrity could have been shaken, if she had traveled along another path. Angela liked to compare a way of life with a roadway. From her home in north central Italy, we might imagine her telling her daughters, "We need to know which road we're on and keep going. We'll never find out what Venice is like if we're walking the road to Rome."

Among her warnings is *not to deal with a bad sort of woman* (Ch. III:1). She does not say "a bad woman." We can know that a particular *sort of* person is bad for us without judging her soul. Angela alerts us not to make a practice of spending time with such companions. If we spend our time with people whose attitudes and activities are at odds with our values, we are choosing an environment that does not nourish our spirits. A plant absorbs what is in the air around it and in the water and soil.

She also warns of what she calls *dangers and various traps and diabolic snares* (Ch. III:7). Her concern is not unlike that of Jesus, who prayed for his disciples, not to be taken out of the world but to be preserved from evil influences (John 17:15). The world is God's creation, full of God's presence. Ursulines walk through it, are a part of it. They hear and see God in it. Nonetheless Angela, like Jesus, acknowledges the forces that can turn us away from God. They can trap us in materialism or selfishness or vanity. They can snare us with counterfeit love or admiration.

All around us are the vendors of these falsehoods, clamoring for our attention, just like the vendors at their stalls in Brescia's piazza on market day. They shout, "Here is a comb that will make you lovely!" "Here is a brooch that will make you look important!" "Buy this! Buy this!" Angela asks us to focus our attention inward, not to give it all to this world, not to give ourselves away to lies and emptiness.

Purity and Asceticism

Chapter III is mostly meant for a woman beginning this way of life. This is the beginning: learning to be authentic; her actions consistent with her commitment. Above all is inner authenticity. Angela's friend Antonio Romano dealt in fabric. When Antonio described a bolt as pure silk or pure wool, a customer could trust that it was so. That fabric was entirely what it was said to be, with no other threads woven in. This is our purity—to be fully and entirely what we pledge to be.

6 However, in every situation each one ought to conduct herself in such a manner that she not commit either against herself or in the sight of others anything at all that may be unworthy of spouses of the Most High.

7 Indeed, above all let her keep her heart pure and her conscience clean of every evil thought,

8 of every shadow of envy and ill will,

9 of every discord and evil suspicion,

10 and of every other bad appetite and wish.

11 Instead, be happy, and always full of charity and faith and hope in God.

The impurities that can stain such a life, according to Angela, are *evil thought[s]* of all kinds, *appetites and wishes* that turn aside from God (Ch. IX:7, 10). How can we remain in Christ's embrace if we sink into *envy, ill will, discord, suspicion* (Ch. IX:8, 9)? These pollute the heart. So this is what the Ursuline must give up. The asceticism of sacred virginity is to be emptied of these impurities. The result? Happiness! Angela encourages us to let our inner space be filled instead with *charity and faith and hope in God*. And to *be happy* (Ch. IX:11).

Many people hear the word "virginity" and think about sex. Angela spoke of *sacred virginity* and thought about love. It is about how our relationship with Jesus Christ opens our eyes to find God in all around us and to bring God to all around us, receiving and giving love.

Deeper into Love: Chapters V and VI on Prayer and Mass

If Chapter III is primarily for the beginner, Chapters V and VI tell how a relationship deepens: through prayer and daily Mass. In Chapter V, "About Prayer," Angela describes a way of prayer that reflects her own experience. This she teaches us. Each day she would go into her room, and into *the deep recesses of [her] heart*. There she would *raise her mind to God*. God *light[s] up* her heart, even its dark corners. Jesus shows her his *brilliant face*. She can take to him her sorrows, and he soothes her *afflicted heart* (Ch. V:15, 16, 19).

When the shadows of sinfulness threaten to overwhelm her, she *cr[ies] out* to him (Ch. V:20-22). He has assured her that he would not allow even her offenses to separate them. She gathers into her prayer her dear *father and mother, all [her] relatives and friends,...the entire world*, all burdened by sin and by its effects (Ch. V:24).

Jesus' blood [was] shed for love of us. For Angela, there is a triple equation: blood = passion = love (in any sequence). Each element stands always for the others, at the Last Supper, on Calvary, in every Mass, and in our own hearts. The fullness of life is poured out in suffering and death, given out of love (Ch. V:25).

Recognizing that proof of love, she yearns to bear witness, to tell everyone about it. How she wishes to *open the blindness* of people who do not see Christ's love for them (Ch. V:31-34)! Perhaps he asks us to heal their blindness by living his love for them, making it visible. Yet how meager and imperfect is the human heart! Angela begs him *to burn* away its impurities *in the blazing furnace of [his own] divine love*, just as the goldsmith burns the dross from gold. Then, by his grace, our *every affection and passion* are able to carry his love to others (Ch. V:36, 37).

In her prayer she gives again, each day, her whole self, each day's offering more complete. Her worthiness or unworthiness has ceased to be important. *Every thought, word and deed* belongs to God (Ch. V:40). That is not the result of her work but of divine love.

Angela prayed intensely in private. She also considered daily Mass so important to *sacred virginity* that she titled Chapter VI "About Going to Mass Every Day." *Our Lord* Jesus' love was poured out for us on the cross. Mass is where we enter that mystery most intimately. He comes to us in body and in blood.

Angela treasured *all the merits of the passion of our Lord* available to those who *participate* in the Mass (Ch. VI:3). Grace, a free gift, is not

12 And let interaction with one's neighbor be reasonable and modest as St. Paul says: "Modestia vestra nota sit omnibus hominibus"; that is, let your manners and prudence be evident to all, and let every action and speech be honest and polite.

13 Not naming God in vain.

14 Not swearing, but only saying with modesty "yes, yes" or "no, no," as Jesus Christ teaches.

15 Not answering arrogantly.

16 Not doing things unwillingly.

17 Not staying angry.

18 Not grumbling.

19 Not spreading gossip.

20 Finally, not doing any act, any deed unworthy especially of one who has the name of a servant of Jesus Christ.

21 Instead, let all our words, acts, and conduct always be to teach and edify those who deal with us,

22 having charity always burning in our hearts.

23 Furthermore, let each one be willing to be ready to die sooner than ever consent to stain and profane such a sacred jewel.

something we can merit. Only the Son deserves to share the divine fullness. He lived it faithfully, a human vessel of God. He lived his passionate love, lived it to the end, and beyond. He still wants to share the grace of divine fullness of life and healing with humanity. At Mass we hear his Word and join in his offering. We commune with him (Ch. VI:5). And just as his spirit flows out to others, so must ours.

Offenses against Sacred Virginity

This is why Angela talks about how to treat others in Chapter IX, "About Virginity." Love treats others with respect and kindness, in deeds and words.

She presents a list of behaviors to avoid, well aware that we cannot claim to be in love with the God that we do not see, as Saint John says, and neglect to love the neighbor we do see (1 John 4). It is easy to imagine that we love God. Ever realistic, Angela takes precautions against self-deception. She itemizes a series of offenses against *sacred virginity*. Besides misuse of God's name and *swearing*, she lists offenses against love of neighbor: arrogance, acting grudgingly, *staying angry*. She knows that we will get angry. Nursing the anger is what damages love. So do *grumbling* and *gossip* (Ch. IX:13-19).

These failings in love may seem small. Why do they matter so much?

In her day, servants of the great Italian lords would wear a badge or a special color showing which important personage they served. Whatever they did reflected on his house. It was seen to be done in his name.

Angela reminds her daughters that we are known as *servant[s] of Jesus Christ* (Ch. IX:20). She alerts us about what is not consistent with belonging to him. How can we represent such a Lord and treat others in ways at odds with his spirit?

Mirroring Christ

What behaviors ARE consistent with this vocation? We might take Angela's list and turn it around. An Ursuline should be reverent, should be a woman of her word, saying *yes, yes or no, no, as Jesus Christ teaches* (Ch. IX:14; Matthew 5:37). She should be respectful toward others, open-hearted, forgiving, cooperative. She should respect others' reputations. To sum it up, she should seek to act as Jesus would in every situation. Jesus was God's human face in Palestine (cf. Colossians 1:15). Angela mirrored Jesus in Brescia. Cozzano summarizes: "...everyone was compelled to say, 'God is here.'"[14] We are to mirror him too, each in our own corner of the world. The result will be teaching by our actions the way of the Gospel.

Similar teaching appears in the Fifth Counsel, where Angela advises the *colonelle* to instruct the women in their tutelage that, *in speaking, their words be...compassionate and leading to concord and charity. Tell them that, wherever they are, they should give good example.... And seek to spread peace and concord where they are. Above all let them be humble and gentle* (Fifth Counsel:12, 13, 16, 17).

Such a presence will build up the spirits of *those who deal with us* (Ch. IX:21). This is the fruit of good example and of something deeper and brighter—charity, flaming charity, God's love, *always burning in our hearts* (Ch. IX:22). Gabriele Cozzano described Angela in just such terms after her death: "...like a sun that gave light to all the others. She was like a fire, a conflagration of love, that set them alight. She was like a throne for God, which instructed them."[15] If we live deeply our relationship with God, we can become points of contact where God touches people, and people experience God. This is what our life means: belonging utterly to God, not just for ourselves, but on behalf of others.

Angela ends this chapter rather dramatically, asking her daughters to be willing to be ready to die rather than *consent to stain or profane such a sacred jewel* (Ch. IX:23). She knows that something which is not worth dying for is not worth living for. She calls that *something* a *sacred jewel*. In sixteenth-century usage, an unmarried woman's physical virginity was often called a "jewel": precious, hidden, and guarded.

However, what Angela has been describing throughout Chapter IX is *sacred virginity*, a way of life consecrated to Christ. She has described what would *stain* it: interior shadows such as *envy, discord, suspicion*. These and other *evil thoughts* can *stain* its purity. She has described what would *profane* it: actions bearing any stamp other than Christ's. Deeds that are selfish, egotistical, self-gratifying, unkind—these *profane* what belongs to God. Such stains and profanations are *unworthy of spouses of the most high* (Ch. IX:6) and *unworthy of one who has the name of a servant of Jesus Christ* (Ch. IX:20).

The Prologue to the Rule claims that our Ursuline vocation is God's invitation. God deigns to invite us. Gratitude is our response, shown by treasuring the precious gift. Christ has drawn us into an intimate relationship. Let us never consent to violate it! Instead, let us treasure it always. This jewel is indeed precious. It is beautiful. It is sacred.

Reflection

❖ This chapter views virginity through different cultural, historical and linguistic lenses. Consider how one of these ideas challenged or deepened your understanding. Does your own context offer further perspectives?

❖ Consecrated celibacy was counter-cultural in Angela's day. How does the world around you view such a choice?

❖ Were you surprised at the "asceticism of sacred virginity"? At the "offenses against sacred virginity"?

❖ Find in this chapter a line that reflects how you have experienced God's love. How do you feel called to share your experience of God with others?

---

[1] In this sense, unmarried girls were often called "virgins" with no intentional physical reference at all. The sleepy girls ("virgins") in Jesus' parable about the supply of oil in their lamps (Matthew 25:1-13) have often been misinterpreted as though their virginity were significant, whereas the significant element was really their readiness for God's coming.

[2] Constance Jordan, *Renaissance Feminism: Literary Texts and Political Models* (Ithaca, NY: Cornell University Press, 1990), p. 53.

[3] Barbara Newman, *From Virile Woman to WomanChrist*, p. 7.

[4] Rosemary Reuther, "Mothers of the Church" in *Women of Spirit: Female*

Leadership in the Jewish and Christian Traditions, Rosemary Ruether and Eleanor McLaughlin, eds. (New York: Simon and Schuster, 1979), p. 73.

[5] Ruth Leibowitz, "Virgins in the Service of Christ: The Dispute over an Active Apostolate for Women in the Counter-Reformation" in Reuther and McLaughlin, eds., p. 134.

[6] Reuther and McLaughlin, p. 17.

[7] Italian girls were generally chaperoned from the age of twelve till marriage. [Shulamith Shahar, *Childhood in the Middle Ages*, trans. Chaya Galai (New York: Routledge, 1990), p. 212.] This practice also ensured segregation in the workplace, into positions of lower skill and lower pay. [Margaret L. King, *Women of the Renaissance* (Chicago: University of Chicago Press, 1991), p. 70.]

[8] Newman, *From Virile Woman to WomanChrist*, p. 13.

[9] Maurizio Pegrari, "I giochi del potere: Presenza ed incidenza del patriziato nella società bresciana del Cinqecento" in *Arte, economica, cultura e religione nella Brescia del XVI secolo*, ed. Maurizio Pegrari (Brescia: Società Editrice Vannini, 1988), p. 225.

[10] Newman articulates reasons for a woman to "escape from...arranged marriage at puberty, a husband sometimes old enough to be her father, the likelihood of physical and verbal abuse, the legal and economic constraints of wifehood, the long series of inescapable, often life-threatening pregnancies" (Newman, *From Virile Woman to WomanChrist*, p. 6).

[11] Newman, *From Virile Woman to WomanChrist*, p. 8.

[12] Caroline Walker Bynum, *Jesus as Mother: Studies in the Spirituality of the High Middle Ages* (Berkley: University of California Press, 1982), pp. 184, 259.

[13] For an interesting chronology of this topic, see Elizabeth Abbott, *A History of Celibacy: From Athena to Elizabeth I, Leonardo da Vinci, Florence Nightingale, Gandhi, & Cher* (New York: Scribner, 1999).

[14] Quoted in Mariani, Tarolli, Seynaeve, p. 176. *Dichiarazione della Bolla*

[15] Quoted in Mariani, Tarolli, Seynaeve, p. 176.

Portrait of a Lady by Luca Mombella (1518 - after 1588). In the Pinacoteca Tosio-Martinengo, Brescia. By permission of the Civic Museums of Art and History of Brescia.

God Alone – True Poverty of Spirit

The Seamstress by Antonio Cifrondi (1657 - 1731). In the Pinacoteca Tosio-Martinengo, Brescia. By permission of the Civic Museums of Art and History of Brescia.

The Lady and The Seamstress: Two Brescian Women

The Lady gazes almost vacantly from Luca Mombello's (1518-1588) *Portrait of a Gentlewoman*. She wears the finest luxuries that sixteenth-century Brescia could produce or import. Mombello does not neglect her face or her graceful hands. But his attention is clearly on her adornments. Pearls, gold, precious stones. Silk fabric, gold thread, gossamer scarf. Brocade, embroidery, lace. Fashionable slit sleeves, trimmed in gold braid. The suggestion of a family crest in the border of her mantle.

The Lady wears these proofs of great wealth. We can be sure that her husband is a rich and powerful man.

But who is the person inside those clothes?

The Seamstress was painted by Antonio Cifrondi (1657-1730) a good deal later, when genre painting had created an interest in subjects of ordinary life and people of the lower classes. Brescian clothing styles had changed somewhat from those that Angela describes in her Rule's Chapter II, "How They Should Be Attired." For example, buttons have replaced lacing on the bodice. But we recognize the simple style, the scarf and the brown color which Angela recommends.

Here is a working woman. Cifrondi is less interested in the details of her work than in the effect of the window's light on the room, on her face and clothing, and on the thread. Simplicity governs the painting's composition, a simplicity suited to the subject.

And she has a pet!

The Context

By an odd reversal, the word *poverty* often leads us to think about riches. Poverty may be called a lack of material goods, if it is defined by contrast.

What was the material context of Brescia in Angela's day? What was the economic situation of the women to whom she addressed Chapter X of her Rule, "About Poverty"? What were her own experiences?

The Brescian Economy and Women

First, Brescia. To look at a map of northern Italy is to realize the crucial position that Brescia occupies, both the city and the larger province (including Desenzano). It dominates a route along Lake Garda to Trent.[1]

It lies on a fairly direct line between Milan and Venice, the two competing poles of regional power. Venice had for several centuries been the
trading center between Western Europe and Asia through the eastern
Mediterranean. When Angela was close to twenty, Christopher
Columbus of Genoa, sailing under the Spanish flag, opened Europe's
consciousness to a whole "new world." Its natural resources, e.g., gold
and dyes, almost immediately began to enter Europe from the west,
through Spain. Some of that trade passed into Italy through Milan.

Brescia, a central point between Venice and Milan, was a plum cov-
eted by the political and economic powers.[2] After French mercenaries
led by Gastone de Foix invaded, sacked and devastated Brescia in 1512,
the city found itself alternately dominated by the French, the Spanish
and the Venetians. Venice gained firm control in 1516-17. Through
much of Angela's life in the city, Brescia prospered. Its main industries
and trades dealt with wool and fabric. Nearby regions contributed iron
and wood products to the rebounding economy. In fact, eight years
after the Sack, Pietro Tron, the mayor, was able to report to the Senate
of the Venetian Republic that this city of 40,000 "did not seem as
though it had ever been sacked."[3]

As in most periods and places, however, prosperity in Brescia was
unevenly distributed by social class and by gender. In fact, the position
of women declined even in the upper classes as their economic functions were more and more restricted. The authority and power which
women of rank had often exercised in a feudal society dissolved in the
urban and commercial economies of the Renaissance era.[4]

Yet women had an economic role. On a farm, even a small farm,
their labor gave them a significant place in the rural economy. This was
also true in the domestic workshop. However, larger-scale enterprises
were beginning to dominate manufacturing.[5] Here, women workers
were separated from the family unit and their work was assigned a
lower value than when it was seen as part of an economic whole. In
the city, more economic functions took place outside the home and
were considered the province of men.

When Angela arrived in Brescia in 1516, the ravages of warfare had
disrupted rural society and driven many to seek employment in the
cities. Because their brothers succeeded to family farms, unmarried
women were marginalized and disproportionately made the journey
to the city. For them, the city offered mostly household work. They

usually lived where they worked. One Venetian parish recorded 250 female "productive workers" in the late 1500s, of whom 245 are listed as *"massare,"* that is, domestic servants or cleaning women.[6]

Women were also involved in textile production at all levels: winding and spinning, weaving, washing and dyeing, sewing, trimming and embroidery. They dominated the field in the Middle Ages. Progressively, though, the more profitable aspects were taken over by male-only guilds, which in Italy restricted women in the fifteenth century and excluded them by the sixteenth.[7] Low status limited women to low-paying work. At the end of the fifteenth century, women's salaries were roughly parallel to men's for similar work. By the end of the sixteenth century, the ratio had plunged by forty percent.[8] The daughters of families in craft production often assisted in the family business or were apprenticed elsewhere, for example, as lace-makers or seamstresses. A single working woman could earn wages, usually saved for her dowry.

Some employed women actually found a greater personal freedom in the city than they had experienced in the tight strictures of village and family life. However, their situation was often marginal and they remained dependent, if not on their own family patriarchs, then on their employers. Some, unemployed and adrift in cities, turned to prostitution. The census of 1500 counted 12,000 prostitutes in Venice.[9] In 1520, Pope Leo X expelled courtesans from Rome.[10] Both Catholic and Protestant reformers attacked prostitutes' recognized place in society, partly for reasons of morality and partly for fear of venereal disease.[11]

Even women of wealthy families had little or no control of material resources and no financial independence, unless they were widowed. (Angela involved widows as "lady governors" in support of the Company of Saint Ursula.) Any inheritance of land or money remained in the control of the patriarch. A woman's dowry passed from father (or uncle or brother) to husband, and the only disposition a woman could make of it was by bequest, i.e., after her death. If a woman wielded any influence outside the family, it was ordinarily indirect, through family position or any sway she had with her husband.

Marriage was the recipe for women's long-term social and economic security.

These were the economic situations of most women in Brescia. Prostitutes and courtesans made up two classes outside established society.

The Growth of Consumerism

Meanwhile, Europe was continuing its transition from feudal to commercial economies. Even landowners moved into the cities to participate in urban commercial developments, for example, from the rural Desenzano region to Brescia itself. Previously, land had conferred wealth and power. Now, money became more and more significant. How to display one's power in terms of money? With luxury consumer goods.

Because industries had not yet developed to create consumer goods for their own sake, luxuries appeared in the form of more and more elaborate versions of basic products, especially clothing. Fabrics and dyes and jewelry offered the most scope for the rare and precious—thus expensive. This period of the Renaissance has left visual records in art picturing men and women of fashion in their brilliant, often fantastical finery. These represent not only personal vanity but economic and social standing.

Angela and the Socio-economic Milieu

Angela herself had made the shift from country to city, though apparently not for economic reasons. She owned a small vineyard near Desenzano, which provided some modest personal income. From 1516, when an errand of mercy took her to Brescia, until about 1532, Angela resided in the large houses of her friends among the urban gentry. The widow Caterina Patengola belonged to a landed family with ties in the Desenzano region. Antonio Romano was a well-to-do businessman, a fabric merchant. Agostino Gallo had been born to a prosperous cloth merchant.[12] He gained local fame as an author whose philosophy of a healthy society endorsed the importance of agricultural life. Gallo sought to rebuild a virtuous, humane community in the aftermath of violence and demoralization.[13]

"Madre Suor Angela" held a place of respect in these homes. Amid their comforts, her personal conduct reflected great simplicity, even abstemiousness. She participated with the other women in customary household tasks. Angela bridged the social classes and financial differences that so visibly divided her fellow Brescians. Women came to her and joined the Company from across the classes. The fact that the majority were from the poorer classes reflects demographics: there were more poor people than rich people.

Angela's approach in Chapter X, "About Poverty," pays little attention to specific material conditions. The first two lines describe poverty of *temporal things* (Ch. 10:1, 2). The rest of the chapter expands upon *true poverty of spirit* (Ch. X:3). That is where she wants to take us. Spirituality must play itself out in the field of our actions and decisions and influence. For sixteenth-century Italian women, economic matters were largely outside that sphere. Therefore we should not be surprised that her chapter on poverty has so little to say about material issues.

Chapter II, "About How They Should Be Attired," does discuss some material details. We will find in these details clues about Angela's creative alternative to consumerism and class divisions. Her Chapter IV, "About Fasting," presents a spiritual practice which supports poverty of spirit.

Angela never measures. She does not give us a quantitative approach to poverty. The life-long *stripping* that she invites us to embrace goes ever more and more to the center. Despite her repetition of the concept of *stripping*, there is nothing meager or sparse in her language. It is redolent of wealth, fullness, delight, joy—in God. Her tone is absolute: *all, total nothing, stripped of everything, God alone, God alone.*

The Rule

The Rich and Naked Truth

Chapter X once again shows us Angela in all her intensity, at once wise and radical.

She tells us that poverty is the rich and naked truth about ourselves, the truth of what we are. We're so afraid of what we are: God's beloved. Each one of us exists because God loved her into being. Perhaps we are afraid that is not enough. In this chapter especially Angela claims that being God's beloved is the only reality that IS enough.

Yet we are blind to this truth, which is deeper than eye can see or senses can feel. Angela invites her daughters to use the eyes of faith and to trust their experience. Faith shows us God in everything and everything in God. The world is luminous with God. Angela's faith led her and leads us to the divine dimension of all that is. Faith underlies her directives on obedience in Chapter VIII, which is based on the belief that the Holy Spirit guides us through the many voices of creation and in our own hearts. Faith shows the sacred nature of the world. Here, in the world, we can touch Christ, in the consecrated celibacy she describes in Chapter IX.

This experience is delightful! Angela seemed delighted so often. Her friends described her glow, her warmth.[14] In Chapter X, "About Poverty," we sense that she experienced God loving her, enriching her, yes, delighting her. To this experience she invites the Ursulines.

True Riches

With few concrete directions, Chapter X nonetheless contains the secret of how to see and experience as Angela did. She seems to ask, "Are you willing to be stripped?" She asks that we *strive* and do more than strive (Ch. X:8); she calls upon us to *embrace* poverty (Ch. X:1). The word *embrace* evokes Saint Francis of Assisi and his joyful love for Lady Poverty. Angela did not intend that Ursulines become Franciscans. Yet she calls upon her daughters to *embrace* poverty. She might be asking, "Do you want the delight I've discovered?" If we answer yes, she is ready to tell us, "Embracing poverty is necessary, then. Yes, joyfully."

Why?

"To be stripped of anything that would come between you and God," she would say.

The Brescian women she spoke with did not have many belongings to be stripped of. What was the poverty to be embraced? Chapter X invited them to embrace their reality, including their lack of possessions. Angela offered a way of life wherein they might consider themselves fortunate to have enough to live with simple dignity and enough to share. And no more.

What that meant in practical, economic terms differed from person to person. Angela herself, inspired though she was by Saint Francis of Assisi, did not renounce all possessions, as Francis had. She owned a small vineyard in Desenzano. It provided her some income, and she paid taxes on it.

1 We call upon each one, finally, to embrace poverty,
2 not only that of temporal things
3 but above all true poverty of spirit through which man strips his heart of every affection
4 and hope for created things,
5 and of himself.
6 And in God he has all his wealth and outside of God he sees himself impoverished of everything, being a total nothing, and with God possessing everything.
7 But Truth says: "Beati pauperes spiritu, quoniam ipsorum est regnum caelorum"; that is, blessed are the poor of spirit, because theirs is the kingdom of Heaven.

The poverty she asks Ursulines to embrace does refer to material possessions, what she calls *temporal things* (Ch. X:2). Things matter, but they are only the beginning. In her Rule's Chapter X, "About Poverty," she talks about *things* (*cose*) and about *material things* (*robba*) and about *goods and wealth* (*bene*). She makes distinctions that raise questions for us: Are the material things I have good for me? Do they contribute to goodness for me? For others? If so, they are really *goods*, true *wealth*: *bene*. If not, they are just *things*, not wealth, no matter what price tag they have. We are better off without them. We need to be freed of anything that might fool us or anyone else into mistaking it for a cause of happiness.

Poverty of temporal things is the necessary beginning of *true poverty*. Angela establishes her priorities without neglecting either dimension. *Above all [is] true poverty of spirit through which [we] strip [our] heart* (Ch. X:3).

How can we strip our hearts? By turning to God instead of relying on any creature to feel ultimately satisfied.

Good people are probably not clinging to evil. But they may be wrapping themselves in created things to feel valuable or important or worthy, to feel good. Things like prices and pleasures. Things like prestige and pride. It is as true today as it was in Brescia's shops in 1535 that things are assigned a value by money. If fabrics are rare or ornaments require skill to produce, they are given a high price. The prices make us think they are more valuable. We think that something with a lower price is less valuable. We're not seeing the thing itself. We're seeing the price. Strangely, people even feel more valuable by having expensive shoes or rare jewels. We wrap ourselves in such things. Angela stresses that no thing can give a person the value that comes from being in God.

If we do wrap ourselves in these created things we are placing our hope in the creature, not in the Creator. We cheat ourselves. We prefer something, when God offers us everything.

Everything—it sounds like a contradiction of poverty. The chapter "About Poverty" is full of such seeming contradictions. It teaches that *true poverty of spirit* opens our eyes to all the *wealth* that can be ours *in God*. The line piles paradox upon paradox: *And in God [s]he has all [her] wealth and outside of God [she] sees [herself] impoverished of everything, being a total nothing, and with God possessing everything* (Ch. X:6).

We may be tricked into thinking of ourselves as though we stood alone, outside of God, unconnected. That's when we feel so small and worthless that we look for something to make ourselves feel good, valuable. But that is not true. We are not outside of God at all. Really, we exist in God. If we were outside of God we would not exist at all. The truth is what Saint Paul affirmed, that in God "we live and move and have our being" (Acts 17:28). In the Creator of all that is. *God alone (solo Dio*, Ch. X:13) is the source. *God alone* offers us the fullness of the *kingdom*. The reality is that we are rich. We possess everything. There is no thing to hanker after, to feel deprived of, to envy.

Cynics may look upon that promise as a trick—heaven. Be poor here and be rewarded later on, in heaven. Angela reminds us, *Truth (Jesus) says: "blessed (Happy) are the poor of spirit, because theirs is the kingdom of Heaven"* (cf. Matthew 5:3; Ch. X:7). Jesus says that the kingdom of Heaven IS, not WILL BE "theirs." Angela follows Jesus in affirming that happiness is found in poverty of spirit. We already have the kingdom of heaven. Here Angela calls Jesus by one of her favorite names for him, "Truth." He shows us the truest reality of our world, its deepest layer, its sacred dimension, which is so much more real than what the surface shows us. And it is good news! Jesus opens our eyes to see that all creation radiates God's love and presence. What is this but heaven? Jesus also told us, "The kingdom of God is near at hand, in your very midst" (cf. Luke 17:21). The secret is that only the poor of spirit are able to see it.

Radical Simplicity: Chapter II on Dress

Anyone who wishes to see this truth needs to practice seeing beneath the surface, or even disregarding surfaces. In her Rule, Angela offers some ways to develop such deeper sight. One way is practicing *simpl[icity]* in dress (Ch. II:1). That is one of the purposes of the Rule's Chapter II, "How They Should Be Attired."

On first glance, the fabrics and colors and styles that Angela discusses in Chapter II seem excessively detailed. What do these minutiae have to do with the spirit? Angela addresses them in order to lead Ursulines to look for and live by the truth, taking no false values as their guide.

It is not surprising that Angela paid attention to fabrics, after having lived fourteen years in Antonio Romano's household on the Vicolo Santa Agata. His fabric business was going on all around her: conversations about shipments, quality, exotic imported dyes, precious golden and silken threads. Customers came and went. Wealthy people were always looking for Chinese *silk* and perfect *velvet* (Ch. II:6).[15]

126

Shopkeepers would get excited about news of a shipment of dyes from the New World through Spain. Fashionable people were hungry for the newest styles and colors.[16]

Many of these Brescians had come to settle in the city from rural areas, some from around Desenzano, where they owned land. In the city money was beginning to be more important than land as a sign of wealth. They liked to display their wealth and social position by what they wore—clothing, jewelry, fancy shoes. The more elaborate the better, with ornaments like braid and flounces on the sleeves.

When a lady's portrait was to be painted, her husband wanted everything she wore to announce his wealth and position.[17] The lady fretted and worried about every detail, from buying fabric to planning her hairstyle. Some families shopped for these luxuries to dress up an unmarried daughter, to make her look more valuable to a prospective husband. Evaluating a woman on the basis of her clothing was standard procedure. A bride's trousseau was not only for her use. Each item declared to her new in-laws the standing of her birth family. The trousseau made up a percentage of the dowry and had to be appraised independently by two clothes dealers as part of the financial transaction between the families.[18]

Courtesans and wealthy prostitutes also dressed themselves to attract attention and business and to suggest that they were worth a high price. Some indulged in luxuries to compensate themselves for their lack of social acceptability.[19]

While all those clients were doing business in Antonio's shop, Angela was often receiving a different kind of visitor in the back of the house. Many were serving girls and women in the neighborhood. Some were seamstresses, their fingers always busy with *embroidery or other similar handiwork* (Ch. II:4). They might have been day-laborers or employed in wealthy families.[20] She heard how they stayed up late, straining their eyes in poor light, to finish *flounces or braid* (Ch. II:4) for their clients or mistresses to wear to a banquet. She knew the toll it took on their health and peace of mind, even on their freedom for relaxation and prayer.

The guidelines in Chapter II, "About How They Should Be Attired," prepare the heart for the profound message of her chapter on poverty: Be simply who and what you are, nothing more. Never anything less. Never the price tag.

Angela emphasizes dressing simply. She recommends that Ursulines wear *linen or cotton,...serge* (Ch. II:2, 3). These were the fabrics available to ordinary people. Colors like *tan, grayish, or a dark blackish* are the fibers' natural colors or the dyes that ordinary people could afford (Ch. II:3).

Angela herself regularly wore a *grayish* dress, the garb of the Third Order of St. Francis, as Antonio Romano noticed in his first meeting with her in 1516.[21] All Third Order members had that privilege, but most wore it only for their burial.

Angela was well aware that Saint Francis's father, Signor Bernadone, was in the same business as her friend Antonio. So Francis knew fabrics, too. He wore coarse gray or brown cloth instead of the fine fabrics his father sold. The color made a clear statement precisely because it was what most ordinary people wore, not what the prosperous Signor Bernadone marketed to his best customers. It was Francis's way of saying that he would be one of God's poor, simple people. He would rely on God, not on commerce, to fulfill his needs.

Angela never expected Ursulines to adopt Franciscan clothing when they entered the Company. Unlike nuns, Ursulines would not wear religious habits. For most of them, there was nothing to change. They were ordinary women and already wore quite simple clothes, not luxurious ones.

But what of the wealthier members? Some Ursulines belonged to the middle and upper classes and continued to live in their families. These women continued to wear what they already had, if there was nothing ostentatious about their clothes (Ch. II:4). When these articles of clothing wore out, they would adopt simple clothing, more like what their poorer sisters had always worn. The result was not that they would all look alike. But all the Ursulines would look more like each other than the wealthy ones would look like their rich relatives.

Thus simplicity in dress could have a major transforming effect. It is not about minutiae at all. Angela had invented a creative new way, a challenge and an invitation. Since clothing was a major signal of social class, this pattern of dress was radical and systemic. The Company does not have classes. The members are sisters.

No one is to have a price tag. No one. That is wealth beyond anything the markets or banks can give.

Of course, the root of this unity goes far deeper than dress. Angela addressed unity more explicitly in her Counsels and Testament.

Social Position

Clothing makes a statement, many statements. Simplicity says that even the members with social rank would not rely on the position that prominent relatives and friends might give them. Recognition and honor can be gratifying, even when they come from merely being linked with someone else. They can be just as false as price tags, though. A complete delusion! Angela, who moved with such ease and respect among all kinds of people, would smile at the foolishness of thinking oneself any more or less important or worthy because of family or social connections. Each person is honorable as a reflection of the Creator. Her chapter "About Poverty" teaches that the more deeply we live that truth, the more satisfied we are.

Family connections must be taken seriously, especially in Italy, where family is everything. Angela is not asking her daughters to renounce their families. How could we renounce the wellspring of our lives? Not at all. Many Ursulines lived with their families, as she did for so many years at Le Grezze. They shared the joys and labors of their flesh and blood. Angela delighted in her own relatives and friends. Even after moving to Brescia, she kept up family connections with visits to the shores of Lake Garda. She traveled with her cousin Bartolomeo. She counseled obedience to one's parents. But flesh and blood is not everything. God is everything.

Yet she calls for some sort of stripping (that word again!) with regard to family. She says to *strive to be stripped of everything and to put all [our] wealth and love and delight not in material things, not in food and over-eating, not in relatives and friends...* (Ch. X:8-11). Stripped of what? Of thinking oneself important because of blood ties or social recognition. Of making them our whole world and neglecting our wider human family. Of filling our hearts with these good loves so completely as to forget their Source. God wants to fill us. We will always be hungry until we turn to the Source.

8 And just so, let each one strive to be stripped of every thing
9 and to put all her wealth and love and delight not in material things,
10 not in food and over-eating,
11 not in relatives and friends,....

Hungry for God: Chapter IV on Fasting

Hungry! Hunger also functions to prepare the heart for *true poverty of spirit*, according to Angela's Rule. At first it seems surprising that she talks about *food and overeating* (*golla*, over-indulgence in the delights of the palate) in this chapter "About Poverty" (Ch. X:10). What does eating have to do with poverty?

It has to do with how we fill ourselves. Some people feel so hungry that they depend on food or other bodily pleasures to fill their hearts. That is their way of seeking to be satisfied, complete. But these attempts do not satisfy. Such people will always need more and more.

In terms of food, Angela seemed to be at the opposite pole. She fasted often and rather rigorously, according to the testimony of her friends, especially Antonio Romano and Agostino Gallo, at whose tables she ate.[22] The length of her Rule's Chapter IV, "About Fasting," indicates that she considered this practice *something indeed necessary and as a means and way* of Ursuline life (Ch. IV:1, 2). It is one of the ways toward true poverty of spirit.

She urges Ursulines to want to *embrace* fasting (Ch. IV:1). *Embrace* is the same word she uses to introduce poverty (Ch. X:1). Fasting is not easy to *embrace*. Even a person who is willing to fast may not readily *embrace* it. Clearly, Angela was enthusiastic about the importance of fasting. Chapter IV shows that she wants her daughters to hunger for its fruit, for openness. Openness is less about being hungry and more about making room for what God wants to give.

Angela knew what God wants to give us—the food and drink we need (Ch. X:15-17), but also *spiritual goods and benefits* (Ch. IV:6). Bodily fasting can help us open up our inner space to God. She never suggests that our fasting earns grace or conquers sin. God alone is the Source of grace. God is the one who does the work: *God, you who rein in vices through bodily fasting, [who] exalt the mind [and] give virtue and rewards...* (Ch. IV:5). Fasting is not an instrument that we can use to make something spiritual happen.

Bodily fasting is not a goal but a *means and way*. It has a purpose. When we fast properly, we focus less on our own impulses and more on openness to God. Then we are more ready for what God wishes to do for us. God will lead us to *true spiritual fasting* (Ch. IV:2).

True spiritual fasting means fasting from sin, from our sinful tendencies. We fast and God works. God is like a vinedresser. In her own little vineyard near Desenzano, Angela would prune so that the vine's vital energy would produce more abundant fruit. When she saw a diseased branch, Angela would lop it off to keep the vine healthy. God will do that for us, *lop off vices and errors* (Ch. IV:2), if we open ourselves to such cultivation. Fasting is one way of praying for spiritual health and fruitfulness.

Vices and errors are forms of evil. Angela says in this chapter "About Fasting" that the *throat—gluttony—was...the origin of all our evils* (Ch. IV:6). The suggestion is that Adam and Eve sinned through eating. They hungered—to be like gods. They did not embrace the rich and naked truth of who they were. They hungered to be what they were not. This gluttony led them to be ashamed of who they were, to hide themselves from God, and to cover themselves up. And humanity has been doing the same thing ever since. Angela asks her daughters not only to fast but to strip themselves.

Fasting helps address this source of evils, this hunger for falsehood. Fasting is a way of praying with the body. It is as though one said, "God, I want to empty myself, asking you to remove my tendencies to sin, asking you to fill me with spiritual gifts, with yourself. That is my hunger, for you to do your work in me."

The chapter "About Fasting" mentions many occasions for fasting, not only in Lent and the Church's other traditional days and seasons. Angela calls upon Ursulines to fast regularly on certain days of the week (Ch. IV:8-17). She knew the fruits of fasting from experience, and she wanted that blessing for her daughters. She wanted fasting and abstinence to be a part of the rhythm of their lives.

Angela's own fasting was quite ascetic. She ate fruits and vegetables, not meat, and drank water only, not wine. Yet this chapter does not prescribe the same pattern for others. She had found the right form of fasting and abstinence for herself and seemed to expect that each member could find her own way. She made no prescriptions. Angela's teaching is never about amounts, never something measurable. She teaches the spirit in which to fast and pray.

An individual's discernment about her own mode of fasting would come in consultation with her spiritual guide and a wise older woman (Ch. IV:18, 19). There were to be no excesses, no damage to one's good health (Ch. IV:20). Angela's own example indicated that the pattern of one's fasting might change in different seasons of life. For example, when she was sick she ate meat for strength.[23] She drank wine at feasts.[24]

From fasting to feasting! One who does not fast will hardly know how to feast. Angela wanted her daughters to mark feast days with special visits (Fifth Counsel:1). When she speaks of celebrating in anticipation of heavenly joy, she says *far festa*, "to make a feast" (Fifth Counsel:25). A festive banquet is also Jesus' favorite image of heaven.

Angela's treatment of poverty speaks much about delights and joys. They are implicit in her instruction not to put all one's *wealth and love and delight* in creatures. True *wealth and love and delight* come from God. She uses words of fullness, not of emptiness. This poverty is a rich experience.

Ultimate Stripping

The challenge to be stripped of ultimate dependence on creatures goes even deeper than material things, social position and self-indulgence. Angela adds another layer in Chapter X "About Poverty," one that is even harder to understand. What could she mean by not putting all one's *wealth and love and delight...in herself, nor in any of her own attributes and knowledge* (Ch. X:12)? This is the deepest stripping of all. She is moving closer and closer to the center, the center of the self.

How very complete is the stripping when we let go of our reliance on ourselves! Most people will achieve this grace only through failure, humiliation, illness or old age. It takes something drastic to pry loose our fingers, which cling so desperately to our control over ourselves, to pride in what we are or have achieved.

We may read those words and ask her, "But if I let go of all those other goods, what is left but my own attributes and knowledge?"

Angela may answer with a question: "Yes, what is left?"

"How can I even understand myself, except with my attributes and knowledge?"

"Probably only if they fail you."

"Fail!" We do not want to think of it.

Failure, humiliation, illness, old age.

And then we wonder, did Angela ever fail?

12 not in herself, nor in any of her own attributes and knowledge,

13 but in God alone, and in the kind and ineffable providence that is his alone.

Cozzano summarizes situations in which Angela "did not succeed in converting" sinners whom she was trying to lead back to God. "[A]t least she tried...to persuade him to do a little good, or a little less evil."[25] Someone who was willing to *shed my own blood (if I could) in order to open up the blindness of their minds* (Ch. V:34) must have felt deeply her failure to reach and help such people.

An early biographer, Mattia Bellintani, tells of such an instance. People often came to Angela for advice. Whenever she paid a visit to her relatives back in Salò, the house was crowded with people wanting to consult her. A certain priest visited her in anguish. He had a mistress living with him. While Angela was in Salò he would come to the house daily, seek her counsel, weep and repent. But afterwards he did nothing different. Nothing she said could help him resolve his anguish or change his life. He died without making peace with his own soul.

On the other hand, Stefano Bertazzoli later claimed that she had helped him to follow his vocation to the priesthood. He was a curious young law student who also visited Angela in Salò, all dressed up with an extravagant feather in his fashionable scarlet hat. Something about their conversation touched his spirit. She reminded him that he could be more than a feathered hat. He looked into his heart then and followed a calling which led him to become a dedicated priest.[26]

Angela's gifts, like ours, were just that—gifts. God makes use of them—or not. They are not the self.

It is hard to strip this far. Nature helps. Vulnerability, illness and old age all teach us to lean on God and on the people around us, not on our own strength. That begins to fail us. Angela experienced these losses, too. Her blindness forced her to depend on her traveling companions during the Holy Land pilgrimage. A few years later, the Gallo family invited her to join them in Cremona as Brescians fled from Emperor Charles V, who was expected to attack Brescia. Flight must have been a frightening experience. No one could feel safe, or in control of the situation.

Furthermore, Angela became ill in Cremona, so ill that she almost died. Girolamo Patengola—Caterina's nephew and Angela's devoted young friend—wrote an epitaph for her and read it to her as she lay on her sickbed, at death's door. It was a poem about her going to heaven. The anticipated joy of heaven seemed to revive her, and she recovered quite suddenly.[27] The experience may have shocked her into realizing that her life had nearly ended without her having completed her work, that is, without beginning the Company. She would have to turn to God for the strength to carry on. When she finally began the Company of Saint Ursula, she was firmly convinced that God had planted it (Last Legacy:6-8).

She had to depend on other people, too. Angela was an old woman by the standards of her day, past sixty. Her body was beginning to fail her. She needed help. Barbara Fontana shared rented rooms with her. No doubt Barbara took care of many tasks in their little home. The lady governors and colonelle became the leaders and spiritual teachers for the Company, assuming her original roles.

Angela no longer depended on her attributes, her own capacities, but on God's *kind and ineffable providence* (Ch. X:13). She knew Goodness beyond anything that words could say. God! The center of all that is! Possessions, food, bodily comforts, relationships, even ourselves—all are good. And all are partial. *God alone* is Goodness. In *God alone* we put our hope.

Wealth of Hope and Joy

Hope is about how we feed our souls. What we think gives meaning to our lives and value to our selves—that is where we place our hope. Where do we look for meaning, value, joy? Different types of people have different answers. Or people may answer differently through the seasons of life. Angela's advice on poverty is for this variety of personalities and ages among the Ursulines. Material possessions lure some people. To acquire treasure, they spend themselves. Others place all their good in bodily satisfactions. They have many pleasures but few joys. A third group know themselves only in the faces of others, according to their relationships. Belonging, being loved, being admired are the only ways they feel whole. Alone, they feel like nothing. Finally, some people look in the mirror and see only their skills and knowledge and successes. They hardly know who they are beneath these attributes.

To each group Angela advises, "Strip your heart of reliance on created things, of whatever sort. Stand naked before God. Embrace yourself just as you are in God. Love yourself as God has created you. Let everything that you wrapped around yourself, that you thought were your riches, that you depended on to fill your needs—let all of that be stripped away. What will you find? Wealth and love and delight! God provides these. God provides all that you need."

God provides what we need *to eat...to drink*, and every *temporal need* (Ch. X:15, 16). We have many needs besides food and drink. And many desires and expectations, perhaps not all of them actual needs. Maybe we need to reevaluate our list of "needs." We may find that we can be happy and satisfied, even without something that we had expected or longed for or lost. Instead of great emptiness, we will find a great full-ness. Instead of yearning for more, we will rejoice in what comes to us. Instead of calculation, we will know gratitude.

Poverty holds a rich treasure, peace of heart. The key to the treasure-box is hope. Jesus assures us, *"Seek first the kingdom of God, and all these other things...will be placed before you"* (cf. Matthew 6:33; Ch. X:14). Live by God's values, and you will have what you need. Angela echoes Jesus' encouragement to live without anxiety: *do not be anxious about seeking what to eat, nor what to drink, since your heavenly Father himself knows well that you need all these things* (paraphrasing Matthew 6 and Luke 12; Ch. X:15). It is a matter of whether the mind/heart/spirit is entangled in anxiety. One of the distinguishing marks of true poverty of spirit is a heart at peace.

The Rule's treatment of poverty ends with joy. Angela expresses no negative attitudes toward the material world. Rather, she urges her daughters to look more deeply into reality. She issues a radical invitation to the heart of all that is. Poverty of spirit flowers when there is nothing to depend on but God. That is good news—maybe by surprise. God loves to surprise us. We think we know what we need. Often God puts something else in our laps, something wonderful.

Angela shows that poverty and joy are about whom we trust. This chapter of the Rule is about hope in its deepest sense: to rely on God alone, to trust that God really does want goodness and joy for us, that God can and wants to and will provide. She *call[ed] upon each one to embrace* the truth that God alone *knows* what we need and *can* provide it, that God loves us and *wants only what is for [our] good and joy* (Ch. X:18).

14 But the Gospel says: "Primum quaerite regnum Dei, et haec omnia apponentur vobis"; that is, Seek first the kingdom of God, and all these other things of yours will be placed before you.

15 And it says again: "Nolite solliciti esse quod comedatis, neque quod bibatis: scit enim Pater vester quia his omnibus indigetis"; that is, do not be anxious about seeking what to eat, nor what to drink, since your heavenly Father himself knows well that you need all these things,

16 as if he would clearly say: "Do not be anxious about any temporal need,

17 since God—he alone — knows, can, and wants to provide them.

18 He wants only what is for your good and joy."

If we put our stock in God, our value and enjoyment are complete and eternal. Angela's list of partial goods (possessions, food, others, self, etc.) climaxes in the ultimate Good, *God alone,... the kind and ineffable providence that is his alone* (Ch. X:13). *God alone, solo Dio.* Angela's tone becomes absolute. She repeats this dramatic phrase: *God—he alone, Dio egli solo* (Ch. X:17) and God wants (*il solo*) *only what is for your good and joy* (Ch. X:18). Other words and phrases echo the tone, actually pervading the chapter: forms of *all* (*ogni*—3, 6, 9; *tutto*—3, 6, 8, 14, 15; *totalmente*—6) and *not any* (*non alcuna*—12, 16). *God alone* is the all in all.

Reflection

❖ Have you experienced that approach to the center of yourself through the stripping Angela describes? Have you found a gift in it?

❖ Angela was a "bridge-builder" among classes in her society. Where do you see a need for bridges?

❖ Consider whether your circle of "relatives and friends" is open to wider circles of relationships and concern. Give thanks for the people in both/all circles and for the different ways in which they show you God's providence.

❖ What would it mean to have enough to live with simple dignity and enough to share—and no more?

❖ Angela's key to poverty is hope. Where do we place our hope?

❖ A consumer economy tries to trick us into buying things to fill our hearts. How?

❖ Do you believe that God wants only what is for your good and joy?

---

[1] James M. Powell, *Albertanus of Brescia: The Pursuit of Happiness in the Early Thirteenth Century* (Philadelphia: University of Pennsylvania Press, 1992), p. 17.

[2] 1509: Defeat of Agnadello, entry of French troops of Louis XII into Brescian territory; the Gambara faction foments such disorder that the General Council of the city submits to France on May 23. 1512: The "Venetian party," captained by Luigi Avogadro, retakes Brescia on February 3, hunts down the Gambara faction and sacks their homes. They withdraw to the castello. Fifteen days later, the French arrive under Gastone de Foix and the Gambara party rushes down from the castello to join the French troops in sacking the city. About 10,000 are killed. In ensuing months all families with Venetian ties are proscribed and imprisoned and their goods confiscated, while the Gambara, Martinengo and other families take the spoils. Public executions and murders multiply and add to the general climate of violence and demoralization.

3 Transcription in the Merician Museum, Centro Mericiano, Brescia; translation by the author.

4 Jordan, p. 15.

5 King, p. 68.

6 King, p. 70. Venetian data represent trends typical of the northern part of Italy, much of which was dominated by the Venetian Republic.

7 King, p. 67.

8 Fossati, p. 27.

9 King, p. 78.

10 Hanelore Sachs, *The Renaissance Woman*, trans. Marianne Herzfeld (New York: McGraw-Hill, 1971), p. 52.

11 King, p. 78.

12 Mariani, Tarolli, Seynaeve, p. 139.

13 Gallo's *Ten Days of Agriculture* was later expanded to "Thirteen" and then to "Twenty" days.

14 Among others to describe Angela's impact on others was Gabriele Cozzano, *Dichiariazione della Bolla*, Appendix 24 of Mariani, Tarolli, Seynaeve, p. 649.

15 Despite Western Europe's increasing impact on imports and style, Italy was still a major source of fabric and fine fashion for Europe, even after 1520. [Doreen Yarwood, *Fashion in the Western World 1500-1990* (London: B. T. Batsford, Ltd., 1992), p. 9.]

16 Vecellio's costume book, published in 1590 in Venice, responded to the growing wealth of the mercantile class and to the interest in clothing as a way to demonstrate it, as travel and exploration sought both new raw materials and new markets. [Vecellio, publisher's note, n.p.]

17 Christiane Klapsich-Zuber, *Women, Family and Ritual in Renaissance Italy*, trans. Lydia G. Cochrane (Chicago: University of Chicago Press, 1985), p. 245.

18 Klapsich-Zuber, p. 221.

19 Shulamith Shahar, *The Fourth Estate: A History of Women in the Middle Ages*, trans. Chaya Galai (London and New York: Methuen, 1983), p. 209.

20 King, p. 67.

21 Romano in the *Processo Nazari*, Appendix 16 of Mariani, Tarolli, Seynaeve, p. 595.

22 Romano in the *Processo Nazari*, Appendix 16 of Mariani, Tarolli, Seynaeve, pp. 595, 596; Gallo, p. 600.

23 Giacomo Chizzola's words suggest that she ate meat when she was sick. [Chizzola in the *Processo Nazari*, Appendix 16 of Mariani, Tarolli, Seynaeve, p. 598.]

24 Gallo in the *Processo Nazari*, Appendix 16 of Mariani, Tarolli, Seynaeve, p. 600.

25 Mariani, Tarolli, Seynaeve, p. 176.

26 Mariani, Tarolli, Seynaeve, p. 180.

27 Gallo in the *Processo Nazari*, Appendix 16 of Mariani, Tarolli, Seynaeve, p. 600.

Part 4

A Spiritual Family

Hl. Ursula with companions, woodcut ca. 1460-1470. The Latin inscription reads "O how beautiful is the chaste generation . . .. In her train, maidens will be led to the king" (Psalm 45 [44 in Vulgate edition]). This image was probably created for one of the many confraternities of St. Ursula. (Timber panel pressure 5, NR. 21 [facsimile edition], courtesy of Stiftsbibliothek, St. Gallen.)

Together

A leader in the midst of her companions, Ursula stands as their inspiration and example. This German woodcut (ca. 1460-70) depicts Saint Ursula as a captain, with an arrow piercing her heart. A witness, not a victim, she shows how to live.

Saint Ursula and her companions—so the story goes—set out together on a journey that would take them from Britain to Rome and ultimately to their final destination, heaven. Ursula was the undisputed captain. She gathered the eleven (or eleven thousand) other women. Her example and encouragement inspired them all to commit themselves to Christ.

When an unexpected revelation told her that martyrdom lay ahead, Ursula convened her companions. Together they considered their options. No one would be forced. These heroines unanimously agreed to continue their pilgrimage. Their influence drew others. Angered by the witness of their faith commitment, pagan soldiers ambushed and killed them.

In this woodcut from around the time of Angela's birth, the companions' solidarity is evident. Together they sail their ship into the future.

The Context

The Company of Saint Ursula came into being in a particular place and time: Brescia, 1535. Brescia, in the easternmost part of Lombardy, had been wrested from the control of Milan and functioned practically as the westernmost area controlled by Venice, the Serenissima.

Angela's world and her place in it were conditioned very particularly by her being a woman, and even more particularly by her being unmarried. She and the other single women who made up the Company did not stand outside their situation and analyze it with sociological or demographic tools. Even the consciousness of history as dynamic and society as changing was only beginning to hatch. No doubt life as they knew it was just life.

All the more amazing, then, that Angela could imagine an alternative way of life. Of course she thought about her circumstances, but not about social theories. She experienced life, its joyful wellsprings and its burdens. She felt where it was painful, especially when the pain resulted from injustice or some other evil. She saw what could be different and how she and others could make a difference. These women could accomplish much for themselves, among themselves. She knew the value of each member, created, loved, chosen by God. She knew the wisdom that women are capable of, taught by one another and by the Holy Spirit. She knew the strength of their companionship, *like a mighty fortress or a tower impregnable* (Last Counsel:15).

For some situations Angela recognized the need for help and resources from women and men with social and economic power. She asked them to use their power, not just FOR the Company's members, as happened in the charity houses, but WITH the members, serving the members' needs as the members saw them. The men could be the Company's agents in places where the members could not act. The Company engaged them on its own terms, to fulfill its purposes. Though weak in social and economic terms, these single women were strong in spirit.

The Rule's Chapter XI, "About Governance," outlines the creative social network that Angela wove. She did not set out to change the basic outer circumstances of society, a concept that would have been foreign to her era. Nonetheless, she created a new way to live inside it—on the basis of women's strengths, shared.

Famous Italian Women

Italy had produced famous women in this very historic moment, women who made a splash through their public roles or unusual accomplishments. Some women carved out spheres of action or influence in their families or even in economic or civic affairs through sheer personal force, but most often behind the scenes.

Vittoria Colonna (1490-1547) was well known in Rome as an intellectual and a poet. No doubt many women felt an inner stirring when they heard about her, an example of what women could do if they had the education and opportunity. Yet these eminent women did not have the great riches of sisterhood that Angela's circle enjoyed, since they were usually at odds with each other, in struggles for power on behalf of husbands or sons.[1] The learned Caterina Sforza (1463-1509) electrified Italy when Angela was young by leading her husband's troops to victory at Forli in 1483, and often fighting on horseback, even during her pregnancies. When widowed, she seized power, briefly, as regent. She was a natural strategist and politician. Caterina was a first cousin of Angela's spiritual son Duke Francesco Sforza II, but much older than he and more involved politically with his father Ludovico il Moro.

In Brescia, before Angela's arrival, Laura Cereta (1469-1499) was respected for her humanistic education. Perhaps Brescian women smiled at how Laura refuted men's claim to greater intellectual powers and moral rectitude. Challenging tradition and perhaps with her tongue in her cheek, she argued that Eve's sin was NOT greater than Adam's, "For where there is greater wisdom, there lies greater guilt."[2] Brescia's Gambara family had an accomplished ancestor, Ginevra Nazarola of Verona, whose widowed mother had arranged for her and her sister Isotta to receive an excellent education.[3] Ginevra married Brunoro Gambara in 1438 and came to Brescia, where, long after her death, her memory remained a beacon of women's possibilities.

The Brescian Veronica Gambara (1485-1550) wrote anti-war poetry. Having moved away at marriage, she was back home in Brescia for her father's funeral in 1512 and was trapped there during its Sack by French mercenaries. As a young widow, she governed her late husband's domain, Correggio. She later established a distinguished salon.[4]

But these were all wealthy women, members of powerful families, like the ones that Baldassar Castiglione (1478-1529) wrote about in *The Courtier*.[5] No matter how educated they were, they were still defined by their roles in the world of men.[6]

Women and Education – Debate and Reality

Some learned men were beginning to write about women. They generally agreed that girls and women should learn to read — to increase their piety and domestic skills — always to make them better wives and mothers.[7]

Angela's reading contributed to her expertise in sacred Scripture; preachers and theologians sought her out. Giacomo Chizzola reported that she could read Latin.[8] She read a great deal, according to Agostino Gallo, apparently mostly "holy books."[9] Besides Scriptural texts, the works of the Fathers of the Church were available in Brescia.[10] Clearly, the male educational experts of the day were interpreting women's capacities from their limited vantage point, and to support their biases. In this as in all else, including the Company's governance, Angela was unconstrained by narrow expectations about women. As feminist historian Millagros Ortega Costa has observed, the sixteenth-century women who succeeded in self-actualization were those who consciously ignored the restrictions of Church and society.[11]

Angela had no formal schooling. On the farm, children learned from their parents all that was needed for rural life. A few of the early Ursulines, mostly the ones who had grown up in towns, may have attended small schools in their neighborhoods.[12] They would have learned a skill for work, like embroidery, and a little bit of reading. A few also learned to write, though Angela never did. This skill was taught separately from reading.[13] Some of the Company's early members from wealthier families learned to read at home, especially the ones with brothers. Families were more likely to hire tutors for their sons.[14]

The members who had been foundlings or were orphaned usually began to be servants very young.[15] A few girls were apprentices, either to a woman artisan or to a craftsman's wife.[16] Families sometimes considered a craft useful for girls who were not expected to marry, such as someone with a handicap.[17] They had no chance for schooling.

Childhood was short, and not always happy. Instead of sentimentality, it inspired economic concerns. Working-class families of modest means, like the Mericis, had a distinct advantage in building familial relationships. In wealthy families, infants were sent away to paid nurses, and girl babies were often sent farther from home than their brothers.[18] Boys were often removed from the family circle at seven, to learn "manly" things.[19]

Some very poor families abandoned their children, girls twice as often as boys.[20] A girl represented a mouth to feed and eventually a dower to pay. Some impoverished country people sold their daughters into service to city families, who might contract to maintain them and provide a dower "for love of God."[21] In this situation, a poor girl was completely dependent. Her employer stood *"in loco patris"* (in place of her father), with parental rights to approve her marriage.[22]

Domestic Service

Domestic service, the main form of employment for women, put female servants into quasi-familial settings, for good or ill.[23] Away from their parents, some even had a little freedom, depending on their situation in the employer's household. Many had to endure harsh masters and mistresses, sexual harassment and rape. Rape was not taken very seriously when the victims were servants.[24] If they became pregnant, they were dismissed for immorality.

Fortunate the poor girl who found herself in the household of a kindly master or mistress like Caterina Patengola! She encouraged her servant Giustina in her spiritual practices and helped her follow her vocation to Santa Croce Monastery.[25]

Servants could attend public events—games and jousts, carnival parades, and other public exhibitions. Religious devotions and street preachers attracted big crowds, servants among them. Of course, a young woman of twelve or older was supposed to be chaperoned[26] unless she had no responsible household superiors who cared about her.

Some serving women had a tiny disposable income. Many received only room and board and were supposed to obtain their accumulated wages at the end of their employment, often in the form of a dowry.

Dowry and Marriage

By the age of twelve, a young woman had to be on the path to marriage. In the upper classes, her marriage had probably already been arranged. In the burgher class, her father had been saving and investing for a dowry to attract an advantageous family alliance. Or he had decided to send her to a convent (which would accept a smaller dower) and to give a larger portion to her sister. A poor girl was working to save money for a dowry. Some employment contracts called not for regular wages but for a dower, which would be paid only on marriage or entrance into a monastery.[27] Because wars had reduced the population of marriageable men, a woman's family used the dowry to compete for potential husbands. The dowry was all-important![28] Without a dowry a woman could not marry, and there was no social category for the unmarried woman outside of religious life.[29]

The dowry represented a daughter's share in the family property. In name, women could possess property, but they had no control over it.[30] Through the dowry, a man passed his daughter's share to the control of his son-in-law for the eventual benefit of their joint progeny. The women were the links in these economic alliances between men. Only a widow might escape male guardianship if she did not remarry or fall under the guardianship of her father, brother, or in-laws. She could sometimes participate in social and economic life on behalf of her minor children, deal in property and appear in court.[31] Southern Europe, where the age disparity between spouses was great, had many widows who survived much older husbands. If they had children, remarriage was unlikely.[32]

Communal Alternatives to Marriage

Some unmarried or unmarriageable poor women found a home in a refuge sponsored (usually) by wealthy urban women. These communities might support themselves with skilled handiwork.

To shelter orphan girls and poor girls at risk in a "*casa delle zitelle,*" lay benefactors such as Isabetta Prato sponsored asylums.[33] For former prostitutes seeking a different life ("*convertite*"), Laura Gambara created a refuge to address their personal and social issues, teaching them skills to make an honest living. Angela's friends Laura and Isabetta combined their undertakings under one roof as a house "*della Carità.*" Refuges like these became alternative family models, with the women in leadership called "mothers" and "teachers."[34]

The urgent situation of *convertite* was overwhelming, since prostitution was swallowing many women's lives in the early sixteenth century. The majority had turned to prostitution as a last resort in their poverty. In 1500 Venice had 12,000 registered prostitutes.[35] There were official civic brothels, though the spread of the disfiguring and ultimately fatal "French disease" (syphilis) was making officials nervous. Pope Leo X issued a decree in 1520 expelling Rome's many courtesans (much involved in the politics of the papal court). People were frightened of venereal disease, and prostitutes had less legal protection than previously.[36] More and more unfortunates were suffering and dying from the scourge.[37] War and rape spread syphilis though Brescia, especially in the horrible Sack of 1512. Concerned lay men founded the Hospital of the Most Holy Trinity as a final home for the afflicted.[38] Many prostitutes left children behind when they died, orphans needing care. Isabetta Prato met a growing need.

A few refuges housed *malmaritate* ("badly married"), too. These women had separated from their husbands. Their circumstances were dire: no home, no social standing, no legal rights. The asylums did more than shelter. They helped women to lives of dignity and self-determination.[39]

Thus not every woman was in a man's power; some widows, prostitutes, *convertite* and *malmaritate* lived on their own or in households of women. However, these were not considered desirable states of life. They were all defined by not having a husband.

Religious Alternatives

For the unmarried woman, the life of a nun was more desirable, and surely of a higher status, than that of a 'spinster.'[40] Nuns could choose to give themselves to God in a community of women. In actuality, most were placed there by their families, just as their sisters were placed in marriages.[41] Many patrician men placed their illegitimate daughters in religious life. Prompted by socio-economic factors in Venice between 1448 and 1505, the number of convents rose from twenty-eight to forty-one.[42] Working-class women generally could not afford the dowries that most convents required to be self-sustaining. However, they could work and reside there as servants.

No wonder that many nuns lacked spiritual commitment, if they had no authentic vocation. Scandals erupted as a natural result, though exaggeration and scapegoating no doubt colored some accounts.[43] In the year of Angela's birth (1474) Pope Sixtus IV tried to close the Benedictine convent of Saint Angelo Di Contorta, which between 1401 and 1487 faced fifty-two prosecutions for sex crimes.[44] Despite official policies about nuns' cloister (*clausura*),[45] sixteenth-century Italy had many "open monasteries" whose nuns had obtained papal exemptions from the observance of cloister.[46]

True dedication motivated some lay women to share a religiously shaped life, without the solemn vows that would have required them to adopt cloister, and without the ecclesiastical authorization—or authority—of bishops, popes or male monastic orders. Saint Frances of Rome had founded such a society in 1425.

Some women gathered as members of a Third Order, either Franciscan or Dominican. After Pope Nicholas IV's declaration *Supra*

Montem gave clearer definition to the Third Order of St. Francis, confraternities developed through Italy. Though the Third Order did provide a cohesive set of shared practices, it was not in itself a life-vocation. Married and single people, priests and bishops could be members. Franciscan spirituality enriched their primary vocations. Angela's membership in the confraternity based at Salò formed her spiritually. But it did not satisfy her sense of need for a company of women in a vocational sisterhood.

Devout women periodically sought other forms of celibate religious commitment outside the recognized structures, under different names, and without organization. Beguines, for example, had arisen primarily in northern European towns in the late Middle Ages. Beguines lived as single women in loosely structured communities for as long as they chose to do so.[47] Restricted by the Council of Vienna (1318), their tide was ebbing by the late fifteenth century.

In Spain, a pious single woman was called *"beata"* (blessed). In Italy the *"umilate"* (humble) were pious lay women dedicated to works of charity. They were often called *"mantellate,"* from the modest mantles they wore. In Tuscany and Umbria, the *mantellate*, *pinzochere* (or *pizzochere* or *bizzoche*) proliferated. *Pinzochere* especially imbibed the strong penitential reforms that were reactions against social and ecclesiastical corruption. They were identified with dramatic penances, including pilgrimages. They shared with Third Order Franciscans a devotion to the Passion of Christ and to Jerusalem and the Holy Land.

As celibate and non-monastic, and so not anchored in society, these women met aversion, suspicion, even persecution.[48] For example, Bellezza Orsini, a *pinzochera*, was arrested after arriving in Rome on pilgrimage in the 1520s, on charges of casting a spell and was grilled by the Inquisition.[49] Similar darts were cast at the first Ursulines, after Angela's death had removed the protection of her recognized sanctity. Her confidante Gabriele Cozzano responded to the criticisms that this life in the world was spiritually, morally and socially inferior, that Angela's very salvation was questionable.[50] Both he and a later observer in 1600 mentioned mockery of the early Ursulines as a painful reality.[51]

Despite the limitations placed on them, single women repeatedly sought to shape their lives more or less on their own terms, by their personal and religious genius. Some initiatives were communal, others individual. By and large, they had to accommodate to the dynamics of oppression or live on society's margins. Rarely did these constructs endure.

Angela's Company did endure, though only after passing through trial by fire after her death, and being somewhat reshaped in the aftermath. The Company had stability through its integration into Brescian society. Angela wove it into the city's fabric through relationships among the members and between the members and the matrons and men whom she involved. Chapter XI, titled "About Governance," could just as well be called "About Community," since the chapter describes a set of relationships. Within a realistic assessment of society, it offers a visionary alternative.

The Rule

Angela's Rule ends with Chapter XI, "About Governance." What does it mean to govern the Company? The answer to this question has evolved over the centuries. It is not within the scope of this work to trace the history of that evolution. These pages deal only with governance as it is described in Chapter XI of the Rule.

Mostly, to govern means to steer the Company. The word has a Latin origin that comes from navigation. Examining Angela's experience of travel may shed light on her understanding of governance, especially as she repeatedly calls the Company's life a *via*, that is, a road or pathway. She traveled much on land and sea. She knew that the *"gubernator"* is not the captain but the one who steers, keeps the ship on its course, so that all the passengers may arrive safely at their destination. And what is the Company's destination? Heaven, of course. That is clear from the Prologue, which ends with *return[ing] gloriously to our homeland, where from all those in Heaven and on earth great glory and triumph will arise* (Pr.:30, 31).

Angela on a Journey

Angela had experienced the joy of returning home from her pilgrimage to the Holy Land in 1524. Her destination had been Jerusalem, and then back home. She had experienced not only those destinations, but the whole route as holy. The journey had included Venice, where the pilgrims embarked after celebrating the Eucharistic feast of Corpus Christi, Christ's Body, with the annual solemn procession to the harbor. Recent warfare and piracy in the eastern Mediterranean, combined with torrential weather that spring, brewed dangerous uncertainties.

Blessing the ship must have been an occasion of intense prayer for safety before the forty-some pilgrims set out.[52]

The single stop in the voyage held a mystery for Angela. At Canea (present Khaniá) on Crete she lost almost all her sight to a temporary eye condition. As time unrolled the scroll of her near-blindness, she could read its meaning. She was able to see the pilgrimage sites deeply with her spirit.[53] God surely touched her in Canea, opening her to unexpected depths of loss and of grace.

On the return trip, God touched her again, when her eyes were healed at Candia (present Iráklion), a port city of northeastern Crete. Praying before a crucifix, she found that she could see again. After the stop at Candia, the returning vessel was blown off course and nearly submerged by a tempest. Preserved from that danger, the voyagers then encountered a fleet of eight Turkish warships. Using gifts and negotiations to lull the Italians into a false sense of safety, the Turkish captain set up an ambush, which the Venetian ship was able to avoid. Angela's shipmates credited their survival to her prayers.[54]

It was a long round trip—six months before the pilgrims were home again. Yet every point of the journey was important. There were moments of deep devotion. Angela wept and kissed the holy ground of Calvary, where Jesus Christ had shed his blood and given his life. But God was not only in the Holy Land. Each place along the way held God's presence. So it is with our lives. The peaks of inspiration and special holy places make it easy to find God. But God is just as present every day, and just as much at home or work as in church.

What does that understanding mean for the Company? Our goal may be heaven. But Angela's Company has a purpose here in this world, too, along the way. It exists to help each member live fully and faithfully here and now, as well as get to heaven. It also exists to share God with our neighbors. The more deeply each one lives her relationship with God, the more clearly she finds God all around her. She begins to glimpse heaven's light. If she reflects Jesus' light through her deeds, others will see it, too.

Governance as Steering and Service

Governance helps this happen. The people entrusted with governance must encourage the whole Company to keep the destination in view. They must build unity and assure that there are resources to get there. They must also help each one individually to walk her own path.

Angela calls governance a service. In her first counsel to women who would exercise this service, she calls them to *learn from Our Lord who, while he was in this world, was as a servant.* She quotes his teaching after he had washed his disciples' feet: *"I have been among you not as the one who is served, but as the one who serves"* (cf. Matthew 20:28, Mark 10:45; First Counsel:7). In the Church, too, Angela points out, special office should mean special service, as *St. Gregory, even though he was Pope, still called himself servant of the servants of God.* This is Jesus' teaching: *"Let whoever is greater among you be as the least"* (cf. Luke 9:48; First Counsel:6-9). In the face of corruption at the highest levels of the sixteenth-century Church, Angela's words voice a reformist spirit. Contemporary history must have shown her what to avoid. She was to structure her Company in a non-hierarchical way.

Those who govern serve by steering, or guiding the vessel that is the Company. They do not decide where to go. Every member helps set the course. Their maps are the Gospel and the Rule. When a situation calls for important decisions, the whole Company must *gather at the feet of Jesus Christ, [who]...will enlighten and teach you what you have to do* (Last Legacy:3-5).

Roles in Governance

While the whole Company is involved, Angela provides for three particular groups to govern. Even though the ultimate body of governance is the Company as a whole, some matters are best handled by people with certain skills. These are three groups of people elected to serve the Company in certain ways. The whole Company elects its *governors*. To govern is not to rule. No one rules the Company.

Though she did not name it as such, the Rule assumes that a chapter of the whole exercises ultimate authority within the Company. The earliest documented meeting of the chapter occurred on March 18, 1537, sixteen months after the Company was founded. The proceedings of this chapter, held in the kitchen of her dwelling, have come down to us. They demonstrate the functions of election and of decision-making. This event put into practice her encouragement to respond to *times and circumstances...to make new rules or do something differently* (Last Legacy:2). The structures were developing even within Angela's lifetime. (The meeting itself is discussed later in this section.)

The Colonelle

Chapter XI sets forth the character and functions of each governance group. First Angela designates *four of the most capable* members (Ch. XI:1). These women are named first because their role is the most important, helping the members as *teachers and guides in the spiritual life* (Ch. XI:4).

Angela calls them *colonelle*.

The office of *colonella* finds its model in civic affairs. Since the word for a neighborhood is *colonello*, neighborhood leaders were *colonelli*. (Merician texts generally use the masculine singular and plural forms, *colonello/i*; this book adopts the feminine forms *colonella/e*, also found in other early documents.) Angela grew up with the office of *colonello* at home in Desenzano, where neighborhoods had local leaders.[55] It was a common facet of urban life. In Genoa, for example, four men were elected in each quarter of town to manage local affairs and keep peace, and four women were elected to supervise morality and settle women's quarrels.[56]

Angela used this way of dividing the members by Brescian neighborhoods, but the colonella described in the Rule has a role more appropriate to Ursuline life. The colonella is designated to visit the Company's members in particular districts or neighborhoods. She must *be a most vigilant [shepherd] and good [servant]* (Prologue to the Counsels:6; First Counsel). Most of all, Angela wants her to love her *dear sisters* almost as though they were *daughters*. Yes, with a mother's love, kind and gentle and firm, knowing each one so well as to discern the best way of dealing with her, not applying the same measure to all (Second, Fifth, and Eighth Counsels).

In 1537 the Company elected as colonelle Barbara de Monteclaro; Margarita de Brixia (Brescia), a local woman; Agnes, a maid in the household of Lady Ursula de Gavardo; and Clara, who lived in the household of Sir Paulo da Angolo.

1 In order to govern said Company it is provided that four of the most capable virgins of the Company ought to be elected,

2 and at least four widowed matrons, prudent and of honorable life,

3 and four mature men who have led upright lives.

Teachers and Guides in the Spiritual Life

The role of women as *teachers and guides in the spiritual life* must have seemed unusual, even bold, in the Church of the sixteenth century. Today some still wonder whether women are capable teachers and guides in the spiritual life. Angela's first members surely had little formal education. Yet they had been educated by experience.

Angela had models in women who had shown her this way. Blessed Stefana Quinzani had been a servant girl in Orzi-nuovi, in the Province of Brescia, before joining the Dominican Third Order and later founding a Dominican monastery. Among the revelations that Stefana reported receiving directly from Christ were the words, "exert yourself and lead an active life.... a life that incorporates both activity and contemplation is more perfect." She cared for the sick and orphans.[57] She was an inspiration to Angela, who probably used to see her when Stefana came to Brescia. Angela visited her in Soncino when she was ill.[58] Stefana exemplified how much women can teach each other. When she died in 1530, it was a sad loss to many who had respected her.

Angela also revered the memory of the charismatic Blessed Osanna Andreasi (d. 1505), who had been Stefana's mentor and her predecessor as spiritual advisor to the Gonzaga dukes. Osanna's biographer reported that, when she could not contemplate as she wished because of so many visitors, Christ told her that he did not want her in a convent "so that she might be a mediator for the salvation of souls."[59] Angela made a pilgrimage to Osanna's tomb in Mantua in 1520.

The example of these holy women supported Angela's intuition about her Ursulines' capacity for spiritual teaching. Who can know the graces and the problems of Ursuline life better than a woman who is living it?

For several years, Angela herself had been preparing the first Ursulines for this role of teaching and guiding. Isabetta Prato gave her the use of a room in her home. They had it decorated in 1533 as an oratory for the women who were beginning to live this life, even before they formally founded the Company in 1535. Here they prayed and planned together. By God's grace, trusting in the Holy Spirit, Angela instructed these women

4 These virgins should be like teachers and guides in the spiritual life.

as the group grew. She had heart-to-heart conversations with each one. Some of these members were ready to serve as spiritual teachers.

The Counsels

Angela's advancing age told her that she would not be with them much longer. She composed for the colonelle a booklet of advice, called "counsels." Gabriele Cozzano wrote it down as she dictated. The Counsels preserve her instruction to the colonelle on how to serve their sisters. With her words and with one another, they would go forward. As always, Angela firmly trusted that the Holy Spirit would continue to instruct them.[60]

The relationships built into the Rule develop in a regular rhythm of personal contact. A colonella should visit each member in her home, about twice a month (Ch. XI:8a) and also on special feast days (Fifth Counsel:1). Visits weave together work and celebration. Being with a member in her home gives the colonella insight into the circumstances of her life.

Angela's own spirit shines through her advice, which blends homey practicality with passionate idealism. She wants the colonella to visit *especially on feasts*, to share joy. What happens on those visits responds to the member's needs. They talk about how the woman is developing habits of life that support the aspirations of her heart. The colonella encourages her to live her Ursuline vocation simply, kindly, gently, giving good example, spreading peace. She teaches the practices of the Rule. If someone is failing to use the *means and ways* that the Rule provides, the colonella must try to help her correct her actions and embrace her vocation whole-heartedly. If a member is weighed down, stuck in humdrum or in problems, the colonella helps her to lift her eyes and spirit, to look ahead (Fifth Counsel). The visits put into action the reality that this woman is not alone in her vocation. She can draw strength from a relationship that supports her values, commitment and spiritual practices.

This service makes significant demands on the colonella, in time and

8a Now, the four virgins should want especially to have this as their undertaking, that is, to visit, every fifteen days

7 or more or less as seems necessary,

8b all the other sisters, the virgins that are in the city,...

energy and self-giving. It must come from deep in her heart and spirit. Angela urges the colonella to *pray to God to enlighten you and direct you,* trusting that God *will help you in everything* (Prologue to the Counsels:7, 15).

Angela calls a colonella a *guide,* first because her teaching is not about ideas or words. It is about living. A guide is one who walks ahead on the path and helps another person find the way. Our path passes through a woman's life, day by day and year by year—through both women's lives. Part of the teaching flows from the wisdom of experience. Part is through example. The teaching must be alive in both of them. A colonella must *live and behave in such a way that [the other members] may see in [her] a model* (Sixth Counsel:1).

To Comfort and Help

According to Chapter XI, "About Governance," Angela expected the colonelle to help these women with their problems, too (Ch. XI:8b-12). It was a function important to the situations of the members in her day, and even now. Unmarried women were very vulnerable to all sorts of injustice. Men often imposed on the younger ones, especially. Rape was common, and it often went unpunished if the victims were servants or poor.[61] According to Venetian law, female servants who had been raped by their employers could get full wages, release from service, and money for a dowry. However, they would find it hard to get another job. Thus many either endured the situation or turned to prostitution.[62] They were all defenseless if employers were abusive or withheld their wages. Some employers or supervisors would not allow them time for prayer or hindered them from fasting or the sacraments (Ch. III:8, 9). If they were sick, there might be no one to care for them.

Mistresses too could be harsh (Ch. XI:10). A contemporary play dramatizes their situation. *The Woman from Ancona* was first produced in Padua in 1533. In it,

9 to comfort and help them if they may be involved in some dissension or in any other trouble, of the body just as of the mind;

10 or to check whether their household superiors may be abusive in any way

11 or may want to hinder them from some sort of good

12 or pressure them into some danger of evil.

Doralice, the mistress of the household, mimics her maids, "The wretched girls say when you scold them, 'You are hard to please...[mistresses] don't let you live.'" But Doralice dismisses such complaints coldly, saying, "But leave them to their misfortune."[63]

Members who lived with their families may not have borne these problems, but they had others. Their parents probably preferred for them to marry. Parents and guardians could use powerful pressure. Or they might make it difficult for a member of the Company to carry out the spiritual practices that supported her vocation (Ch. XI:10-12). Some parents continued to present their Ursuline daughters as marriageable. They pushed them to attend dances or other situations that were not consistent with their dedication (Ch. III:9).

What can a colonella do about such problems? First, helping a member bring them into the light is a powerful support to the woman's own integrity and resolve. Then the colonella guides and supports her in facing the problems and trying to work them out.

If that effort is not successful, then and only then the colonella is to *refer [the situation] to the matrons* (Ch. XI:13). It was important to Angela that the persons directly involved manage as much as they could, as close to the situation as possible. Her guiding principle is called "subsidiarity" today. If the woman and her colonella cannot manage, the colonella is to seek help from the matrons. Together they should try to offer a solution. The Company supports each member faced with any danger, problem or threat to her dignity or her vocation.

The Matrons

Matrons, usually *prudent* widows *of honorable life* (Ch. XI:2), manage whatever business the Company requires and represent it publicly. They foster healthy community spirit. They collaborate with the colonelle in assisting members who face difficulties. The matrons have been mentioned earlier in the Rule. In Chapter I they meet the guardians of prospective members (Ch. I:7). In Chapter III they help members whose families *wish to hinder* their spiritual practices (Ch. III:8-10). In Chapter IV they assist members in discernment about healthy fasting (Ch. IV:19, 20). A Brescian matron of the upper class could be an advocate for justice. She could speak to a guardian or an employer as a peer, with an influence that a daughter or a servant did not have.

Why did Angela specify *widowed matrons* (Ch. XI:2)? For one thing, these sixteenth-century widows often had experience in managing large households and extensive properties. Someone like Isabetta Prato, who was widowed in her thirties, developed administrative skills. A widow had an independence unknown to unmarried women or to those with husbands. She was often freer to devote herself to good works than married women were. For example, Isabetta's care for orphan girls and Laura Gambara's for prostitutes eventually combined under the name "La Carità," and Laura turned her home over to this good work.[64] Would Laura's husband have agreed to this arrangement when he was alive?

Through friendship with Angela, these women took an interest in the Company of Saint Ursula. They became part of the Company's governance when the members elected them to serve for terms of several years.[65]

Closely as they are connected, matrons are not members of the Company. They have their own vocation in their homes and families, usually as mothers and grandmothers. Angela honored their calling. When the oratory in Isabetta's home was decorated in 1533, holy widows were among the saints painted in the frescoes. One was Saint Paula, a wealthy Roman and an impressive scholar. She built two monasteries near Bethlehem, where she and her daughter Eustochium assisted Saint Jerome in his biblical translations. The young widow Saint Elizabeth of Hungary was Isabetta's patron saint. (Angela may also have harbored a special fondness for her as a fellow member of the Third Order of St. Francis.) The fresco shows Saint Elizabeth assisting young girls, as did Isabetta. Her image provided both a tribute and an inspiration to Brescia's charitable widows.

The Service of Administration

Angela involved women whose zeal, competence and experience suited them to serve the Company as a whole. She expressed her own heartfelt instructions to the matrons in her *Testament*, a document of eleven spiritual "Legacies" which she dictated to Gabriele Cozzano. The *Testament* specifies the matrons' functions, including organizing monthly gatherings and engaging preachers (Eighth Legacy). They are to handle any money that comes to the Company, assuring that it is used *for the good and the development of the Company* (Ninth Legacy:4) or for alms (Ninth Legacy).

In their own families the widowed matrons had been responsible for young people. For young Ursulines, the older women were helpful mentors about practical matters. Angela urged the matrons to act *like mothers, being solicitous about...their spiritual sisters and daughters* (Ch. XI:5). That is how Angela herself loved her daughters! She sought to assure that the matrons understood their role in this way. These women had been her dear friends for years. She and they had opened their hearts to one another. She trusted them to act as she would act. But what about the future? Angela bequeathed to the matrons her trust to serve the Company according to her instructions. Her *Testament* would foster the same spirit in future leaders (Prologue to the *Testament*:25-30).

5 And the widows should be like mothers, being solicitous about the well-being and usefulness of their spiritual sisters and daughters.

Nourishing the Community

As spiritual mothers, the matrons must nourish the community. Above all, they must build up harmony and unity of hearts and wills. They must uproot any *weeds of discord or other scandal*, and *on no account let such a seed grow in the Company* (Tenth Legacy:15). They must pay attention to the Company's spiritual health. If poisonous ideas and values begin to compromise the Company's integrity, the matrons must deal with the situation.

Such weeds might sprout up if a member is unfaithful to her commitment. If she neglects the practice of the Rule, she affects the whole Company by compromising its spiritual health. The Rule contains the *means and ways* for living the vocation. *There is little or no difference between freely saying: "I no longer want to serve God" and not wanting the ways and the rules necessary to be able to keep oneself in this* (Pr.:14). Each member's fidelity supports every other member in her Ursuline vocation. If her colonella cannot guide a negligent member back into faithful living, one of the matrons must try, as Angela prescribes, with *all possible gentleness. And above all, be on [her]guard not to want to get anything done by force, because God has given free will to everyone, and wants to force no one, but only proposes, invites and counsels.... I do not say, however, that it will not be necessary occasionally to use* reproaches and severity, at the place and time, according to the importance, condition and need of the persons, but we must be moved solely by charity and by the sole zeal for souls (Third Legacy:7-15).

It is possible that a wayward member does not respond to the matron's efforts. Once again, Angela directs that, if the matron has *gently counseled and warned one of them three or at most four times, about some notable fault, and [sees] that she does not want to obey, [the matron will] leave her alone and stop sending her the [colonella]* (Fifth Legacy:1-4). This action makes clear that not living the life of the Company is the same as withdrawing from it. It shows the member that her faults are not hers alone. They damage the common good. The hope is that she will wish to return to her relationship in the Company.

One who is sorry and does want to return *must be received, but on condition that she ask pardon of the Company and of her colonella. And as a penance, she should be given to fast one Friday on bread and water* (Fifth Legacy, 9-11). This is for her own well-being, and for the Company's. One who damages spiritual health must act in some way to restore it. Fasting is a way of experiencing that intention in her own body. Asking pardon is a way of experiencing it in the body of the community. Asking pardon and doing penance should lead to forgiveness and reconciliation.

The matrons are to be involved with individual members not only when there are problems. In fact, they would be of little use if their relationships were limited to problems. Angela *beg[s]* them to *have engraved on your mind and heart all your dear daughters, one by one, not only their names but also their condition, and character, and their every situation and state.... [T]his is how real love works.... [I]f you love these dear daughters of ours with a burning and passionate charity, it will be impossible for you not to have them all depicted individually in your memory and in your heart* (Second Legacy). In this spirit of love, the matrons will be able *to lead them with love and with a mild and kindly hand* (Third Legacy:1).

Well-being and Usefulness

The Rule says that the matrons are to be *solicitous about the well-being and usefulness of their spiritual sisters and daughters* (Ch. XI:5). Matrons and colonelle may seek to support a member with difficulties of any sort: ill health or emotional suffering or injustices. Together they try to help her find a solution.

Also, as noted in the Rule's Chapter IV, "About Fasting," matrons have a special function. No Ursuline ought to fast without advice. Fasting will not be the same for every person. Each one is to discern a pattern of fasting that is spiritually nourishing to her. She must consult her spiritual guide and also a matron. A wise older woman can advise her with a woman's experience of a woman's body. If anyone tends to go to excess, the matron may have to *relax and diminish these fasts as seems necessary* so that she will not *indiscreetly hurt [her]body* (Ch. IV:18-20).

Usefulness touches several aspects of life. For example, if a member is having difficulty supporting herself with dignity, the matrons may help her to be trained for a job. Or they may consult with other women or men of their own class (today's 'networking') to find a suitable opportunity, a job *where she can live virtuously and well* (Ch. XI:28). They also counsel members to help them be useful within their families.

The Service of Witness

The nine matrons named in Angela's Testament were titled "*Madonna—Lady.*" They were all from the upper classes: *Countess Lady Lucrecia [Lodrone], principal mother...the noble matrons, Lady Genepra di Luciagi, Lady Maria di Avogadri, Lady Veronica di Bucci, Lady Orsolina di Gavardi, Lady Giovanna di Monti, Lady Isabetta da Prato, Lady Lionella di Pedeciocchi, Lady Caterina di Mei* (Prologue to the Legacies:2). They served a Company in which many, if not most members were working women. A company of women! Single women! Self-governing! The Company was indeed different from the society around it. To survive and to safeguard the freedom and vocations of the members, the Company needed these women of influence.

The matrons provided credibility for the all-but-unimaginable idea of women choosing a life of celibate consecration in "the world." Religious life, in a monastery, might be acceptable as a sacred place, a safe place for a woman. Most people accepted the proverb that a woman needed "either a man or a wall." In truth, an unmarried woman was less secure than

13 And if they themselves [the colonelle] would not be able to provide for them, they should refer it to the matrons.

her married sisters. (The dangers of childbearing and abusive husbands were little recognized, though.) And there were always suspicions about a single woman's chastity.[66] Many poor and dependent women fell prey to men with power over them. Poverty pushed others into prostitution. There is a way of thinking that presumes these situations arise from moral inferiority in women and that women need men to guide and control them. Well-known matrons of honorable life (Ch. XI:2) were to act as spokespersons. They would testify that the Company was stable and virtuous.[67]

This service of witness would soon be even more critical, after Angela's death. Her fellow Brescians may have been doubtful about this *newly begun life* (Pr.:2). But because they had known her for over twenty years, they were willing to trust her Ursulines. After her death in 1540, trust would give way to skepticism. Already, the parents and guardians of some members were unhappy about their daughters' choice to be Ursulines. They considered it their duty to provide for a young woman to be married, just as Angela's aunt and uncle Biancosi had tried to provide for her. When she was gone, the matrons' influence would be needed even more to sustain the Ursulines in the face of opposition.

The matrons were already involved with the candidate's family even before a woman was admitted. This contact was both relational and strategic. The governors of the Company—women and men— were to visit the parents or guardians of someone wishing to become an Ursuline (Ch. I:7). Angela wanted the matrons to be acquainted with the candidate's family and to understand *[her] condition, and character, and...situation and state* (Second Legacy, 1-3). They also went to verify the woman's freedom to join the Company. What if her father had made a contract of engagement for her or had promised her dowry to a monastery? Such complications would be dealt with at once. If the woman and her family were at odds, it would be far better to resolve the issues before she was admitted to the Company.

In the light of Angela's emphasis on freedom, why ask anyone beyond the woman herself? This measure was part of a strategy to protect the woman's choice. The governors would verify that her guardians *do not have any legitimate cause* to keep her from following her vocation. *[I]f by chance they should afterwards want to prevent her*, the governors served as witnesses on behalf of her freedom (Ch. I:7).

Another need for the matrons' influence arose when families and *other worldly superiors* might seek *to pressure [Ursulines] into...dangers* or sought *to hinder them from fasting or prayer or confession or other kinds of good things.* Angela urges a woman under pressure to *be quick to refer this to the lady governors...so that they may take care of it* (Ch. III:8-10). A matron could offer helpful leverage (Ch. XI:13).

The Men – *Like Agents*

6   And the four men should be like agents, and yet fathers, in the ongoing necessities of the Company.

14 And if even they cannot take care of things, it may be desirable to call together the four men as well so that all together they may agree to offer a remedy.

15 If it should happen that any one of these sisters, because she is an orphan, would not be able to have what is hers,

16 or, being a housekeeper or a maid or in another station, might not be able to obtain her pay,

17 or some other similar thing should happen so that it would be necessary to go to court, and to seek what is right

32 or arrange an agreement (which is the best that can be done),...

The third group of *governors* described in the Rule is masculine. In addition to the colonelle and matrons, the Rule provides for *four mature men who have led upright lives* to be elected by the Company (Ch. XI:3) to *be like agents* (Ch. XI:6). The colonelle and matrons would call upon them if a member faced a problem that they themselves *[could] not take care of* (Ch. XI:14) and in *ongoing necessities of the Company* (Ch. XI:6). It is noteworthy that Angela describes the men governors as *like agents*. Clearly the principals, the decision-makers, are the Ursulines themselves. Again, the governors are the Company's servants.

Women were excluded from some spheres of action. For example, Italy's law courts and businesses were usually closed to women. If a need arose for legal action, an unmarried woman over eighteen could bring a suit or appear in court, but it was more usual for her to be represented by a male relative or a lawyer.[68] Angela mentions potential legal issues. A woman's brother or uncle or other relative might withhold her inheritance. If she had no family members to take up her case, she would *not be able to have what is hers* (Ch. XI:15). Or a housekeeper or maid or other worker *might not be able to obtain her pay* (Ch.

XI:16).[69] Some employment contracts called not for salary but for a dowry, to be paid to a husband or monastery.[70] An Ursuline in this dilemma could languish unpaid in perpetual bondage. There are many ways for a defenseless person to be victimized. Sometimes, the mere fact that she has supportive friends will prevent injustices.

The men would *go to court* for an aggrieved member if necessary. The desirable outcome would be an *agreement (which is the best that can be done)*. Angela's peacemaking spirit emphasizes the priority: first seek peace, seek to repair the relationship, *arrange an agreement* (Ch. XI:17, 18). Perhaps the woman could do that on her own, but perhaps not with the same degree of influence. She was not on the same footing as the authorities in her family or job. Strategically, the men's ability to represent the Ursuline in court could have an impact on the negotiation, even if the matter never actually went to court. Like the matrons, these men had social standing and influence in Brescia.

As useful as these positions in the Company's governance would be, they remained vacant for the first few years. No men were elected at the chapter meeting in 1537. The minutes read, "election was not yet carried out...since no provision had yet been made about them."[71] When the Company did elect four men, they were gentlemen of influence and experience in business and law, Gabriele Cozzano, Giulio Balteo, Giovita Boni (all notaries) and Girolamo Girardetti fu Bernardino.[72]

Like Fathers

Twice the Rule states that the four men are to be *like fathers* (Ch. XI:6, 19). Looking back to the sixteenth century, we might fairly ask, "Didn't fathers rule?" Not in this company of women! These men had to be ready to serve when a need arose and only then, ready to serve and not to control. They had to be able to collaborate respectfully with the colonelle and the matrons (Ch. XI:14).

For the daughter of Giovanni Merici, *like fathers* apparently meant that, *out of charity, [they] should want to...help according to the need that exists* (Ch. XI:19). Angela was looking for men whose integrity had been proven by their *upright lives* (Ch. XI:3) as much as for skill and experience. It was equally important that

33 then these four men, out of charity, like fathers, should want to take hold of this task, and to help according to the need that exists.

they share the Ursulines' spirit. They would have to be eager to work for justice on behalf of people who had been abused.

Even though their service involved confrontation and struggle, they must seek first to achieve justice in peaceful ways that restored damaged relationships (Ch. XI:17, 18). Angela may well have learned this principle too from her father. He confronted his older brother Carlo, who (since their father was dead) had probably negotiated Giovanni's marriage arrangements with the Biancosi family and seems to have kept control of Catherine's dower after the wedding. On January 26, 1476, Giovanni lodged a notarized petition on his own and his wife's behalf to obtain the dower from Carlo. However, the case was not tried, since the brothers worked out a compromise by February 29.[73] Shortly before his death, Giovanni Merici acted as mediator between his brothers-in-law Biancosi and Cimbaldo, resolving a dispute that had reached the docket of Salò's mayor.[74]

The involvement of lay men with the Company alerts us to notice that nothing in this chapter on governance mentions clergymen. There are no ecclesiastical roles in Angela's conception of the Company. She provided for the members to choose a priest to serve as a confessor, but he was not a part of the governance (Ch. VII:12).

Spiritual Family

It is no accident that familial words color Angela's language: *my very dear sisters....like mothers....like fathers*. She clearly understood the Company as a spiritual family.

Angela was fortunate to have grown up as she did in her family, sisters and brothers living and working together with their parents. Their home was a warm and stable place. She knew the love and care of a father and mother till her teens, when they died. She was close to her sister, certainly. Her relationship with her brothers is unknown. Perhaps when her brothers had married and she was living at Le Grezze, they may have stayed close and helped each other. Clearly, Angela wants all her *very dear daughters and sisters* to care for each other lovingly.

They would not live or work together, as the family on the farm had done. No, but Angela called them to be *sisters in the blood of Christ* (First Counsel:1). She understood this sisterhood to be organic, alive, based on a common relationship with Christ.[75] As we know from the

Rule's treatment of prayer, Angela saw his blood as the emblem of his love. This family is to be based on Love himself. This is Jesus' way. He affirmed relationships transcending natural ties (for example, "whoever does the will of God is my brother and sister and mother" – Mark 3:35; cf. Matthew 12:50).

Angela is ever a mother. Her sense of spiritual maternity appears at the very beginning of the Rule. The Prologue, *in the manner of letters*, is addressed to her *beloved....most beloved daughters and sisters* (Pr.:3, 4). From heaven, she promises, she will *see them and know them better. And I can and want to help them more* (Fifth Counsel:36, 37). She will be *always in your midst, helping your prayers* (Last Counsel:20).

The same warmth pervades the Counsels. Angela entrusts to the colonelle her role of motherly care and urges them *to cherish [the members] day and night, and to have them all engraved in your heart...* (Prologue to the Counsels:11). They should *be an example and mirror for their daughters* (Sixth Counsel:8). She is leaving the matrons *in my place as my heirs* (Prologue to the Testament:29). Her Legacies to them echo and re-echo the refrain: *be good and true mothers* (Ninth Legacy:3).

The loving title that Brescia gave her, "Madre Suor Angela" ("Mother Sister") bears witness to the reality and impact of her motherhood. She embraced all without distinction: the duke and the scullery maid, the attractive and the difficult. In her they found life. Calling her "the Madre," Agostino Gallo claimed, "not only I didn't know how to live without her, but also my wife, and all my family."[76]

To the women of the Company, she offered a truly *new life*.

Subsidiarity, Collegiality, Unity

In this family of adults, people filling the specialized roles are to work together. Each month the matrons and colonelle gather. They consider how the Company is navigating, whether it is on course, corporately and in the life of each member. The colonelle report whatever needs they and the women they guide cannot manage. The group seeks a solution (Ch. XI:13). Angela wants them to plan and act in unity. The matrons are to be responsible for matters involving the whole Company, and she urges the colonelle to obey these decisions (Third Counsel:1-3) and to support the matrons when talking with the members. Colonelle are to be bridges, linking individual members with the matrons and with the rest of the Company (Third Counsel:7-12).

Yet the colonelle do not answer to the matrons in carrying out their own service. The colonelle are responsible in matters that affect the members individually, such as personal guidance and even protection when that is needed (Fourth Counsel:1-3). The matrons must listen to them in these matters. In fact, Angela gives to the colonelle her own authority. *If you see [the matrons] slow to provide, be insistent; and in that case, in my name even be importunate and troublesome* (Fourth Counsel:4, 5). If the matrons still do not respond, she encourages the colonelle to *talk in confidence with some person who is good and faithful* (Third Counsel:13), who can help them meet a member's pressing need.

The matrons should call the men together only in a situation requiring their influence or skills. Then the whole group will consider the situation *so that all together they may agree to offer a remedy* (Ch. XI:14). This principle would now be called "collegiality." Each group has its own area of responsibility; all collaborate to carry it out, animated by the same *praise and love of God and zeal for the good of souls* (cf. Prologue to the Counsels:18; First Legacy:3). Acting in this spirit, they will be able to work together for the good of all.

The Chapter – All Together

The ultimate governance is the Company as a whole. It gathers formally as a chapter to make decisions. The chapter elects members to be the colonelle, widows to be the matrons and men to act as the agents.[77] The Company can also remove them, if they would be *unable to carry out [their] duty or behaved badly* (Ch. XI:20,21).

20 If one of the positions of the government is vacated either because of death or because of removal from office, then the Company may want to convene and elect some others in order to provide the correct number.

21 Again, if it happened that someone were unable to carry out her [or his] duty or behaved badly, let that person be removed from office.

Besides electing, the Company also acts together to decide important matters affecting the whole. For example, in early 1537 a new situation developed. Angela's dear friend Girolamo Patengola, Caterina's nephew, had died and left a bequest to the Company. Girolamo had written a congratulatory verse for Angela in Cremona, when she seemed to be on the threshold of heaven, yet now he had arrived there ahead of her. After Girolamo's death, it became apparent that the Rule had not provided for any member to act as the legal representative of the Company. There was no one authorized to accept Girolamo's bequest in the Company's name. So on March 18 the chapter convened to elect such a person: a treasurer. After prayer, the Company's unanimous decision was to elect Angela "mother, minister, and treasurer" for life.[78]

The process illustrates Angela's legacy to her spiritual heirs: how to respond when new situations call for changes and *new rules or do[ing] something differently*. Then let their *principal recourse be to gather at the feet of Jesus Christ...and offer most fervent prayers. For in this way, without doubt, Jesus Christ will be in your midst, and as a true and good master, he will enlighten and teach you what you have to do* (Last Legacy:2-5). Angela trusts her daughters to do what changing circumstances may require, *prudently and with good advice* (Last Legacy:2).

Governance guides the Company, but in what areas? The sphere of governance in the Rule includes matters involving the Company's shared life. Since our members usually live and work and pray separately, there is little to organize. God *has join[ed us] together* (Pr.:4) in a vocation which is realized in each one's heart and life. Governance provides for the few needs we have in common, like gathering to nourish our spirits and our sisterly unity.

Governance is one of the *means and ways* for living with integrity. It provides a community of support for individual members. It helps Ursulines to have the freedom to follow their vocation, the mutual support to flourish in it and the resources to live it with dignity.

Quiet Revolution

The new Company of Saint Ursula was a quiet revolution. Groups of women did not generally govern themselves like this. Most monasteries of women were subordinated to the abbot of a men's community or to male diocesan authorities. It might have been difficult to begin in this unusual fashion except for the assistance of the Reverend Lorenzo Muzio, vicar of Brescia's absentee cardinal-archbishop Cornaro. On August 8, 1536, Muzio granted his approval of the Rule at the diocesan level. Brescians revered and trusted Angela. Muzio's approval and the city's respect averted opposition at first. She realized, though, that the Company's greatest difficulties lay ahead, when her personal influence would be removed by her death. People were uneasy with such a revolutionary situation, however quietly it came.

The Rule turns assumptions upside down. Ultimate control is in the hands of the many, not the few. People from different social classes collaborate as peers. Wealthy and prominent people serve the poor and lowly and work for justice for them. Men do not control women but act as their agents. Instead of clergymen interpreting God's will for them, women gather to seek divine guidance and make their own decisions. They act as spiritual teachers for one another.

Angela would not have used the term "feminism," but her work shows the consciousness that feminist historian Gerda Lerner identifies by the following characteristics:

1) awareness of oppression as a group,
2) recognition that the oppression is not natural but is "socially determined,"
3) sisterhood,
4) women-defined goals and strategies,
5) "the development of an alternate vision of the future."[79]

Sherrin Marshall applies the twentieth-century term "liberated" to women who "pursued...new activities and created definitions of spirituality not limited by gender."[80]

Each Need That Arises

The first part of Chapter XI sets up this revolutionary governance structure described in the first twenty-three verses, explored above. The last part of the chapter, however, seems to stray from the topic of governance, if one thinks of governance merely as organizational. Here the Rule begins to deal with problems such as homelessness among the members and goes on to illness and death. If we recognize governance as the mechanism for steering the right course, this part too fits into Chapter XI.

The Rule talks about what to do if a member is in need, especially if she has no home (Ch. XI:24-28). Angela assumes that matters like housing and finances are part of the journey. As we have seen, *those who govern* are responsible to manage any money or other property that may come to the Company, as God may allow (Ch. XI:22; Ninth Legacy). They should use these things *prudently* (Ch. XI:23) *for the good and the devel-*

opment of the Company (Ninth Legacy:4) and *especially to assist the sisters, and according to each need that arises* (Ch. XI:24).

Meeting needs is part of being on the right course. How we live, how we treat each other along the way, is just as important as getting to the destination. In fact, if we are not living in a heavenly way, we will never get to heaven. If we are, "The kingdom of God is among you" (Luke 17:21), because Jesus is the Way (cf. John 14:6). The way we care for each other—that is his Way, especially how we care for the ones in need.

Homelessness

Angela offers examples drawn from experience. A member might find herself without family. Perhaps a relative has died and there is no familial household which can accommodate her. Often servants were dismissed if sick and old.[81] Angela herself had no family in Brescia. She had left her rural home near Desenzano; it is possible that the Merici family no longer owned their farm.[82]

There were many women like her in the city. Most had come looking for work. Such a person might seek a job where she could live in as a *housekeeper or a maid* (XI:28), or as a lady's companion. For fifteen or more years Angela had lived in the homes of hospitable Brescians. Her life with Caterina Patengola was not unlike being a lady's companion, except that Caterina must have seen her more as a sister in spirit, in the family of Saint Francis. Later Angela

22 If by God's will and provision it should happen that some money or other material things would be held in common, remember that good management is needed for them,

23 and they should be dispensed prudently,

24 especially to assist the sisters, and according to each need that arises.

25 If there should be just two sisters who are left alone, without father and mother and other superiors, then in charity let a house be rented (if they do not have one), and let them be assisted in their needs.

26 But if only one is left alone, then one of the others should want to take her into her home

27 and offer her the assistance which seems right to those who govern.

28 However, if she would want to go to be a housekeeper or a maid, those that govern ought to take care of this, so that she may be settled where she can live virtuously and well.

lived in Antonio Romano's household and then in Agostino and Cecilia Gallo's. Though she helped with the women's work, she was seen as a guest, not as a servant.

Angela had the good fortune to be invited by kind people. However, the plight of a homeless member could be extreme. The Rule says that *those who govern ought to take care of this* (XI:28) to ensure the member's dignity and well-being. Many a person without a home felt desperate enough to accept an unsuitable, even dangerous position. Ursulines were not to be reduced to such dire choices. The matrons could help find an appropriate situation. They were also protectors to these women, who might otherwise be defenseless.

Thus governance includes protecting the weak from injustice. That is part of Jesus' way.

What about a homeless member who did not want to be a housekeeper or a maid? What if she supported herself with some trade, as a lace-maker or a seamstress, say? Angela offers several solutions which could be implemented with the help of those in governance.

If two sisters...are left alone,...let a house be rented...and let them be assisted in their needs (Ch. XI:25). Again, Angela speaks from experience. After some months in the Gallo household, with the stream of Brescians who showed up to visit her on a daily basis, she had decided to move out. A sojourn near the monastery of Saint Barnabas, apparently alone, did not last long. By 1532 Angela and Barbara Fontana had settled into an apartment next to the Church of Saint Afra on Via Francesco Crispi, which they shared till Angela's death in January 1540. This was her living arrangement at the time she composed the Rule.

[I]f only one [sister] is left alone, then one of the others should want to take her into her home (Ch. XI:26). Did Angela recall her own beloved sister, dead so many years? Her gentle challenge and invitation—*should want*—builds upon her sense that this is what sisters would *want* to do for each other. Time and again, throughout the Counsels and Testament, Angela emphasizes her prayer for her daughters to have this loving unity. *There will be no other sign that you are in the grace of the Lord than that you love one another and are united together* (Tenth Legacy:10). Interestingly, this part of Chapter XI uses the word *sister* more than any other section of the Rule.

Those who govern have a role in this arrangement (Ch. XI:27). The homeless woman's colonella brings her need to the attention of the others. They may know who could welcome this sister. Maybe some further support may be needed, too, to lighten the burden involved. A working woman could contribute to the household expenses. An elder might require financial support. Governance, then, fosters the spiritual family in very specific ways.

Old Age, Illness

From homelessness, Angela moves on to the needs of old age and illness (Ch. XI:29, 30). Again, her life informs the Rule. Only she in this young Company had experienced these diminishments. In 1535, at sixty, she was old; life-expectancy was closer to forty. She was learning about the last part of life. She must have leaned upon Barbara Fontana to do the heavy tasks in their little home, though there is a tradition that she drew water at the fountain along Via Francesco Crispi.

Angela had survived a terrible illness in Cremona. She urges that, *if any of the sisters is ill, she should be visited and assisted and guided day and night, if she is in need of this* (Ch. XI:30). She wants her daughters to be present with one another in their frailty. No doubt Barbara's presence strengthened Angela under the burden of her years.

Illness and age taught Angela how it feels to need assistance and that it is difficult to accept help graciously. She knew that it can be even harder to accept someone else's guidance and that some elders, when their minds begin to grow dull, actually do need to be guided. Thus the Rule directs that, if members are *so old that they cannot support themselves, they should be graciously willing to be assisted and guided as true spouses of Jesus Christ* (Ch. XI:29). *Spouses of Jesus Christ* echoes a phrase used repeatedly in the Prologue. It sets a tone that pervades the Rule and colors this consideration of elders. Let all treat each other with the respect that befits such a calling. Assistance, even supervision, should be given with gentleness and reverence.

There is a second meaning: the old and sick should behave as *true spouses of Jesus Christ. They should be graciously willing to be assisted and guided*, the Rule says. Graciously. Accepting assistance with grace, returning

29 Should they be so old that they cannot support themselves, they should be graciously willing to be assisted and guided as true spouses of Jesus Christ.

30 Finally remember that if any of the sisters is ill, she should be visited and assisted and guided day and night, if she is in need of this.

a grateful smile. Someone who has lived intimately all these years with Jesus must surely have learned from him who is "meek and humble of heart" (Matthew 11:29). That is Jesus' way. If we belong to him, it will be our way, too.

We begin to see that "About Governance" is less about organization and more about relationships. Maybe it could have been called "About Community."

Death

From a discussion of illness and age, Chapter XI follows a natural progression to one who *is about to die* (Ch. XI:31). The Prologue had foreshadowed this conclusion by ending with words about *heavenly glory* (Prologue:30, 31). The Company's sisterly companionship goes right up to death, it seems. And beyond!

Angela treated the moment of death with spiritual fervor in her two other works, the Counsels (Last Counsel:23-25) and the Testament (Last Legacy: 20, 21). In the Rule's Chapter XI, she takes a different tone. Here she refers to a member's last will and testament. She encourages a dying member *to leave some little thing to the Company* (Ch. XI:31). Since few of the early Ursulines had much property to leave as an estate, their bequests were not primarily economic considerations. Women of the period often used wills *as a sign of love and charity* (Ch. XI:31). With very little control over even their own property during their lifetime, women could make choices about disposing of it after death. Italian Renaissance women customarily willed most of their property to their families, as did men. Yet documentary studies show that women were more likely than men to make additional bequests to others, usually to other women or to favorite charities.[83] Through their wills, they demonstrated affection and exercised choices that were not often available to them in life.

Angela's bequests were of her rosary, prayer book and other devotional objects, left to close friends. Her formal *testament* took the form of words to the Company's matrons. She called the sections of that document her legacies, *recommendations...like legacies which, as my greatest desire, I leave you to carry out faithfully* (Prologue

31 If she is about to die, let her want to leave some little thing to the Company as a sign of love and charity.

to the Testament:30). These words were her final spiritual gifts, to be used on behalf of the Company when she had gone.

Yet she promised that she would never be gone: *I shall always be in your midst* (Last Counsel:20). Speaking as though from heaven, she assured her daughters that *I see better and hold more dear and pleasing the good things which I see you constantly doing, and...even more I want and am able to help you and do you good in every way* (Prologue to the Counsels:24, 25). Death is not the end of life. It is the beginning of a new life.

Celestial Glory

The relationships of the Company continue after death, Angela makes clear. When a woman dies, our companionship does not end. Angela directs Ursulines to accompany a sister lovingly to her burial, *going two by two in charity, each one with a candle in her hand* (Ch. XI:32). We carry the light for her—the light of Christ. She first received it with her baptismal candle. She held it with the candle she carried in the commitment ceremony when she gave herself to him in the Company.[84] Holding a candle, we accompany her with our prayers as she takes this final step. Prayer is our way of supporting her, till Jesus draws her to himself, into heavenly glory (Ch. XI:35, 36).

Still in companionship, *with the other virgins* (Ch. XI:36)! *God has join[ed the Ursulines] together* (Pr.:4). In heavenly life that unity will be even deeper.

What an unexpected ending for a chapter on governance! But this is the destination the Company has been steering toward. The Rule's first chapter is "About the Manner of Receiving" a new member, the beginning of her Ursuline life. Where else could that life end, but in heaven? Where else could this Rule end, this the guidebook for the journey?

The Prologue has laid out the same pattern. In the Prologue we glimpse the whole Rule. The Prologue begins with God's call (Pr.:4) and ends with our *return gloriously to our homeland, where from all those in Heaven and on earth great glory and triumph will arise* (Pr.:30, 31).

That glory, that light and joy, is the destination. It is not a reward, it is nothing we could ever earn or merit. All is gift, all is grace. *Our sweet and kind spouse Jesus Christ* (Ch. XI:35) called us to belong fully to him. In the moment of death he will *pull* us to himself. He will crown us *with that golden and brilliant...crown* (Ch. XI:36). He is the crown. He is the glory.

Reflection

❖ If you thought of your life as a journey, what sorts of people would you want to be traveling with?

❖ Angela looked realistically at her world and then looked again, imagining how it could be. Consider an aspect of our world, or of your own life, that you would like to re-imagine.

❖ The roles fulfilled by colonelle, matrons and men call for collaboration in a shared spirit, for common goals. Where are you challenged to collaborate with people who are different from you?

❖ Angela's creative vision saw transformed relationships as a basis for greater justice. What might her insight offer us in today's social settings, be they local, global or ecclesial?

❖ Domestic servitude remains the lot of women and girls in many countries. A member of the Company tells her own story: An aunt brought her from Africa to Canada, supposedly to visit. In the aunt's large home, she cleaned, cooked, did laundry and cared for four children, all without pay. After two years, the young woman asserted herself, and the aunt tried to get her into trouble with immigration authorities. Alone and penniless, she was dependent on the aunt. Meanwhile, however, she had met Marcella Hinz, an Ursuline, who took the young woman into her own home and assisted her in finding work. Through this encounter, a vocation which had been sown in an ardent Catholic family in Africa bloomed into a life-commitment in the Company of Saint Ursula in Canada.

❖ "I've often heard them say that they don't deserve better treatment or pay. A major task we face is convincing the women that they are individuals of worth."
- Irene Otiz, a Mexico City social worker, quoted in "In Latin America the Gender Gap Kills" by Barbara Fraser and Paul Jeffrey, Part 7 of Latin America Today, a series in *National Catholic Reporter* (Oct. 8, 2004), 11.

---

[1] Gerda Lerner, *The Creation of Feminist Consciousness from the Middle Ages to Eighteen-seventy* (New York: Oxford University Press, 1993), p. 119.

[2] Quoted in Lerner, p. 148.

[3] The sisters' instructor was Marino Rizzoni of the famous Guarinian school of the Veneto. [King, p. 195.]

4 Convents, small courts in northern Italy (e.g., Ferrara, Mantua, Urbino), and the families of humanists (e.g., Thomas More) were the rare settings in which intellectual education was available to a very few women. [Sachs, pp. 8-18.] There are records of household schools in some Italian towns (Verona, Turin and Florence), where it is estimated that about 4% of girls learned basic skills. In Venice in 1587, a generation after Angela, 12% to 13% of all girls and 33% of boys could read. [King, pp. 168, 172.]

5 Castiglione frames the contemporary debate about women in a dialogue format, articulating views on equality between the sexes and views of women's natural inferiority, especially in intellectual matters.

6 Even in the upper classes, the Renaissance can be viewed as a period of regression for women. The cities' increased economic activity did not include them. The new power structure denied them the authority and leverage that women of feudal rank had often held in the Middle Ages. The Venetian Francisco Barbaro wrote in *De re uxoria* (1416) about the well-ordered family as the guarantee of civic stability. He saw this order as chiefly dependant on "controlling the activities of women in relationship to the production and distribution of wealth." [Summarized by Jordan, p. 41.] Leon Batista Alberti's *De re uxoria* (1441, Book II of his *Della famiglia*) describes the husband's process of tutoring his new young wife into submission. [Quoted by Jordan, p. 52.] The heritage of Roman law in some areas, including Brescia, did give women some legal rights. For example, they could own property but ordinarily had to depend on a male guardian to administer it. [Sherrill Cohen, "Asylums for Women in Counter-Reformation Italy" in *Women in Reformation and Counter-Reformation Europe: Public and Private Worlds*, ed. Sherrin Marshall (Bloomington: Indiana University Press, 1989), p. 173.]

7 Matteo Palmiere (1526) expressed the common view that women should not be educated in things for which they have no use in their domestic duties. [Jordan, p. 68.]
Some writings on the subject, contemporary with Angela, are
  • Juan Luis Vives' *Instruction of Christian Women* (1532): prescribes only enough reading and writing to fit a girl for her domestic role and for chastity and obedience; he tutored Mary Tudor, later Queen of England [King, pp. 164-166.];
  • Bruto's *Institutione di una faniculla nata nobilimente* (1555): concerned that "I cannot make myself believe that [a woman's literary education] could be good"; study can hurt "the beauty and innocence of her spirit" because she is intended by nature for domestic work [Quoted by Jordan, p. 146.];
  • Erasmus's *Christiani matrimonii instituto*: argues for girls' education, "for study busies the whole soul...a means of impressing the best precepts on a girl's mind and of leading her to virtue" (Ch. 17). In a somewhat schizophrenic way, he argues for equality in marriage, yet contends that

a wife is naturally inferior and to be instructed and ruled by her husband [Jordan, pp. 58-64.];

● Cornelius Agrippa's *De nobilitate et praeexcellentia foeminei sexus* (1509): argues for women's innate superiority in a tone that may be either serious or satirical, and for egalitarian treatment [Newman, *From Virile Woman to WomanChrist*, pp. 224, 227.];

● Andrea Alciati's *Custodiendas Virgines* (Bologna, 1530): assigns to the goddess Pallas (wisdom) the role of preserving girls' virginity, i.e., through education, especially religious instruction [Zarri, "From Prophecy to Discipline: 1450-1650" in *Women and Faith: Catholic Religious Life in Italy from Late Antiquity to the Present*, p. 94.];

● Firenzuola's *Fair Ladies of Prato* (c. 1540): posits equality of the sexes on the Platonic view that the differences are material, therefore non-essential. [Agnolo Firenzuola, *On the Beauty of Women*, trans. and ed. Konrad Eisenbichler and Jacqueline Murray (Philadelphia: University of Pennsylvania Press, 1992), p. xxxiii.].

[8] Chizzola in the *Processo Nazari*, Appendix 16 of Mariani, Tarolli, Seynaeve, p. 598.

[9] Gallo in the *Processo Nazari*, Appendix 16 of Mariani, Tarolli, Seynaeve, p. 601.

[10] Mariani, Tarolli, Seynaeve, p. 113.

[11] Milagros Ortega Costa, "Spanish Women in the Reformation" in *Women in Reformation and Counter-Reformation Europe: Public and Private Worlds*, p. 108.

[12] Shahar, *Childhood in the Middle Ages*, pp. 215, 216; King, p. 168.

[13] Mariani, Tarolli, Seynaeve, p. 112.

[14] Brescia was rich in the new fields of antiquities and classical studies and in its use of the new technology of printing, beginning in 1473. [Belotti in Belotti, ed., p. 50.] Between then and 1500, its printers produced 260 works, mostly literary and predominately Latin classical texts. With this output, Brescia stood fifth among Italian centers of learning. (Or sixth, according to P. Veneziani [quoted by Belotti, p. 50, note 80].) Its ancient Roman ruins became the first publicly held archeological site in Italy, thanks to scholarly awareness among the city's leaders. [Bruno Passamani, "Il culto dell'antico e gli studi antiquari a Brescia tra i secoli XV e XVI," in *Arte, economica, cultura e religione nella Brescia del XVI secolo*, p. 343.]

[15] Shahar, *Childhood in the Middle Ages*, p. 240; Judith M. Bennet and Amy M. Froide, eds., *Singlewomen in the European Past 1250–1800* (Philadelphia: University of Pennsylvania Press, 1999), p. 9.

[16] Shahar, *Childhood in the Middle Ages*, p. 187.

[17] Bennet and Froide, p. 9.

[18] King, p. 25; Klapisch-Zuber, p. 105.

[19] Shahar, *Childhood in the Middle Ages*, p. 186.

[20] Klapisch-Zuber, p. 105.

21 King, p. 28; Klapisch-Zuber, p. 107, based on research in Tuscan records. "Sale" was illegal, but the practice was widespread.

22 Klapisch-Zuber, pp. 173, 174.

23 In Venice, later in the 16th century, records indicate that, of 584 "productive workers" in one parish, 250 were women. Of these, 245 were "massare," i.e., "domestic servants or charwomen." [King, p. 70.]

24 Penalties for rape differed, applied according to categories of victims: women of "honest lives" (virgins, wives, widows) or of "indecent lives" (servants, slaves, prostitutes). [Trevor Dean and K. J. P. Lowe, *Marriage in Italy, 1300-1650* (New York: Cambridge University Press, 1998), p. 95.]

25 Mariani, Tarolli, Seynaeve, p. 133.

26 Shahar, *Childhood in the Middle Ages*, pp. 212, 213.

27 Klapisch-Zuber, p. 166.

28 The size and importance of the dowry peaked in Renaissance Italy in the fifteenth century. Even in the poorer classes, it "became the sign of a proper marriage. The practice guaranteed parental control over their children's marriages" [Jutta Gisela Sperling, *Convents and the Body Politic in Late Renaissance Venice* (Chicago: The University of Chicago Press, 1999), p. 3.] or religious life.

29 King, p. 28.

30 King, p. 48.

31 Jordan, p. 71.

32 Maryanne Kowaleski, "Singlewomen in Medieval and Early Modern Europe: The Demographic Perspective," in Bennet and Froide, p. 78.

33 Despite the generosity of these wealthy women, obtaining voluntary contributions to help support the girls was a serious need, which Laura and Isabetta laid before Brescia's City Council in 1533 and again in 1534. [Belotti in Belotti, ed., p. 94.]

34 Monica Chojnacka, "Singlewomen in Early Modern Venice: Communities and Opportunities," in Bennet and Froide, pp. 227-230.

35 King, p. 78.

36 King, p. 78; Cohen, p. 168.

37 Sachs, p. 52.

38 Opened in 1525. [Mariani, Tarolli, Seynaeve, p. 219.]

39 Cohen, pp. 182, 183; Marshall, p. 5.

40 Shahar, *The Fourth Estate: A History of Women in the Middle Ages*, pp. 39, 40.

41 Repeated efforts to assure the freedom of religious vows, e.g., by the Fourth Lateran Council in 1215, required a legal age of consent: twelve for girls, fourteen for boys. But if the family had already invested her dower in the convent, a girl had no real alternative. [Shahar, *Childhood in the Middle Ages*, pp. 191, 193.]

42 Sperling, p. 27.

43 Timoteo da Lucca, a reforming friar, charged in 1497 that convents were "whorehouses and public bordellos." [Quoted in King, p. 85.]

44 King, p. 85.

45 The papal constitution *Periculoso* ("dangerous") of 1298 and the papal bull *Apostolicae Sedis* of 1309 imposed perpetual cloister on all nuns. [Mario Sensi, "Anchoresses and Penitents in Thirteenth- and Fourteenth-Century Umbria," in Bornstein and Rusconi, p. 67.]

46 Katherine Gill, "Open Monasteries for Women in Late Medieval and Early Modern Italy: Two Roman Examples," in *The Crannied Wall: Women, Religion, and the Arts in Early Modern Europe*, Craig A. Monson, ed. (Ann Arbor: The University of Michigan Press), p. 16.

47 Beguines ebbed after high membership in 1449: 1000 in Cologne, 1500 in Basl, 2000 in Paris. [Fossati, p. 29.]

48 Gill in Monson, p. 42.

49 Gill in Monson, p. 21.

50 Cozzano, *Risposta*, Appendix 23 of Mariani, Tarolli, Seynaeve, p. 631.

51 Girolamo Lombardi on Ottavio Gondi, quoted in Mariani, Tarolli, Seynaeve, p 321.

52 Mariani, Tarolli, Seynaeve, p. 190.

53 Gallo in the *Processo Nazari*, Appendix 16 of Mariani, Tarolli, Seynaeve, p. 599.

54 Romano in the *Processo Nazari*, Appendix 16 of Mariani, Tarolli, Seynaeve, pp. 596, 597.

55 Mariani, Tarolli, Seynaeve, p. 81.

56 Shahar, *The Fourth Estate: A History of Women in the Middle Ages*, p. 211.

57 Gabriella Zarri, "Living Saints: A Typology of Female Sanctity in the Early Sixteenth Century," in *Women, Family and Ritual in Renaissance Italy*, trans. Lydia G. Cochrane (Chicago: University of Chicago Press, 1985), pp. 235, 236.

58 Mariani, Tarolli, Seynaeve, pp. 211-213.

59 Zarri, p. 235.

60 The Italian text of the Counsels, divided into a prologue and nine sections, labels them *arricordo* ("reminder" or "counsel") and *precetto* ("precept") inconsistently. To avoid confusion, the references herein will all be termed "counsels."

61 King, p. 77.

62 Chojnacho in Bennet and Froide, p. 224.

63 Ruzante (Angelo Beolco), *La Anconitana: The Woman from Ancona*, trans. Nancy Dersofi (Berkeley: University of California Press, 1994), p. 61.

64 Mariani, Tarolli, Seynaeve, pp. 152-154. Both women belonged to noble families at the peak of power in Brescia's ruling class. The Gambara clan was second only to the Martinengos in controlling the city council between 1486 and 1516. Isabetta Prato was born into the Bargnano family, which stood eleventh among the thirty-five ruling clans in the same period. [Pegrari in

Arte, economica, cultura e religione nella Brescia del XVI secolo, p. 233.] Both clans could be classified as "rural nobility," i.e., their base of power was in land before they entered the scope of urban politics.

65 Apparently some early Ursulines participated in the good works initiated by these widows, especially by instructing orphan girls. [Mariani, Tarolli, Seynaeve, p. 220.] Thus there was a mutuality through sharing their gifts in service.

66 Shahar, *The Fourth Estate: A History of Women in the Middle Ages*, p. 27.

67 Women without parents or without men were vulnerable to accusations of heresy. [Lerner, p. 79.]

68 Shahar, *The Fourth Estate: A History of Women in the Middle Ages*, p. 14.

69 Wages due only at the end of employment were often postponed. [Klapisch-Zuber, p. 174.]

70 Klapisch-Zuber, p. 166. On those terms, an Ursuline would never be paid.

71 Mariani, Tarolli, Seynaeve, p. 310 (translation from Latin the author's).

72 The first such election to be documented dates to 1555. The Company also elected three men of the local nobility as "protectors." [Mariani, Tarolli, Seynaeve, p. 312.]

73 Belotti in Belotti, ed., p. 49, note 75.

74 Belotti in Belotti, ed., p. 48.

75 Mary Germaine Thorburn, OSU, "The Christology of Angela Merici," unpublished paper, 1975.

76 Gallo in the *Processo Nazari*, Appendix 16 of Mariani, Tarolli, Seynaeve, p. 599 (translation the author's).

77 The Company also chose or elected the confessor (Ch. VII:12).

78 *Atto d'elezione di Angela Merici*, Appendix 6 of Mariani, Tarolli, Seynaeve, p. 580.

79 Lerner, p. 274.

80 Marshall, p. 7.

81 Klapisch-Zuber (study of Florence in this same era), p. 175.

82 From records showing a Zuan Merigo (Angela's elder brother?) working in the port for the Commune of Desenzano and his son being employed as a digger for seven days in 1509-1510 (presumably to pay their taxes in labor rather than in cash), Gianpietro Belotti speculates that after Giovanni Merici's death the family farm was no longer prospering. He also suggests that it may have been sold around or after 1516, though the property records for the relevant years are lost. By 1523, Angela was the only Merici owing property in Desenzano—her vineyard. [Belotti in Belotti, ed., pp. 72-74; cf. Mariani, Tarolli, Seynaeve, p. 124.]

83 King, p. 55.

84 Mariani, Tarolli, Seynaeve, p. 384.

Part 5

The Trellis

The Trellis

Photograph courtesy of Hector Bedolla

Healthy growth requires healthy beginnings. That was true in Angela's vineyard near Desenzano. Vines know, somehow, from deep in their viney roots, how to twine as they grow, always twining around something. It is the vintner's responsibility to provide the trellis. If the vine twines along the trellis, it will be lifted to the sun. If it runs along the ground, with no guidance, it will tangle among all sorts of other growth. No one confuses the trellis with the grapes, but a good trellis is an important means to cultivate good fruit.

Chapters I to VII set out behaviors and spiritual exercises that form the trellis lifting the Company's vines to the sun. These practices foster deep personal commitment. They are grounded in the relationship with Christ that the Prologue talks about.

A. Setting Out on the Path: Chapters I - III

The first three chapters of the Rule deal with very basic matters in the process of incorporating new members. They are about a new Ursuline's first steps along her path. Their significance is great, though, since how she takes these first steps strongly influences how she will walk the whole way. Issues of clothing and behavior may seem external, superficial, even trivial. Yet Angela's deeper message is not merely about what to do, but about how and why. Each of these first chapters prepares the new member for a particular aspect of her core commitment.

Chapter I, "About the Manner of Receiving," assures the members' freedom. That is the basis for *holy obedience* to God. Chapter II, "How They Should Be Attired," calls for choices based on true values, consistency between inner spirit and outer appearance. Authenticity is the basis for *true poverty of spirit*. Chapter III, "About the Manner of Interacting in the World," deals with the delicate balancing act of being in the world, yet not swallowed by it. If their commitment permeates their actions, God's love will shine through these women into the world. That is the sign of *sacred virginity*.

Chapter I, "About the Manner of Receiving" – Freedom

The manner of receiving involves discerning God's call, supporting the freedom to answer it and honoring relationships. The Company seeks to foster the inner and the outer freedom of a prospective member. It opens a way for her to give herself fully to God.

Chapter I is directed both to the members and to the governors. The Rule uses two verbs, *entering* and *be admitted* (Ch. I:1) to point in two directions: to the woman who wishes to enter and to those who must consider whether and how she is to be admitted. It names some criteria for this vocation. The woman approaching the Company must look into her own heart for these. The governors must seek to understand her. One of the most important services the governance can perform for the Company is assuring the quality of its future membership.

The chapter begins with the woman's suitability for the Company, that is, her situation in life and interior dispositions. Angela emphasizes the candidate's freedom to make this choice and sets up a procedure intended to honor the member's relationships while supporting her if she faces opposition from her family. The chapter ends with preparation for her eventual commitment.

Criteria for Admission

Angela begins by saying that a prospective member *ought to be a virgin and should have the firm intention of serving God in this sort of life* (Ch. I:1, 2). How are these qualities determined? Regarding the first criterion, Angela's concern was not physical. Most simply, being a *virgin* refers to the candidate's state of life.

Is this woman unmarried? If she has made the vow and entered the vocation of marriage, she is not free for this way of life.

Does she have a young child? Then motherhood is her first commitment. (The reception of Marta della Pizza during Angela's lifetime raises, but does not answer,

1 First of all, remember how each one who will be entering or be admitted into this Company ought to be a virgin

2 and should have the firm intention of serving God in this sort of life.

3 Then, she should enter it happily

4 and of her own will.

the question of a widow whose children are adults. Marta's mother, known as "la Pizza," was a colonella.[1] In the Rule this office is reserved to the Company's members. Later, widows sometimes filled the position. Was La Pizza—mother and widow—a member? We do not know.)

Is the candidate known to be chaste? Her life must show that she can embrace consecrated celibacy.

Angela's second criterion is *the firm intention of serving God*. God, *serving God*, must be her focus, because it is the focus of Ursuline life. This most important, deepest qualification is spiritual. Is the Spirit stirring in her heart? Does she yearn to live intimately with God? If that desire is calling her to sacred virginity, she may be suited for it.

[T]he firm intention of serving God in this sort of life, the third criterion, may seem self-evident. Why else would one wish to join the Company? But a wish is not a *firm intention*! A wish may last but a moment; a *firm intention* endures. A wish flutters about in our thoughts and emotions. A *firm intention* shapes our actions. This intention must be tested over time. When Angela was in Salò with her aunt and uncle Biancosi, the Franciscans guided her in adopting consistent practices of spirituality and behavior. Her family and the Franciscans and she herself came to recognize her *firm intention of serving God*, at first in the Franciscan Third Order. Angela applied the same considerations to the women who would become the Company's first members. They began to learn the practices of Ursuline life for several years before they actually began the Company in 1535. Angela came to know them well as she visited them and gathered them in Isabetta Prato's home for prayer and discussion. She could observe their *firm intention of serving God*.

Angela expects a candidate to have clarity about *this sort of life*. Many, many good people serve God. Every vocation is a way of serving God: marriage, ministry, single and religious life. Each person is called by God, and each is suited to answer in a particular way. That is one's vocation. Vocations are not interchangeable. We can hear Angela urging clear discernment, "You want to serve God. Wonderful! Of course! But in *this sort of life*?" To discern that, a woman can try gradually to live this way. "Be earnest," Angela might tell us. "Be honest. Honest with everyone, with the Company. Mostly with yourself. Listen. Listen for deep inner sounds of happiness." Each woman's music will be her own. Does her happiness purr or bubble or laugh? How does happiness sound at her heart's core?

No one should expect that this life will make her happy, though. The question is whether, on this path, she can find happiness. No way of life or person or community will make us happy. But we have the best chance of finding and making our happiness in the sort of life that we are best suited for, created for. If the Company is a woman's authentic vocation, she will draw energy from its practices and joy from Ursuline companionship. If not, she will be uneasy and lonely. A new member *should enter [the Company] happily and of her own will* (Ch. I:3, 4), Angela's fourth criterion. If this is the place God calls her to, she will be able to find happiness here. *[God] wants only what is for your good and joy* (Ch. X:18).

Freedom to Choose

She should enter, Angela emphasizes, of *her own will* (Ch. I:4), her fourth criterion. A woman's *own will* did not figure importantly in six-teenth-century Italy's families or society. Yet Angela sees it as the only way to undertake this life and the only way to live it.

Most women's families chose for them, often happily, often not.[2] Sometimes those choices coincided with their own, sometimes not. Italian court documents show disputes over parents' attempts to impose their will by force or beatings.[3] And even if marriage or religious life proved difficult, social institutions supported and shaped these states of life. The Ursulines would have only each other and the guidance of the Rule. External pressures were and are immense, not only to marry, but to live by selfish or worldly values. Only free choice, coming from deep personal commitment and upheld by grace, can sustain one who takes this path.

There is also an intrinsic reason for Angela's insistence on freedom. The *holy obedience* described in Chapter VIII requires the inner freedom to listen to the Holy Spirit—in many voices but most especially in one's own heart. Members must also be able to act on what they hear. People who have already demonstrated their liberty of spirit can be expected to live *holy obedience.*

Angela's fifth criterion is that the prospective member not already be committed to marriage or monastery. Why would someone seek to enter the Company

5 Third, she should not have made a promise to any monasteries nor to earthly men.

if she has already *made a promise to any monasteries [or] to earthly men* (Ch. I:5)? That seems like a contradiction. Exactly! She cannot make up her mind! Maybe her family chose a state of life for her, and she agreed but has changed her mind. In the upper classes especially, a Renaissance Italian family often engaged a daughter when she was very young. That had to be resolved before she was fully free. Vows made in religious life would be an obstacle, too. One who has committed herself to a man or a community is responsible to reach a mutual resolution of that commitment before she can undertake a new one. Each person has the responsibility to choose freely, make her choice known clearly and act accordingly.

Steps toward Entrance

Assuming that she has chosen to join the Company, the Rule tells her to speak to her *father or mother or other superiors* (Ch. I:6). She could perhaps come quietly into the Company, since membership does not require her to change her residence or to wear different clothing. But that would not be honest. A member must be able to live her truth. If it is difficult...well, the years ahead will require honesty and courage. She will need to practice and demonstrate these qualities now.

She must *first ask their permission* (Ch. I:6), the Rule says. "*First*" signals an important sequence. Several possible steps follow. We must remember that nearly every unmarried Italian woman of Angela's day lived in some social unit headed by a person in authority. By far the best start for her new life was to get everyone's agreement. That honored her relationships and involved her relatives in supporting her choice, smoothing the road ahead.

The next step is having *the governors [women and men] of the Company talk with them* (Ch. I:7). This visit served more than one purpose. Angela wanted the Company's leaders to know and understand each Ursuline, *not only their names, but also their condition, and character, and their every situation and state* (Second Legacy:2, 3). What better starting point than visiting her home and family?

6 Fourth, if she has father or mother or other superiors, she should first ask their permission

7 so that the governors of the Company, [women and men] may talk with them so that [they may verify that] they do not have any legitimate cause, if by chance they should afterwards want to prevent her from entering into this holy obedience.

The Company is like a family, too, a spiritual family, not just an associ-ation. A member brings to it her whole self, including her relationships. No one exists in isolation.

Another purpose for the visit came into play if the family was unwilling to endorse the vocation, a situation that Angela herself had faced as a young woman in Salò. The best way would be persuasion. The governing people could help. Besides offering moral support, they could answer questions and provide credibility. Their maturity and social standing might assuage parental fears for an unprotected daugh-ter's future. And if there was *any legitimate cause...to prevent her* (Ch. I:7), it had to be dealt with.

Such a *legitimate cause* could be a contract of engagement to marry or the payment of her dowry to a monastery. The role of the govern-ing women and men was to guarantee the woman's actual freedom, to verify that the parents *do not have any legitimate cause, if by chance they should afterwards want to prevent her from entering* this way of life (Ch. I:7).

Parents and guardians did sometimes change their minds. They probably loved their daughter and wanted the best for her. They felt responsible to arrange a marriage or place her in religious life. They may have gone along with her desire to become an Ursuline, thinking that she would eventually "come to her senses." When their concern for her future became pressing, they might insist on a monastery or a marriage. Religious life was seen as "real" consecration. A nun seemed more stable and secure than an Ursuline. Or an advantageous family alliance through marriage might seem more compelling to the parents than their daughter's personal choice. They might invoke duty as a rea-son for her to marry. In such a case, the Company's "governors" would stand up for her. They could testify that there had been no legitimate obstacle to her choice.

Inner freedom is essential for a full response to God's invitation. In a world where women's freedom had no structure of support, Angela created it, a revolutionary act.

Beginning to Learn this Way

Next the Rule cites *at least twelve years of age* (Ch. I:8) as the threshold. In the twenty-first century, we ask, "How much freedom and under-standing can be expected at twelve?" At twelve, a sixteenth-century girl was often engaged to marry. Some even married at this age and were mothers a year later. If someone thought that God was calling her to this celibate vocation, twelve was the proper age *to be taught the truth of this unique way of life* (Ch. I:9). No one so young could actually become a member. This was a learning time, for her and for the Company, as they became acquainted. Not till she was fifteen would the Company consider accepting her formally into a process of preparation. She would make a commitment between eighteen and twenty.[4] Her sisters were probably already married by those ages.[5]

As the Rule describes it, the learning begins through contact. The Company welcomes the candidate to gatherings (Ch. I:9). The teaching is not so much instruction as it is personal formation.[6] She can develop habits of life and spiritual understanding, leading her to experience *the truth of this unique way of life* (Ch. I:9). Again, we are reminded that "truth" is one of Angela's favorite names for Jesus Christ. Our way, our truth, our life: Jesus is all. The candidate learns to know him and to recognize his voice.

8 Fifth, she should be at least twelve years of age.

9 Remember, however, that those of a younger age can be received into the group so that they may be taught the truth of this unique way of life.

Reflection

❖ What are the sources of joy for you in living your vocation?

❖ Angela creatively developed a way and involved others to support the freedom of women who would otherwise have been trapped in social and economic systems. Do you see an area where you could apply your creativity or your supportive assistance to do something similar?

❖ How does your on-going growth in your own vocation help you to know Jesus better as the truth of your life?

Chapter II, "How They Should Be Attired" - Integrity

Once women are actually admitted, they start to live according to the Rule for several years before making promises. The transition to commitment is gradual. Values like those taught by Chapter II must be learned. Therefore, and for reasons of practicality, they *can wear those same clothes which they are wearing when they enter* (Ch. II:4).

Modesty

Angela uses two Italian words with the same root, *honeste, honestade,* in the first line of her chapter on clothing: *the apparel and the garb ought to be modest (honeste – plural form) and simple, as truly demanded of virginal integrity*

Old costume of marriageable maiden. Woodcut by Cesare Vecellio (1521-1601), #66 in Vecellio's *Renaissance Costume Book*, Dover Publications, Inc. (www.dover-publications.com).

1 Once more remember, indeed, how the apparel and the garb ought to be modest and simple as truly demanded of virginal integrity.

2 Indeed, each one should go about with her bodice suitably laced up, and on top shawls or scarves of cloth such as linen or cotton, not too thin and certainly not transparent; and so should the shawls be.

3 Now, their clothes ought to be of simple cloth or serge, dark in color or dark tan or grayish or a dark blackish color as is convenient for each according to what she can do.

(*honestade*) (Ch. II:1). Today, *honest* means true to one's word, speaking or acting truly. In several languages, this basic word was applied in the sixteenth century to chaste women, for example, wives true to their marriage vows.[7] They are "honest"; they have honor, that is integrity. *Honestade* could also mean integrity with or without reference to issues of chastity.[8] The issue had a special urgency in Angela's day, when it was widely assumed that single women, who belonged to no man, belonged to every man. An Ursuline's clothing would reinforce the Company's credibility for chaste commitent, as well as her own.

In relation to Ursulines' clothing, then, one meaning of *honesta* is "modest." Angela's main point is that our clothing be consistent with our commitment. This is the *integrity* she speaks of. Clothing makes a statement. In these words she has told us that our clothing should speak the truth of our lives: our *sacred virginity*, our complete belonging to Christ. Very low-cut, open bodices filled in with some sheer white material were typical for women of all classes and ages.[9] Her direction to have *the bodice suitably laced up, and on top scarves* (Ch. II:2) means that there is no place for self-display, whether for vanity, seductiveness or status.

Simplicity

Having lived for fourteen years in a cloth merchant's household, Angela naturally paid attention to fabrics: *scarves of cloth such as linen or cotton....clothes of simple cloth (panno) or serge (sarza)* (Ch. II:2, 3). These were the common fabrics that ordinary Brescians wore. Her dear friend Antonio Romano and the other cloth merchants imported beautiful *silk* and *velvet* (Ch. II:6, 7).[10] These were the expensive luxuries of the wealthy. They made a statement about their wearer. They said, "Notice me. I am rich. I am powerful. I belong to an important family."

Angela's interest in simplicity appears also in her references to color. When she calls for dark tones: *dark...or dark tan or grayish* (Ch. II:3), she is referring to shades that were usual among the working classes. Vivid colors were not available to ordinary people. Italian merchants imported dyes, which had been a staple of the Asian trade through Venice for centuries. Exotic dyes, like fine fabrics, were consumer luxuries that broadcast one's wealth, lavished on oneself. Upper class clothing burst into even more brilliant variety in the sixteenth century. Spanish explorers were bringing mysterious elements from the "new world" and even from Asia, along the western route.[11]

Meanwhile, local Italian dyers constantly worked and experimented to develop new dyes, as Angela would have known well in the Romano household. Angela suggests fabrics *dark in color or dark tan or grayish (beretino) or a dark blackish color.* She is not seeking to be vague. Good black dye was nearly unknown at the time. Dyers constantly experimented on how to achieve a good black through elaborate stages of shades of gray dye. The more often a fabric was dipped in the gray dye, the closer it approached true black and was accordingly more expensive.[12] Most people could not afford the luxury of bright color or of deep black and used cloth in its natural shade or one of the ordinary dark dyes. Generally, working people wore duller and grayer colors.[13] In describing Angela's funeral, Brescia's chronicler Pandolfo Nassino recorded that her body was garbed in *grayish* (using the Italian word *beretino*) clothing, typical of the Franciscan Third Order.[14] These details are not merely an historical exercise, any more than her citing of clothing styles in this chapter of her Rule was a fashion exercise for Angela. They might all be summarized in one word, "Simplicity!" Simplicity to the point where dress is not a major concern. Simple, dignified, modest. She cites details to show her daughters in concrete terms how to put simplicity into practice. In a world with different practices, we must find our own ways. We look at her examples closely enough to understand why she includes them, then apply her values to our own society and economy.

Solidarity

4 But the sisters can wear those same clothes which they are wearing when they enter this rule, but only for as long as these clothes last. However, of course, any type with flounces or braid on the sleeves or of any special cut or with any embroidery or other similar handiwork is never called for.

*5 They ought to wear a cincture cord as a sign of exterior mortification and perfect interior chastity. [*Verse 5 has been identified as an insertion made after Angela's death. The cincture was imposed by some of the matrons in an effort to refute criticisms that the Company was not religious enough. Those opposing the cincture saw it as inconsistent with their fully lay vocation in the world. Furthermore, the word "chastity" does not appear elsewhere in Angela's Rule.]

In this spirit, then, we read Angela's firm words that *any type with flounces or braid on the sleeves or of any special cut or with embroidery or other similar handiwork is never called for.*[15] Why single out these styles to prohibit? Why *sleeves*? Sleeves were a major fashion item in late fifteenth- and early sixteenth-century Italy. Many women had a basic dress (or a few) with several sets of detachable sleeves, one more elaborate than the next.[16] They competed with one another by means of *flounces or braid.*[17] Competition like this separates people by envy or by economic layers.[18] The attention paid to extravagant styles also distracts attention from truly significant matters, including the wearer!

Angela treats *embroidery* as extravagant. There was a cost, besides the specially dyed embroidery threads. Embroidery and lace and open work really were *work* (*lavori* in Italian, Ch. II:4). Most of this labor was done by seamstresses or servants, usually overworked and underpaid.[19] What one woman wore, often with pride, another woman had created, often with pain.

Shoes were another matter for vanity (Ch. II:6). In his *Abiti antichi e Moderni di Diversi Parti del Mondo*, Cesare Vecellio describes sixteenth-century Venetian women as shortening their dresses enough to show off their fashionable shoes.[20]

It is not surprising that Angela considered *silver and gold...undesirable* (Ch. II:6). Metallic threads and beads were a way of wearing one's wealth.[21] A bride's family might dress her that way to impress the wedding guests. A husband might use his wife's clothing to show off his wealth. Christ's spouse too should be dressed in such a way as to manifest his riches. In the words of Saint Paul, "Put on then, as God's chosen ones, holy and beloved, heartfelt compassion, kindness, humility, gentleness, and patience, bearing with one another and forgiving one another…. And over all these put on love, that is, the bond of perfection" (Colossians 3:12-14).

Old costume worn in Venice and other parts of Italy. Woodcut by Cesare Vecellio (1521-1601), #71 in Vecellio's *Renaissance Costume Book*, Dover Publications, Inc. (www.doverpublications.com).

Vanity

Angela is thinking of Christ's spouses when she rules out *transparent scarves* (Ch. II:7). According to custom, every woman wore some sort of scarf over her bodice, since the dresses were so low-cut. But some fabrics were so thin that they could be called *transparent.* As for *gathers on the camisoles* (Ch. II:7), why do some women try to make their breasts seem larger than they are? The attention these women attract does no good to them or to those who look at them.

One of Angela's basic pedagogical methods is to list concrete details and finish with a summary phrase. She has listed *undesirable* features of clothing. At the end of the chapter comes the summary: *Finally, no styles or varieties or anything at all transparent or other signs of vanity that could mar one's conscience or that of others and may be contrary to virginal integrity* (Ch. II:8, 9).

Vanity has two common meanings; both apply here. One is emptiness, the foolish assignment of value to something that has no enduring value:

6 Silk is not acceptable, even less velvet and silver and gold; no slippers and shoes if they are not black and of a modest style.

7 No colored scarves and kerchiefs, none of silk or any other kind that is too thin and transparent; no gathers on the camisoles.

8 Finally, no styles or varieties or anything at all transparent or other signs of vanity that could mar one's own conscience or that of others

9 and may be contrary to virginal integrity.

Vanity of vanities, says Qoheleth, vanity of vanities! All things are vanity! (Ecclesiastes 1:2)

The second meaning of vanity is self-absorption, based on appearances, especially on false images of the self. Both forms of vanity *mar one's conscience.* False values are the enemy of *true poverty of spirit.* To be stripped of them is the best way to reach the truth of oneself in God.

Integrity

The *conscience of others* also matters, when we decide what to wear. None of us is alone. Members of the Company are part of their larger community. We cannot control what others do or think, but we should not seek to wear clothes that are intended to puff us up in pride or evoke envy or lust in those who see us. That would be *contrary to virginal honestade* (Ch. II:9). These last words of Chapter II hark back to its beginning. Angela begins and ends this discussion of clothing with *integrity*.

By the chapter's end, we have seen Angela apply this spiritual concept in very concrete and challenging ways. *Honestade* is the integrity of truth: the inner and outer realities are the same. Chapter II is to remind a new member to wear clothing that speaks the truth that she now belongs to Christ, not to the world of commerce or competition...clothing that says we are one Company, not separate social classes, much less that some of us take advantage of the hard labors of our poorer sisters...clothing that shows our self-respect and respect for others, with no mixed messages about our complete self-gift to God. This is the *honestade*, honesty, integrity of wholeness and simplicity, of being completely God's.

Reflection

❖ Select a key idea to reflect about in your own choices around clothing:
> modesty,
> simplicity,
> solidarity,
> vanity,
> integrity.

❖ Angela understood the cost of certain fashion items in terms of the labor of poor women. What do you think she might say today about clothing assembled in sweat shops or maquiladoras?

Woodcut by Cesare Vecellio (1521-1601), #111 in Vecellio's *Renaissance Costume Book*, Dover Publications, Inc. (www.doverpublications.com).

Chapter III, "About the Manner of Interacting in the World" – In the World but Not of the World

In the Prologue, Angela says that *God has granted you the grace of separating you from the darkness of this poor world* (Pr.: 4). Yet members never leave the world.[22] They will live out their vocation—in the world—by interacting. There is nothing new about where they are. But now they interact with that world from a new place, an interior point of reference, their espousal to Christ.[23] Now they must be a light in that world, glowing from within. Their light is Christ. Words and deeds must show him to the people around them: families, neighbors, the *world*.

Learning Balance

Chapter III reverberates with echoes of Angela's teenage experiences in Salò. Then she was trying to translate her interior reality into consistent outer actions. Some of her impulsive deeds show her struggles. According to early biographers, Angela rubbed ashes in her blond hair when she was told that its beauty would attract suitors. She is said to have tossed some soil on the delicacies offered at a picnic rather than indulge her palate.[24]

Eventually Angela was able to balance the tension between her inner focus and the distractions or detours that opened up around her. The Franciscan Third Order provided guidance and personal support. She learned the regular spiritual practices that would steady her steps. She learned to trust herself, or rather to trust God's active presence strengthening and guiding her. The subtext of Chapter III is her trust that her daughters too can balance the tensions of being in the world yet not of it.

Yet most of what Angela talks about in Chapter III, "About the Manner of Interacting in the World" is what *not* to do. That is because the transition from one way of life to another requires attention to the behavioral changes that the new member needs to implement. Gradually, each faithful Ursuline grows in the habits that will *let all [her] words, acts and conduct always...teach and edify those who deal with [her]*, the ideal of *sacred virginity* expressed in Chapter IX (Ch. IX:21). The negatives, the "do nots," in Chapter III point out habits that must give way to new ones. Angela comments on behaviors inconsistent with the new life, on unhealthy activities and on actual dangers to a woman's physical or spiritual well-being. (The sidebar text of the Rule is presented thematically here, not in strict sequence.)

Witness of Actions

Angela calls upon the new Ursuline to behave consistently and to give a clear picture of her commitment. One challenge was to convince her family of her vocation, when her parents' greatest hope was for an advantageous marriage. Family and social life made this a priority. Mediterranean societies had virtually no place for unmarried women in Angela's time. Records from the rural area near Lucca in the late fifteenth century, Angela's youth, show that .5% of the population remained single throughout life.[25]

Another pressing issue reached beyond the family. Single women were at risk of being equated with prostitutes.[26] (This was a particular problem in towns, where poor rural women migrated seeking work to earn a dowry. Towns therefore had a surplus of single women.[27]) Actions, like the clothing described in Chapter II, carry messages. Angela cautions her daughters, *when walking on the roads or streets, to go about with eyes lowered, and wrapped modestly in shawls* (Ch. III, 5). Revealing clothes could seem an advertisement of one's body.

Some situations are no longer suitable for the woman who has made a commitment to Christ. For example, *standing on balconies* (Ch. III:4) was an acceptable way for a young woman of the sixteenth century to receive the gaze and attentions of suitors, even their serenades. It was a traditional setting for flirtation and courtship. A spouse of Christ is no longer available for courtship, though. Likewise, Angela's warning not to stand *at doors or in the streets* (Ch. III:4) is a reminder that someone loitering in public places appears available for whatever may come along. *[D]allying* and *look[ing] curiously* (Ch. III:6) can invite flirtation.

Ruzante's comedy *The Woman from Ancona* (Padua, 1533) illustrates situations familiar to Angela. The play opens with a

2 ...not in any way to listen to the private messages of men or of women, especially in secret.

4 ...to avoid standing on balconies, even less at doors or in the streets, neither alone nor in the company of others, for many reasons.

5 ...when walking on the roads or streets, to go about with eyes lowered, and wrapped modestly in shawls,...

conversation between a young man on the street and the courtesan Doralice, sitting at her window.[28] In another scene, servants carry messages between Doralice and a lover, who later comes to court her as she sits on her balcony.[29]

Angela also warns against *private messages...in secret* (Ch. III:2). In her day, this meant love letters, flirtatious exchanges or secret meetings. Given the strong parental control exercised over most marriages, some lovers took matters into their own hands and arranged to elope, often abetted by a matchmaker. Abduction, seduction or rape could result in marriage between the parties, since the woman's family could no longer present her as marriageable to anyone else.[30] *[P]rivate messages* were often the only way for such communications to reach unmarried women, since they were usually chaperoned.[31] Lower-class women were most vulnerable to seduction and rape, since they had less protection before and less recourse after the fact. The Italian word *imbassade* (*private messages*) carries a negative, malicious connotation.

However they are communicated, secrets lead to dark places. Angela would urge: "Let us live in the light! For our own sake and the sake of all around us! Would it be just to lead another on into an intrigue? Most of all, our fidelity is at stake." In Chapter IX, "About Virginity," she sums up this integrity: *Finally, not doing any act, any deed unworthy especially of one who has the name of a servant of Jesus Christ* (Ch. IX:20).

Healthy Habits

Yet some of the activities prohibited in Chapter III sound harmless to a modern ear. What could be unsuitable about going to weddings (Ch. III:3)? Angela's concern was not about the religious ceremony. However, the wedding feast was where Italian families of her day brought sons and daughters together to match them up for marriage. Like dating in a later century, these pre-marriage activities were innocent in themselves, but not appropriate for the person who had made a celibate commitment.

[D]ances and jousts (athletic contests based on war games, Ch. III:3) served the same purpose, for daughters of protective families. For young working women with less protection they could be truly dangerous. Again, Ruzante's play offers an example contemporary with Angela. Doralice's maid relishes the chance to advance her flirtation with a

3 ...not to attend weddings, and even less dances and jousts and other similar displays of worldly pleasures.

6 ...and walk quickly, without dallying or stopping here and there, nor standing about to look curiously at anything

7 because from everywhere come dangers and various traps and diabolic snares.

young man by dancing with him at a holiday feast. These events, much frequented by groups of young men, often involved excessive alcohol; women can be vulnerable when such crowds get out of hand.

Besides direct challenges to their consecrated celibacy and outright threats to safety, Angela realizes that more subtle dangers can compromise spiritual health. She alerts new Ursulines to several unhealthy habits. *[D]allying* and *looking curiously* can make them vulnerable to *dangers, traps and...snares everywhere* (Ch. III:7). Angela is telling us that wasting time can lead to filling the mind with empty, foolish things at odds with our values. If we go everywhere that curiosity draws us, it can be hard to stay on our chosen path. Cultivate interests that nourish your well-being, she tells us, not those that tug you off your path. Her words direct us inward. We can spend the coin of our selves, the precious coin of our time—our very life—casually or with deep intention. Let not a restless spirit waste our life-time on momentary attractions or meaningless sensations!

Friendship

Another danger is people seeking to take advantage of those who are easily led. This chapter begins with *remember: first not to deal with a bad sort of woman* (Ch. III:1). Angela acknowledges the effect of companionship. Friendship is powerful, for good or ill. So much of each person is potential, and companionship develops our qualities, our very self. Our associates model different behaviors and draw out and reinforce our potential self. Angela recognizes the negative influence of *a bad sort of woman*, someone whose habits tend toward sinful ways, like materialism, malicious gossip, promiscuity, dishonesty, over-indulgence. Speaking to the colonelle in the Seventh Counsel, she is explicit: *idle women who do not like to live chastely, and who willingly enjoy hearing about vanities and worldly pleasures* (Seventh Counsel:4, 5).

Of course, our lives are not isolated. But we can choose whom to seek out and spend time with. Implicitly, Angela challenges us to cultivate friendships which reinforce the healthy tendencies that lead to fullness of life. The very existence of the Company testifies to her endorsement of positive relationships. Members find sisterly support for the best in one another.

1 In addition to this, remember: first not to deal with a bad sort of woman.

The "World"

Angela prohibits *displays of worldly pleasures* (Ch. III:3). Yet Ursulines are meant to *interact in the world*, in the ordinary flow of life. There is a seeming contradiction in English between the negative implications of *worldly (mondani) pleasures* and the positive sense of *interacting in the world (secolo)*. It raises a major issue, one which goes to the very heart of the Ursuline vocation.

What did Angela mean by the *world*? Of course, *world* is an English word. We say "world" to translate two different Italian words, *secolo* and *mondo*, which have two different meanings, descending directly from Latin. Angela drew upon the New Testament in the Vulgate translation of the Bible, the Latin version with which she was familiar.

First let us look at the word *secolo*, which appears in the title of Chapter III: "About the Manner of Interacting in the *World*." *Secolo* derives from the Latin *saeculum*, referring to all that belongs to the cycles of time. It is the common term for a century and carries no positive or negative meaning. All the functions that belong to time are implied: the times of ordinary life, events of the marketplace or the home, the cycles of history.

The other word, *mondo*, has a different sense. It is derived from the Latin *mundus*, which refers to the place and experience of earth alone, supposedly cut off from heavenly or spiritual realities. In the Vulgate edition of the Bible, *mundus* has negative, anti-spiritual connotations. ("Do not love the world [*mundum*] or the things of the world [*mundum*]" 1 John 2:15.) In the Prologue Angela counsels gratitude to God for *the grace of separating you from the darkness of this poor world (mondo)* (Pr.:4). A world blind to God is deep in shadow and in misery. When she warns against *worldly (mondani) pleasures* (Ch. III:3), she means experiences that work against the spirit, tendencies away from goodness, the opposite of heavenly values. *[W]orldly pleasures* are those which appeal to selfishness, pride, lust and anger.

Displays which entertain people by fostering these impulses are not good for anyone. She urges her daughters to avoid them, avoid polluting their spirits. Take *jousts* (Ch. III:3)—games of warfare. They fostered violent spirits. Her spiritual father Saint Francis had turned away from such amusements after his conversion. She had learned from his example that we are better off when we nourish our spirits, rather than poisoning them.

Earlier in these pages, we considered the perspective that Angela's path to heaven runs through the world, not away from it. She heard God's voice, experienced God's providence, found God's face in her surroundings. She found the world to be a sacred setting. Part of the Ursuline vocation is to interact in the world, the *secolo*, ordinary life, while not being swallowed by the world, the *mondo*, the darkness.[32]

Support under Pressure

Angela recognized the problems faced by new Ursulines. When they sought to avoid inappropriate or unhealthy situations, *mothers or other worldly superiors [might] want to pressure them into such things or similar dangers* (Ch.III:8). For example, marriage-minded parents hoped that a wedding reception would build momentum toward an engagement. Saint Bernardine of Siena (d. 1444) complained of mothers "displaying their daughters like wares on the market to prospective bidders."[33]

8 Sixth, that if mothers or other worldly superiors should want to pressure them into such things or similar dangers

9 or should want to hinder them from fasting or prayer or confession or other kinds of good things,

10 be quick to refer this to the lady governors of the Company so that they may take care of it.

[O]ther worldly superiors could have benevolent intentions, just as Angela's aunt and uncle Biancosi had when they tried to take Angela to dances. There may have been—and still are—less kindly motives. Some people misuse authority and try to put women in harm's way for selfish purposes. People in authority might *wish to hinder them from fasting or prayer or confession or other kinds of good things* (Ch. III:9). These *good things* are the *means and ways* that support each member in her vocation. An Ursuline needs these spiritual practices. They nourish her capacity to live poverty of spirit, sacred virginity and holy obedience.

There was little recourse for Brescian women in subordinate positions (the situation of almost all single women). But Angela developed a response system for these problems. The Company's matrons, mature widows of good standing, stood ready to support members whose *superiors* pressured them into inappropriate situations or opposed the practices of their new life. A member had only to *be quick to refer this to the lady governors of the Company so that they [might] take care of it* (Ch. III:10). One of the matrons would visit the parents or employer. She would back up the Ursuline. Her words and prestige would carry weight. The Company's organizational structure provided a creative way to safeguard members' vocations and to sustain them in their chosen life.

Beacons on the Path

Chapter III is the third and last of the Rule's chapters on incorporating new members. Each shows how a new member is to enter into the Company's ways. Yet each chapter also inculcates ideals that remain beacons on her life-long path. Chapter I calls for the freedom that makes *holy obedience* possible. Chapter II teaches simplicity and authenticity, the groundwork for *true poverty of spirit*. Chapter III challenges her to shape her behavior by *sacred virginity*, by her relationship with Christ.

Reflection

❖ Savor the blessings that come from true friendships.
❖ Plan for the strengthening of healthy habits.
❖ Do you habitually waste time or energy in ways that are at odds with the Gospel?

---

[1] Mariani, Tarolli, Seynaeve, pp. 299, 300.

2 While Brescian law allowed women above twenty to marry without parental consent, Lombard tradition (*mundualdus*) required the consent of a special protector for a woman to enter into any legal contract. [Dean and Lowe, pp. 89, 91.]

[3] Dean and Lowe, p. 9.

[4] The edition of the Rule printed by Damiano Turlino in 1569 specifies eighteen to twenty as the age of commitment, probably reflecting actual practice. [Mariani, Tarolli, Seynaeve, p. 380.]

[5] Average ages at marriage ranged from twelve to eighteen, with working-class women marrying at the later end of the scale. [Average of thirteen in Florence, 1430: Klapisch-Zuber, p. 109; thirteen to seventeen: Shahar, *The Fourth Estate: A History of Women in the Middle Ages*, p. 180.)

[6] The Italian text uses *amaestrar*, which suggests discipleship, not *insegnar*, which would suggest instruction.

[7] Christine de Pizan, Venetian by birth, who wrote in Latin and French, described the scriptural Judith as "the honest woman, who will forever be praised on this account...." [Christine de Pisan, *The Book of the City of Ladies*, trans. Earl Jeffrey Richards (New York: Persea Books, 1982), Part II, 30.1.] See entries for *honesty* and *honest* in the *Oxford English Dictionary*, specifically for *honesty* "#3b: Chastity: the honour or virtue of a woman. Obs." with citations from Chaucer et al.; and citations for *honest* "#1. a. Of persons: held in honour...respectable.... #3. Of persons: Having honourable motives or principles.... a. In early use in a wide sense: of good moral character;.... b. *spec.* Chaste, 'virtuous'; usually of a woman. *arch.*" with many fifteenth-century citations. English usages at that time derived closely from Italian. The word and its opposite, *inhonesto*, was also used of men. Later in his life, Ignatius of Loyola related that his reputation in his hometown as a youth was of being "*inhonesto*" in his dress and even worse in his habits (*Scripta* I, p. 596).

[8] The wider use of *h/onesta* is illustrated by the Italian phrase *onesta cortigiana*, or "honest courtesan," used to describe courtesans who achieved respect for intellectual or literary accomplishments. Chastity was not involved, but they were seen as having intellectual integrity. Two sixteenth-century Venetian examples are the poets Gaspara Stampa (1523/24-1554) and Veronica Franco (1546-1591); each was called *onesta cortigiana* by contemporaries.

9 Carl Köhler, *A History of Costume*, ed. and augmented by Emma von Sichart and Alexander K. Dallas (New York: Dover Publications, Inc., 1963), p. 280.

10 Silk came from as far as Asia, though the Florentines had silkworms as early as the thirteenth century, and Marco Polo had smuggled silk worms from China to Venice in the fourteenth.

[11] Spaniards were importing logwood (blue to purple) [William F. Leggett, *Ancient and Medieval Dyes* (Brooklyn: Chemical Publishing Co., Inc., 1944), p. 53.] and cochineal (red) from Mexico beginning in 1523, two years after Cortez's conquest. [Leggett, pp. 10, 86.] Dyes were so valuable that treasure-seeking pirates often seized them. [Stuart Robinson, *A History of Dyed Textiles* (Cambridge, Massachusetts: The MIT Press, 1977, first published in Great Britain by Studio Vista Ltd., 1969), p. 30.] They sparked economic and even military rivalries among Venice, Genoa, and Florence. [Leggett, p. 58.]

[12] Macquer Hellot and Le Pileur d'Apligny, *The Art of Dyeing Wool, Silk and Cotton*, trans. from the French, a reissuing of the edition first published in England in 1789 by R. Baldwin (London: Scott, Greenwood and Co., 1901), pp. 153-161. Cities which relied on the dye industry maintained and heavily guarded their dye reserves. [Hellot and d'Apligny, p. 417.]

[13] Robinson, p. 30. In 1540 Giovani Ventura published *Plictha de L'arte de Tentori*, recipes of the Venetian Dyers Guild, which became a standard reference. It illustrates the costliness of dyes, noting three groups of dyers: "plain dyers," the largest; specialists in certain "high" colors on expensive materials; and silk dyers, "regarded as individual artists and not of a guild." [Robinson, p. 28.]

[14] Nassino in *Memoria della morte*, Appendix 7 of Mariani, Tarolli, Seynaeve, p. 582 (translation the author's).

[15] *Ippolita and Angela* Sforza-Visconti (two sisters) of Milan included several items of cutwork or openwork in their 1493 inventory of valuables. [Pat Earnshaw. *Lace in Fashion from the Sixteenth to the Twentieth Centuries*, second edition (Guildford, Surrey: Gorse Publications, 1991), p. 10.]

[16] Mila Contini, *5000 Years of Fashion*, trans. Olive Ordish (Milan: Arnoldo Mondadori Editore, 1977), pp. 67, 69.

[17] Braid was used to ornament the edges of slashes in the sleeves, more and more popular in the 1530s. [Yarwood, p. 9.]

[18] Cesare Veccelio's engravings illustrate sixteenth-century fashions: #69 (about 1500) shows a low neckline and full sleeves; #68, which he described as the "more modest, 'reformed' dress of olden days," shows a veiled woman with simple sleeves, no embroidery or other handiwork; #73, "Venetian woman about 1530," shows slit sleeves and a laced bodice.

[19] In the sixteenth century, Italian women lost the right to work in gold and silver. Legally prohibited from the crafts that had a higher potential for profit, they were allowed to embroider. [Contini, p. 77.]

[20] Quoted by Contini. It must be noted that Vecellio's work was published in 1590; the surmise that shoes were similarly fashionable in the 1530s is presumed.

21 Bianca Maria Sforza had eighty-three shifts: fifty plain, twenty-five embroidered with black silk, and eight embroidered with silk and gold. [Contini, p. 72.]

[22] This seeming contradiction appears not in Italian but in English, where both *secolo* and *mondo* can be translated as "world." The Roman Union translators of the Rule resolved the problem by translating *secolo* in the title of Chapter III as "public." The situations discussed are indeed in the public sphere. We think that there is a value to the more comprehensive translation "world" and will discuss the distinctions.

[23] The Italian word *conversar* (*interact*) in the chapter's title includes but is not limited to what we mean in English by "conversation." In Italian, however, it has a much wider significance, implying all sorts of interactions.

[24] Mariani, Tarolli, Seynaeve, pp. 109, 110.

[25] Kowaleski in Bennet and Froide, pp. 42, 44.

[26] Karras in Bennet and Froide, p. 127.

[27] Kowaleski in Bennet and Froide, pp. 50, 57.

[28] Ruzante, p. 47.

[29] Ruzante, pp. 75, 137.

[30] King, pp. 30, 34.

[31] Readers familiar with William Shakespeare's play *Romeo and Juliet* will recognize here the role of Juliet's nurse, a servingwoman, in carrying messages between the lovers.

[32] This awareness must have been part of the motive driving the educational mission of the Ursulines who first accepted cloistered life. Their commitment to a mission in the world developed into schooling for young women.

[33] Quoted in Dean and Lowe, p. 16.

B. Spiritual Practices

A Study in Contemplation

Saint Angela Merici by Pietro Rizieri Calcinardi (1801-1894). In Le Grezze.

Her steady gaze on the crucifix is an invisible stream. Along it moves her spirit, to this sign of ultimate, self-giving love. She is ground-ed here, in this relationship. The figure of the Crucified is the source of the light with which her face glows. He has reached out to her, and she has answered. Her prayer began with words, found in the open book lying under her arm. Now it is a wordless exchange, a timeless moment, a presence, each to the other. Her hands, her posture are relaxed in this easy intimacy. The pilgrim staff of her spiritual journey rests on the floor. She has reached her goal.

Pietro Rizieri Calcinardi's oil painting captures Angela at prayer. It is as though the painter could glimpse her spirit. Prayer fills her being. It shapes her body, along the diagonal line of her back to the head, to the face that seems to open up into light.

Himself a son of Desenzano, Calcinardi painted in the mid-1800s, three centuries after Angela. In Desenzano's Church of St. Mary Magdalene, he decorated a chapel dedicated to her. He painted six scenes from her life, following well-known biographical accounts. This painting is different. It draws not upon events but upon an experience of prayer. Calcinardi had been working in the chapel of the Ursuline sisters on the Via S. Maria. Perhaps he was exposed there either to her teachings or to her legacy alive in her spiritual daughters.

Chapters IV - VII

Chapters IV to VII spell out practices that weave the fabric of life in a pattern of spirit: regular fasting, daily Mass and prayer, monthly Confession. Three keynotes of these chapters pervade the whole Rule as well as Angela's other works. First of all, the pattern is Christ-centered: at the heart of Angela's prayer is her relationship with Jesus Christ. Daily Mass sharpens this focus. Secondly, the Trinity is the matrix of Angela's reality. She understands the Father, Son and Holy Spirit as the sources of divine providence, love and guidance (cf. chapters on poverty, virginity, and obedience, respectively). Third, Angela's spirituality is ecclesial, that is, engaged with the Church's life of prayer: the sacraments (Eucharist, Confession) and the daily prayers known as the Divine Office.

Both simple and profound, her teachings lead the beginner along while probing the depths and heights with a saint's intensity.

The Context

Pre-Reformation Church Reformers

Angela's spirituality developed against a particular historical background, in response to the issues of pre-Reformation and Reformation

European Catholicism. Looking at these currents will help us to understand and appreciate her. It will also encourage us to develop a spirituality that responds to the authentic currents of our own era.

Angela Merici was baptized in 1474/5 into a Church sorely needing reform. For well over a century critics and reformers had been crying out against ignorance, superstition and corruption. The clergy and hierarchy were providing minimal leadership. Brescia's bishops rarely resided in their diocese.[1] (While Angela lived there, the bishops were Paolo Zane 1481-1531; the sickly Francesco Cornaro 1532-38, who nominated his twenty-one-year-old nephew Andrea; Andrea 1546-1551, who took possession of his see eight years after his uncle's death.[2])

Strong voices arose from people who were seeking to accomplish reform from within. This effort was part of Angela's milieu. The area around Desenzano had long been rife with reformist concern. Going back several centuries, accusations of heresy made about the nearby monastery of Leno may have actually reflected the region's reformist stance. "Heretic!" was a slur often hurled by defensive clergy.[3] Desenzano had been accused of sheltering heretics, and Brescia had once been called "the home of heretics," perhaps because the reformist preacher Arnold (twelfth century) had been born there.[4] Brescia shared in the fervor stirred up by such reformers as Bernardino da Feltre, who preached there in 1493, 1494, and 1496.[5] Angela alludes to reformist dynamics in her references to maverick preachers (Seventh Counsel:12-22) and in her advice to *pray, and get others to pray, that God will not abandon his Church, but reform it as he pleases* (Seventh Counsel:23).

Among the internal reformers were the layman Geer Groote (1340-1384), the Dominican friar-preacher Girolamo Savonarola (1452-1498; preached in Brescia in 1494), and the cleric Desiderius Erasmus (1466?-1536). Erasmus, who opposed the principle of monastic enclosure, had a circle of sympathizers in Brescia among the Emilii and Maggi families.[6] In 1517 the monk Martin Luther (1483-1546) broke with the Church, some years after passing through Brescia, where he was said to have stayed at the monastery of St. Barnabas, on his way to a disillusioning visit to Rome.[7]

Devotio Moderna

Geer Groote had catalyzed a movement labeled *"Devotio Moderna"* (Modern Devotion). Its constructive results extended from Groote's native Low Countries throughout Europe and reached Italy before Angela was born. Groote focused on ardent devotion to Christ and the primacy of love for God and neighbor, made visible in service to others. He took a moderate approach to ascetic practices such as fasting and other penitential exercises, at a point when some spiritual teachers were more rigorous. He paid little attention to phenomena such as visions, which are not intrinsic to the basic Christian vocation. Groote's followers, called "Devouts" (Brethren of the Devout Life), spread his call for conversion of heart. They taught humility and popularized methods of mental prayer that are more affective (that is, in touch with emotion) than intellectual. Personal piety, meditation and good works marked their spirituality.

Devouts supported themselves largely by copying and selling books, especially publications about Christ's Passion, Mary and the Our Father and Hail Mary.[8] A Devout named Thomas à Kempis (1379-1471) wrote *The Imitation of Christ* just as the moveable-type printing press (first used in 1454) made mass distribution possible. *The Imitation* was a best-seller which put spiritual teachings into the hands of Christians in all vocations, not only into those of clerics and religious. Fully Catholic and within the Church, the Devout movement operated without direct hierarchical control.[9]

New Forms of Life

Attuned to the needs of their world, lay women such as Saints Frances of Rome (1384-1440) and Catherine of Genoa (1447-1510), both married, devoted themselves to caring for the poor and sick. Deeply contemplative and even visionary experiences fueled their zeal. Catherine was the "spiritual mother" of Ettore Vernazzo, who founded the Oratory of Divine Love in 1497. Members of this *Divino Amore* movement were among Angela's friends in Brescia. This link between Catherine and associates of Angela is not direct. However, it illustrates the confluence of the spiritual currents flowing through Italy.

In Angela's surroundings, new spiritual families were multiplying. They were religious and lay, all inspired by a fervent response to their times, especially through works of charity.[10] New lay movements took inspiration from the apostolic life described in the New Testament and from the example of the early Church. Working actively in the social arena, they combined active and contemplative lives in the world.[11]

Holy Women

Besides the emerging groups, the first half of the sixteenth century saw a high number of charismatic holy women active in Italy.[12] Many were within range of Brescia. We met two of them in discussing the Rule's chapter on governance: Blessed Osanna and Blessed Stefana. Osanna Andreasi, the "heavenly oracle" of Mantua (1449-1505), belonged to the Dominican Third Order and revered the Dominican reformer Savonarola (d. 1498). Like him, she deplored "...the state of the Church.... Oh, how many evils loom, especially against the Church, for the...habit of sinning."[13] Living in her own home, she dedicated herself to charitable works.[14] Her sense of Christ's Passion was so deep that she felt the pain of his wounds and of the crown of thorns and had a visionary experience of Jerusalem.[15] Angela honored Osanna's memory and visited her tomb in Mantua in 1520.

Stefana Quinzani (1457-1530), called "the root of Lombardy's health,"[16] was also a Third Order Dominican and Osanna's disciple. Coming from Orzi-nuovi, Stefana had settled in Soncino, where she cared for the sick and orphans and founded a Dominican convent. In ecstasies she experienced the Passion of Christ[17] and received the stigmata.[18] Her relationship with him was marked by a nuptial ring invisible to others.[19] Stefana succeeded Osanna as "spiritual mother" to the Gonzaga dukes. She visited in Brescia, and Angela visited her in Soncino.

Brescian Laura Mignani (1480-1525) was an Augustinian nun and the spiritual mother of Bartolomeo Stella and others connected with the *Divino Amore* movement and with charitable initiatives in Brescia, as elsewhere. She lived in the Santa Croce Monastery, which had been founded during the episcopacy of the reformist bishop Domenico de Dominicis (1464-1478) and continued to be a center of spiritual leadership.[20] Santa Croce was also the home of Caterina Patengola's former servant Giustina (Sister Candida, d. 1515). Countess Lucrezia (Gonzaga de Novellara) Gambara linked her powerful Brescian family with reformed branches of the Augustinian and Dominican orders and had a strong relationship with Stefana Qunizani.[21]

The themes of *Devotio Moderna* and the example of holy women coincided in many points with Franciscanism, which nourished the roots of Angela's spirituality. Her words and her life attest to her earnest conversion of heart; to her affective, Christo-centric prayer; to an apostolic dynamic realized in service. Devotion to the Passion, so important to her, addressed a widespread spiritual need in a century of warfare, with its anguish and painful aftermath. The Sack of 1512 had plunged Brescia deep into such suffering, shortly before her arrival there. Ten thousand lives were lost in a single day. Destruction and disease continued to afflict the population for years to come. Angela's appreciation of Jesus' suffering taught her the love that flowed from the Cross, a compassion that she shared with suffering people around her.

The historian of spirituality Louis Bouyer describes Angela's historical moment this way: "The spiritual evolution of the Middle Ages had ended by producing an acute consciousness of the apostolic response of the Christian, whatever his [sic] state of life....it is interior prayer that gives strength to the apostle, just as it gives the contemplative an apostolic aim and range."[22] Brescian historian Gianpietro Belotti assesses the Bresican Renaissance as attempting to create a new synthesis between humanism and Christian culture.[23]

A Spirit-time

Certain cycles turn throughout Church history, it seems. When corruption infects the clerical and hierarchical structures, the Holy Spirit works all the more powerfully through lay Christians. Liturgical practices, seemingly the province of the clergy, subside. Personal piety among the laity surges. This dynamic opens up a place for women as spiritual leaders. Osanna and Stefana served both women and men as advisors and were widely respected for their personal holiness and their teachings.

Attention to the Holy Spirit's movement in the heart sparks a charismatic, affective spirituality. This was the case in the late fifteenth and early sixteenth centuries in Europe. Angela resonated to these chords struck by history, as we see in her Rule's four chapters on spiritual practices and in her Counsels and Testament. For her ardent personality, relationships and emotions were natural avenues of supernatural grace.

She exemplified the pre-Reformation laity, aware of abuses and seeking authentic interior renewal. Far from rejecting practices that had been corrupted, she affirmed the integrity of their correct use. Liturgical theology was at a low ebb in these years before the Council of Trent. Angela's words on the Eucharist, for example, are sparse. Yet her teaching on the sacraments transcends abuses. She rooted her spiritual practices in the Church's life, tapping its deep underground waters.

God's word as conveyed by sacred Scripture was as precious to early Catholic reformers as it became to Protestants. A tug of war ensued over who had the right—the control—to interpret it. To over-simplify the issues yet indicate the dynamics: the Catholic Counter Reformation would retain Latin and thus a clerical grip even on read-ing the Bible, whereas Protestants were more likely to trust the Holy Spirit to guide individual readers in interpretation. An extreme but real situation illustrates the point: in 1548, the Inquisition heard the case of a Venetian woman who had been accustomed to have the Bible read aloud to her on Sunday mornings.[24]

Just before that vise was closed, Angela Merici became regarded as an expert in Scripture, untutored as she was. Agostino Gallo watched "preachers and theologians" come to her in his home in the Vicolo San Clemente "to ask her for a statement on many passages of the Psalms, of the Prophets, of the Apocalypse, and all of the New and Old Testaments, and hear from her such explanations that they remained amazed."[25] These eminent persons knew that her knowledge and insight came from the Holy Spirit. Gallo himself attributed her expert-ise to her sacramental and private prayer, contemplation, reading and good works—in other words, a thoroughly integrated spiritual life. Angela was so much at home with Scripture that its words and spirit permeate the Rule and her other works.

The scriptural wind was rising, and with it an interest in the prim-itive Church pictured in the Acts of the Apostles. Reform-minded Catholics harked back to the simpler Christianity of apostolic times. Angela thought in these terms as she counseled, *Keep to the ancient way and custom of the Church.... And live a new life* (Seventh Counsel:22). Gabriele Cozzano used the word "apostolic" to describe the Company's "life according to that lived by the Apostles and early Church."[26]

Angela was authentically a woman of her time. She drew from its spiritual wells and ministered to its spiritual thirsts. Each generation lives spiritually in tune with its own age. Contemporary Ursulines must fine-tune their spiritual heritage from Angela to the spiritual needs of our day.

Spiritual Practices

The practices outlined in Chapters IV to VII of the Rule involve both personal spirituality and Church liturgy. They receive attention in the

Rule because they are integral to authentic Ursuline life. They are the structural supports for its healthy growth. Each practice makes an essential contribution to the vocation. We can say generally that the chapter "On Fasting" supports *true poverty of spirit*; "On Confession" supports *holy obedience*; "On Prayer" and "On Attending Mass Every Day" support *sacred virginity*. This pairing does not subordinate the sacraments to individuals' commitment but shows why these universal Catholic practices belong in the Company's Rule.

Fasting – The Context

A special word must be said about fasting, since it is approached so differently today. Christian attention to this spiritual practice first focused primarily on men, beginning with the Fathers of the Desert. Recent scholarship has uncovered specifically female dimensions of fasting, especially in Europe during the Middle Ages and early Modern Era. In *Holy Anorexia*, Rudolph Bell explores the numerous instances of extreme fasting by Italian holy women between 1200 and 1500. He concludes that young women seeking self-definition apart from patriarchy (including clericalism) or seeking to conform themselves to an ideal (sanctity) often pursued their goals through excessive fasting, as their bodies were the only arena they controlled.

Medievalist Carolyn Bynum challenges Bell's thesis in her *Holy Feast and Holy Fast: The Religious Significance of Food to Medieval Women*. She too studies the phenomenon of young women devoting themselves to fasting and almsgiving in order to make themselves less marriageable, either rejecting their sexuality or seeking to define their lives differently from their families' plans (e.g., Columba of Rieti, d. 1501) or outside clerical control.[27] However, she looks at the same women through the lens of medieval spirituality rather than that of modern psychology. Furthermore, she explores the relationship of hunger to Eucharist, e.g., as central to Saint Catherine of Siena.[28]

Food shortages also helped shape ideas about fasting, which made food available for the poor and hungry.[29] Rules of all sorts—for religious orders or lay confraternities, for women or men—contained guidelines about fasting. Angela Merici's Rule is typical in its attention to fasting as a spiritual practice. It offers wise moderation and guidance to women who might have been affected by the motives and extremes so common to their era.

Chapter IV, "About Fasting"

Angela Merici's friend Agostino Gallo reported that she often spoke "so warmly" about fasting.[30] She begins Chapter IV of her Rule by telling her daughters to *remember that each one should want to embrace bodily fasting* (Ch. IV:1). We might wonder at this enthusiasm. How could she be so enthusiastic about fasting?

Remember...want...embrace bodily fasting. The many recommendations that follow demonstrate Angela's conviction that fasting is a powerful way of bringing one's whole self into prayer. The mind *remembers* reasons for fasting. The will *wants*, chooses to do it. The affections (emotions) *embrace* the practice, and, of course, the body carries it out. Fasting is a way of praying with the body, with one's whole being.

Angela's Fasting

Many recoil from all the days Angela sets forth for fasting. It seems so severe! How much—or how little—did Angela herself eat?

Agostino Gallo and Antonio Romano were the two witnesses who had observed her most closely, since she lived under their roofs and ate at their tables. Their testimonies suggest that she fasted and abstained according to the Church's usual practices (as carried out in Lent by all healthy adult Catholics until a few decades ago).[31] This means one full meal per day and another light meal, often split between breakfast and lunch (or a light breakfast and a light supper, if dinner was the mid-day meal); nothing between meals. As a member of the Franciscan Third Order, Angela surely fasted on the days prescribed in its Rule. Her own Rule varies somewhat from the Franciscans' and may reflect her own pattern. She may have fasted more often than was required.[32]

Typical abstinence would involve meatless Fridays or, partial abstinence, with meat only at the main meal. The distinction was almost meaningless in the sixteenth century, since meat was a luxury, as it is in much of the world today. Abstinence from meat means eating like most of the world.

Angela herself was a vegetarian: "fruits and vegetables," according to all witnesses.

1 Yet again remember that each one should want to embrace bodily fasting too as something indeed necessary....

Giacomo Chizzola testified that she would "never...eat meat, except in a time of sickness."[33] According to Gallo, "she never drank wine, or other beverage, except always water. It is true that on the great feast of Christmas and of the Resurrection, to solemnize it more fully, she drank at dinner a single 'finger' of wine...."[34] Nothing in her words indicates that she expected others to imitate this diet.

True Spiritual Fasting

Angela never defines or quantifies the fasts she encourages her daughters to observe. She gives no details about types or amounts of food or drink. Here, as always, she looks at the big picture, the spiritual picture. It might be said of Angela that she was never concerned about the numbers. She did not intend for Ursulines to replicate her form of fasting. Rather, each one should find the way of fasting that is most spiritually nourishing for her, the way that leads to *true spiritual fasting* (Ch. IV:2). Mimicking another person's way can be mechanical, a habit carried out without attentiveness. Authentic fasting involves attentiveness. It engages the whole self in the prayer, a body-prayer. As a bodily practice, fasting helps us deepen our spiritual focus. Thus it serves as a *means and way to the true spiritual fasting through which all vices and errors are lopped off from the mind* (Ch. IV:2).

Lopped off— a vivid word, an unusual word! It is exactly how Angela describes Judith's beheading of her people's enemy Holofernes in the Preface of the Rule (Italian *tronchare*, Pr.:30). Holofernes' head and our vices—both *lopped off*! To save her people, Judith struck two vigorous blows and *lopped off the head of Holofernes* (cf. Judith 13:8-10). She had to, for survival. In her vineyard Angela had learned the urgency of lopping diseased branches off her vines. If she did not act quickly and forcefully, the vine itself could be infected. It could die. Can we be any less vigorous when *vices and errors* threaten our spiritual health and even survival? Jesus told us about the divine Vine-grower, who "takes away every branch...that does not bear fruit" (John 15:2). He described God pruning the healthy vines so that they might bear more fruit.

2 ...and as a means and way to the true spiritual fasting through which all vices and errors are lopped off from the mind.

3 To this we are invited very clearly by the example of all saintly persons,...

Angela says that *we are invited* to true spiritual fasting *very clearly by the example of all saintly persons* (Ch. IV:3). We learn by example. Who are these examples of true spiritual fasting? The saints? Well, many saints, of course. But look around—look for unselfish people. Look for people who put God and their neighbors first. These people want to focus on what is healthy for their spirits. They probably practice some spiritual disciplines. The word *disciplina* means a way of learning.[35] Fasting can be a way of learning that our impulses and enjoyments do not come first. If we can learn this with *pasta* and *vitello*, we can hope to learn it with anger and vanity, with laziness and lust.

The Example of Jesus

As usual, Angela found that the example *above all* others is *the life of Jesus Christ* (Ch. IV:4). Yet Jesus was criticized for going to banquets. His enemies even called him "a glutton and a drunkard" (Matthew 11:19). He had to defend his disciples for not fasting as much as John the Baptist's disciples and the Pharisees did. "But the days will come, and when the bridegroom is taken away from them, then they will fast in those days," Jesus concluded (Luke 5:35).

Angela must have been thinking of the only explicit Gospel example of Jesus' fasting, his forty days of prayer and fasting in the desert.[36] It was at the beginning of his mission; even Jesus had to learn. The Holy Spirit drove him into the desert to teach him, to prepare him for his ministry. The fasting and prayer were his preparation. His mission was to make God present in ways that people could see and hear and understand. Nothing must stand between him and God or cloud the image of God that he mirrored.

In those forty days, Jesus opened himself completely to God. Fasting can be a prayer for openness. It involves being empty, being open, being hungry. It is a way of saying to God, "Here I am, opening myself for what you can do in me. Please help me to be emptied of self-centeredness, of vices. Let me be open to your grace instead. I'm hungry for you. Fill me. Remove anything that stands between us, or turns me in upon myself; remove whatever prevents me from bearing your fruit."

4 ...and above all the life of Jesus Christ, the only way to Heaven.

At the end of the forty days, Satan came to tempt Jesus. He offered the hungry man, on the threshold of his public ministry, a chance to use power to gain bread and riches and glory. But Jesus would use power only in service. He had learned through his fasting that nothing is so satisfying as "every word that comes forth from the mouth of God" (Matthew 4:4). Instead of false satisfactions like glory or possessions, he preferred God's word.

In the desert Jesus had learned how to nourish his spirit. We can use fasting and abstinence to discern among the things we take into our bodies, and also among those we take into our minds, hearts and spirits. Do they nourish us? Nourish our life and growth in a healthy way? Fasting and abstinence can lead to freedom. They can free us from compulsions to fill ourselves with useless or even unhealthy things. Then we will be better able to choose what is truly good for us and to enjoy it. If we link these practices with consuming God's words, we will be well nourished indeed.

The Divine Vine-grower

5 So holy mother Church clearly sings this in the hearing of all the faithful, speaking to God thus, "Qui corporali ieiunio vitia comprimis, mentem elevas, virtutem largiris et praemia"; that is to say, God, you who rein in vices through bodily fasting, [who] exalt the mind [and] give virtue and rewards;....

So—does fasting accomplish this? Does fasting bring about holiness? No. Only God does that. Fasting is one *means* to open ourselves to God's work in us. Angela's words move from Jesus' example to the Church's teaching. She quotes the Preface of the Mass proper to Lent: *So holy mother Church clearly sings this in the hearing of all the faithful, speaking to God thus... God, you who rein in vices through bodily fasting, [who] exalt the mind [and] give virtue and rewards* (Ch. IV:5).

The divine Vine-grower uses our spiritual practices to prune vices, nourish virtue, lift our thoughts to the Light, and to reward us far beyond any joys we could imagine. Angela links fasting with prayer: *Since indeed through fasting one mortifies the appetites of the flesh and one's own feelings, just so through prayer one beseeches from God the grace of the spiritual life* (Ch. V:4). All spiritual practices have this purpose: letting God work in and through us.

6 ...since gluttony was indeed the origin of all our evils, so may fasting and abstinence appropriately be the beginning and the means of our spiritual goods and benefits.

Photograph courtesy of Hector Bedolla

Adam and Eve – Hungry to Be Gods

In all her enthusiasm for fasting, Angela gives no critique of eating, no cultivation of pain or negation of the body. Thus it seems quite a leap for her to say in the Rule that *gluttony was indeed the origin of all our evils* (Ch. IV:6). Adam and Eve ate some fruit, an act of disobedience (Gen. 2:16, ff.), but how could Angela call it *gluttony*?[37]

Adam's and Eve's appetite was to be like gods. The tempter told them, "[T]he moment you eat of it your eyes will be opened and you will be like gods" (Gen. 3:5). They were not satisfied with being human. Humanity was not enough for them. Their eating is a figure of their hunger to be something they were not, to be gods, to put themselves in the place of God in their lives. *[O]ur spiritual good and benefits* (Ch. IV:6), Angela makes clear, come from the divine Gardener, who wants us to enjoy the garden's fruits and to see their true Source. Fasting reminds us that we are not God. When we fast, we use our bodies as well as our minds to learn this truth. Fasting is *the beginning* if we allow it to turn us to God, instead of trying to be God. Rejoice in being human! (This spirit permeates the Rule's Chapter X, "About Poverty.")

7 But the sacred canonists, too, say: "Indictum est ieiunium abstinentiae, lex a Domino Deo, prevaricatio legis a diabolo"; which is, by the Lord God are fasting and the laws of abstinence commanded, and the transgression of laws is provoked by the devil.

8 For this reason we call upon each one to fast, especially on these days of the year: First, all those days which holy mother Church commands, which are all the days of Lent, the four seasons [i.e., Ember Days], and all the obligatory vigils.

9 In addition, all of Advent.

13 ...fast the three days of Rogation, or litanies, that the Church celebrates before the Ascension to implore divine help for the Christian people.

When they had eaten, Adam and Eve hid from God, the very source of their being. How terrible! They were ashamed of their bodies and tried to cover themselves up. How sad! Gluttony turned to shame, as it usually does.

Fruits of Goodness

The Rule posits that fasting and abstinence are God's law and opposed by the devil (Ch. IV: 7). God's command not to eat the fruit of the Tree of the Knowledge of Good and Evil was a command to abstain from evil. *[T]ransgression...is provoked by the devil* (Ch. IV:7), who led Eve and Adam astray and is always trying to lead us to what is not good for us. Angela moves from this concern about goodness and evil to the fasts prescribed by the Church, seeming to suggest that fasting in solidarity with the Church offers an antidote to sinful tendencies. Both the Bible and the Church establish fasting as a regular part of life and as a special kind of prayer, leading to what is good for us.[38]

Indeed, regular spiritual practices are good for us. They bear a fruit that leads us to align more fully with God. What might be the fruits of this practice? With body and with spirit, let us practice fasting—from anger, from pride, from lust, from envy, from laziness, from over-indulgence of any kind! Let us ask God to fill us with peace, patience, kindness, generosity, joy! These fruits will nourish every part of our being.

With the Church

Angela calls *upon each one to fast* with the Church. First she refers to *all those days which holy mother Church commands, which are all the days of Lent, the four seasons* [i.e., Ember Days] *and all the obligatory vigils* (Ch. IV:8). For the six weeks of Lent, the whole Church focuses intently on the things of the spirit, recalling Jesus' forty days in the desert and approaching the sacred remembrance of his Crucifixion and Resurrection. Fasting is an excellent way to focus our attention. Ember Days (no longer widely practiced) renew that attentiveness throughout the year. They are the Wednesday, Friday and Saturday of a given week in each of the four seasons.

[T]he three days of Rogation, or litanies (Ch. IV:13) constitute another series of Church fasts observed from the Middle Ages until the late twentieth century. On these three days of prayer right before the feast of Christ's Ascension, the whole Church together prayed for God's help. Rogation Days were observed with processions and litanies, especially the Litany of the Saints, calling on all heavenly friends for assistance. For rural families like the Mericis of Desenzano, prayers in springtime especially focused on an abundant harvest.

On the vigil of a great feast, fasting helps us focus on the meaning of the celebration to come. If we prepare attentively, there is all the more joy when we feast. Without some fasting, we can hardly appreciate feasting. Angela definitely wants her daughters to celebrate feast days (Fifth Counsel:1). Advent provides a whole season of such preparation. Fasting during *Advent* (Ch. IV:9) sharpens our anticipation for Christmas, for celebrating Christ Incarnate.

Regarding the Incarnation, Angela has offered an interesting scriptural exemplar in Chapter V, "About Prayer," the elderly widow Anna. For years Anna had *continually served God in fasts and prayers* (Ch. V:3). Her practices prepared her to celebrate the Incarnation. She recognized God's presence when a young couple brought their baby into the Temple. She saw God Incarnate, "and she spoke about the child to all who were awaiting the redemption..." (Luke 2:38). Like Anna, the aged Angela had learned to see clearly, to recognize God's presence in her world and to proclaim it.

Up to this point, Angela's list of fasts reflects the general practices of Christian living in her world. They are not specific to the Company.

Ursuline life is first the life of a faithful, earnest member of the Church. For her daughters, though, Angela sees fasting as a rich source of even more spiritual energy.

Carnival

To the list of fasts she adds *the forty days immediately after the Epiphany* (Ch. IV:10).[39] Angela explains her rationale. These weeks include carnival season, when *the senses and appetites and lustful desires...lord it over the world at this time especially* (Ch. IV:10). Her imagery evokes traditional parades featuring a "king" of carnival. Carnival sets up a lord (*signore*), a false lord of desires, swaggering (*signorezzan*) through Brescia's streets. Court records show that criminal prosecutions peaked in this season when anonymity gave cover to lawless behavior.[40] One example can be seen in the 1515 civic register of Azpeitia, Spain. A magistrate arrested a twenty-four-year-old for misdemeanors that were "outrageous, committed at carnival time, at night." The offender was Iñigo de Loyola.[41]

Fasting is to be a spiritual counterweight. Unlike the public displays of carnival time, *more than apparent to everyone* (Ch. IV:11), fasting is quiet, almost invisible. Angela wants her daughters to fast not only for themselves, but also for their neighbors, their city. Each Ursuline, in her own family and community, can be the quiet presence of one who worships the true God, not the false god of pleasure. Angela counts on this spiritual energy *to keep in check the senses and appetites and lustful desires.*

10 ...fast the forty days immediately after the Epiphany to keep in check the senses and appetites and lustful desires which lord it over the world at this time especially.

11 Also, to ask for mercy before the throne of the Most High for so many debaucheries which are committed by Christians during times spent this way, as is more than apparent to everyone.

Furthermore, fasting in carnival time, before Lent, would itself be a prayer to *ask for mercy* (Ch. IV:11). In this time when bodily over-indulgence leads to so much sinful behavior, we offer a body-prayer for our fellow Christians. May they open themselves so that God's mercy may reach them! May *so many debaucheries* not dull their spiritual senses entirely! May they use the coming Lent to turn back to God! The zealous outward dynamic so intrinsic to Angela's spirituality operates here. It is epitomized in the Rule's Chapter V, "About

Prayer," where she cries out, *Lord, on behalf of those miserable wretches who do not know you...my heart is wrenched, and willingly would I shed my own blood (if I could) in order to open up the blindness of their minds* (Ch. V:31-34). Fasting is one way she can reach out to the spiritually blind.

Together

In prescribing fasting for the novena between Ascension and Pentecost, Angela reveals a further richness of fasting joined with prayer, its communal dimension. Up to this point, the focus of fasting has been largely personal, though experienced within the Church. The next several lines open up its meaning within the Company: *fast every day after the Ascension and together remain in prayer with as much strength of spirit as possible till the day of the sending of the Holy Spirit, that is till the Easter of May, beseeching that great promise made by Jesus Christ to his chosen and well-disposed people* (Ch. IV:14-16). Jesus Christ promised the Holy Spirit to his *people*. The fulfillment first came on Pentecost to the disciples who "were all in one place together" (Acts 2:1). Ever after, he promised, his Spirit will be present wherever "two or three are gathered together in my name" (Matthew 18:20).

Ursulines are to pray and fast corporately, Angela directs. Once again, prayer and fasting combine, opening hearts to a divine gift, but now as a community. She urges her daughters to join *with as much strength of spirit as possible* and in confidence. Just as individually these practices open us to God's gifts and presence, so will it be *together*. This is a powerful call. It depends on unity. It builds unity. No wonder that, throughout the Counsels and Testament, Angela so urgently calls for union and concord!

Grace-full Rhythm

Besides the prescribed fasts of the Church and the particular seasons of spiritual need, Angela tells her daughters to

14 ...fast every day after the Ascension

15 and together remain in prayer with as much strength of spirit as possible till the day of the sending of the Holy Spirit, that is till the Easter of May,

16 beseeching that great promise made by Jesus Christ to his chosen and well-disposed people.

12 ...after the octave of Easter fast three days out of the week, on Wednesdays, Fridays and Saturdays.

17 ...after the Easter of May, return to the aforementioned three days of the week till Advent.

225

fast on Wednesdays, Fridays and Saturdays after the octave of Easter till Ascension and through the Ordinary Time of the Church year (Ch. IV:12, 17). She wants fasting to be part of the regular rhythm of our lives. She knows its graces and benefits and teaches Ursulines to live in this stream of grace.

However

Finally, having listed so many reasons and occasions for fasting, Angela ends this chapter with a crucial *However*. Her own enthusiasm now seasoned by maturity, she recognizes that younger members might go to extremes. This was a particular danger. For centuries some young women had made extreme fasting the emblem of their spirituality, as though renunciation itself were a sign of holiness or a path to God. Cultural and religious factors contributed to the phenomenon, including the limitations that patriarchy placed upon young women.[42] One can renounce only what one has. While their pious brothers might renounce property and sexual adventure, young women controlled almost nothing that they could give up. Only food. A cult had grown up around this way of asserting personal autonomy and of accomplishing feats of heroism in the only field open to them: sanctity.[43]

18 However, because one does not want anything unreasonable, you are admonished that no one ought to fast without advice, especially that of her spiritual father

19 and of the lady governors of this Company, who may have to relax and diminish these fasts as seems necessary,

20 because he who indiscreetly hurts his body, "Esset offerre holocaustum de rapina"; that is, would be sacrificing stolen goods, so say the sacred canons.

However, because one does not want anything unreasonable, you are admonished that no one ought to fast without advice... (Ch. IV:19). Each Ursuline should find the form of fasting that is healthy for her. Each person is unique in her body-spirit dynamic and in her combination of health, age and work. Fasting must be integrated into her whole life. Her spiritual director's advice will help to balance her perspective. No doubt Angela could remember what it was like to throw common sense to the wind when she was young, to make grand gestures for God. The Franciscans at Salò had helped her to find her path to God through ordinary life. This was to become the Ursuline way. Each Ursuline's offering to God is the self that is God's gift to her. How wrong it would be to damage that gift by starving herself! No one has the right to do such damage. *[She] who indiscreetly hurts [her] body...would be sacrificing stolen goods* (Ch. IV:19, 20).

The Role of the Matrons

Though extreme fasting and celibacy do not necessarily go together, they may have seemed to reinforce each other in the lives of some people—both men and women. An ideal of unbodied holiness had long driven much of the fasting tradition, with the aim of subjecting body to spirit by harsh punishments. This perspective no doubt offered a seemingly holy mechanism for some people alarmed by their own sexuality and other appetites.

Angela recognized the pitfall. Her corrective measure was to involve the matrons in the members' discernment about appropriate fasting. To be sure that wisdom and individual discernment prevail, the chapter ends by providing that *the lady governors of this Company...may have to relax and diminish these fasts as seems necessary* (Ch. IV: 19). They were wives, mothers, widows. They knew marriage, sexual intercourse, pregnancy, birth, nursing, parenting and bereavement. They gave counsel out of their own experience and their understanding of a woman's body. They could recognize extremes and know what would be healthy. These wise older women would have the last word.

The matrons could be counted on to respect the significance of fasting within the Ursuline vocation. Sometimes parents or others who oppose an Ursuline's chosen life may *wish to hinder [her] from fasting* or other spiritual practices. Angela urges her daughters to *be quick to refer this to the lady governors of the Company so that they may take care of it* (Ch. III:9, 10). The matrons support the member in carrying out these practices.

Why is fasting so important to the Ursuline vocation? Because it helps us to pray with the whole self. Because it teaches us to be hungry for God and the things of God and to put nothing between ourselves and God, nor in the place of God. Because it leads us to

...not live by bread alone,
but by every word that comes forth from the mouth
of God (Matthew 4:4).

[T]rue poverty of spirit is built on this foundation. In Chapter X, "About Poverty," Angela teaches her daughters to put all [their] wealth and love and delight in God alone, not in material things, not in food and over-eating, not in relatives and friends [i.e., social position and power] not in herself, nor in any of her own attributes and knowledge, but in God alone (Ch. X:9-13).

Finally, when she speaks of not sacrificing stolen goods (Ch. IV:20), Angela puts fasting into the perspective of "sacred virginity," by which one gives herself fully to God. That is the nature of "sacrifice," a gift to God. The giver has no right to damage the gift. Health and wholeness are part of the gift, not to be stolen by extremes of fasting.

In some sense, fasting opens us to mystery. We will never completely understand it. But we can experience it.

Reflection

❖ Consider one idea about fasting that challenged you. Why was it challenging? What is your response?

❖ Fasting and abstinence occupied a privileged place among the spiritual practices of Angela's day, especially for women, since they dealt with one of the few areas of life within women's control. Other areas of life may present further opportunities today. For example, might occasional or regular abstinence from media open up inner space and offer the nourishment of silence?

❖ Angela suggests that fasting practices can be linked to the needs of our day.

❖ Have you adopted any practice of fasting that has opened you to new sources of nourishment?

❖ With Angela we might think of fasting not as a penance for sin, not as "giving up" something wrong or unhealthy, not as a spiritual athletic regimen, but as a way of praying with the body.

❖ If you have ever fasted in solidarity with another person or group, reflect upon that experience and its fruits.

Chapter V, "About Prayer"

Always, Angela says in the Rule. *Pray always.* Jesus, whom she names Truth, said that *it is necessary to pray always* (cf. Luke 18:1; Ch. V:5).

And pray all ways. This principle is woven through Chapter V, "About Prayer," indeed throughout the Rule. She teaches us to pray with our whole self: body and mind, heart and spirit. With every part of us! Thus we will grow to become fully and deeply one with God and self. We will experience the depth and breadth of our self and of God working in us.

Yet we cannot pray always, not formally, not at every moment. Chapter V shows how to let prayer frame our days, in a rhythm that keeps us in touch with God all day. This practice will keep us spiritually sensitive. We will be aware of God's guidance through the day's events, of God's providence in the day's gifts and of God's presence in our neighbors. Sacred virginity, the core of Ursuline life, is all about this awareness. The mission of the Company might be described as living so deeply our relationship with God as to find God everywhere and to reflect Christ to everyone around us. Chapter V guides us in developing patterns of prayer that support this vocation.

Prayer and Fasting

The Rule's Chapter IV teaches that body and spirit must unite in fasting, that fasting is a way of praying with the body. Chapter V begins with a transition from fasting to prayer per se. *Prayer with fasting is good* (cf. Tobit 12:8, Ch. V:2). Prayer is like fasting. It is not our accomplishment, not what we do for God. It is our way of opening ourselves, *beseeching from God the grace of the spiritual life* since we have *constant need for God's help* (Ch. V:4, 5).

Both prayer and fasting help to focus us. Body and spirit lean Godward. As we saw in the discussion of fasting above, Angela invokes the example of the elderly prophet Anna, who *continually served God in*

1 Remember again that each one be solicitous about prayer, mental as well as vocal,

2 which is the companion of fasting; but Scripture says, "Bona est oratio cum ieiunio"; that is, prayer with fasting is good.

3 And one reads in the Gospel about Anna, daughter of Phanuel, who in the temple day and night continually served God in ieuniis et orationibus [fasts and prayers].

4 Since indeed through fasting one mortifies the appetites of the

flesh and one's own feelings, just so, through prayer one beseeches from God the grace of the spiritual life.

5 ...one needs to pray always with spirit and mind on account of the constant need for God's help, and for this reason does Truth say, "Oportet semper orare"; that is, it is necessary to pray always,....

6 ...yet again let us advise frequent vocal prayer

7 through which corporeal sentiments are stirred up

8 and one is disposed for mental prayer.

fasts and prayers (cf. Luke 2:37; Ch. V:3). Anna recognized God's presence in the child Jesus, carried into the Temple by his parents. Anna could see. Anna also demonstrated that prayer is not merely private, not for ourselves alone. She lifted her voice, burst into thanksgiving. She spoke to everyone, bearing witness to what she had seen—God right there among them, carried in the arms of Mary and Joseph—Jesus, the human presence of God. Angela's life of prayer made her want to be a witness, too. She wanted to help everyone see (Ch. V:34).

As she has throughout the Rule, Angela once more offers encouragement: to *want to pray,* to *be solicitous about prayer* (Ch. V:1), to *want to say...the Office...and the seven penitential psalms every day* (Ch. V:9). She assumes that we want the fruits of prayer. If we are sincere, we will also want to embrace prayer as *the means* to cultivate the fruit (Pr.:13).

Vocal Prayer

The first form of prayer described in Chapter V is vocal. *[O]ne needs to pray always with spirit and mind...yet again let us advise frequent vocal prayer* (Ch. V:5, 6). We often talk as though our bodies and emotions and minds and spirits were separate realities. They are not. Angela respects our wholeness. Vocal prayer can put words around our unvoiced aspirations. Words can be the vessels that give shape to our spirits' yearnings. Often, *through [words] corporeal sentiments—*emotions*—are stirred up, and one is disposed for mental prayer* (Ch. V, 7, 8). We move through the words and feelings to non-verbal forms of prayer such as meditation and contemplation. Whether the words then cease, or whether they continue to flow, they serve the spirit.

The Office: Praying with the Church

The discussion of vocal prayer begins with the Office and Psalms. Litanies and many other vocal prayers were popular in Angela's time. Myriads of personal and private practices were in vogue. Angela focuses, however, on liturgical prayer, part of the official prayer of the universal Church, the Office. The Divine Office (from Latin *officium*, meaning duty, in this case a sacred duty of honoring God) is a sequence of Psalms, Scripture readings and prayers said at specified times throughout the day by clerics, nuns, monks and many lay Christians. Angela knew its value from her own experience as a Third Order Franciscan.[44]

In praying the Office, we join the whole Church in the circling hours: Matins, or the Office of Readings, about 2 a.m.; Lauds, or Morning Praise, around dawn; Prime, Terce, Sext and Nones through the day (around 6 and 9 a.m., midday and 3 p.m., respectively); Vespers in the evening, near sunset; and Compline at night, before retiring. Angela seems to consolidate Matins and Lauds into *Matutino*, probably influenced by the Franciscan Third Order Rule, which does the same.[45] Only monks and nuns were expected to rise around 2 a.m. for Matins. Others would incorporate some of its texts into their praying of Lauds in the morning or say it the evening before.

Even alone in our own rooms, through the Office we are part of the Church at prayer. We draw upon the riches of each liturgical season, entering the mysteries of Advent, Christmas, Lent, Eastertide and the great feasts, sharing these experiences with the rest of the Church. A further benefit of the Office flows from praying mostly in the words of Scripture—Psalms and other passages and the Gospel canticles. While our

9 That is why each one should want to say devoutly and attentively at least the Office of the Madonna and the seven penitential psalms every day.

10 Because by saying the Office one talks with God, as the blessed martyr Alexander used to say.

11 Those who do not know how to say it will arrange to be taught by the sisters who do know.

voices speak, our spirits listen. The words lead us forward. Psalms help us to pray from deep in the heart, and to join our hearts with others.

The Office leads us along ways that individual dispositions might not find. It leads from "I" to "we." Why should one who is happy pray "Out of the depths" (Psalm 130:1)? Because others are suffering, and a prayer offered in solidarity with their experience reaches out to them with deepened sensitivity. Or why should one in the depths sing "Give thanks to God, who is good" (Psalm 118:1)? Because that is when we most need such words to lift us beyond what we can reach on our own.

The Penitential Psalms: Praying with the World

Along with the Office, Angela includes daily recitation of the seven so-called "Penitential Psalms" (Psalms 6, 32, 38, 51, 102, 130, 143). These seven prayers share a common focus; they help us express contrition, asking God to

Wash away all my guilt;
    from my sin cleanse me,
For I know my offense;
    ...blot out all my guilt (Psalm 51:4, 5, 11).

They also vividly describe helplessness in the face of evil forces such as war, violence or injustice, or interior enemies such as vices, addictions and destructive compulsions. They plumb the emotions, particularly of sorrow:

I am wearied with sighing;
    all night long tears drench my bed;
    my couch is soaked with weeping (Psalm 6:7).

They voice remorse and loneliness:

Foul and festering are my sores
    because of my folly....
Friends and companions shun my pain;
    my neighbors stand far off (Psalm 38:6, 12).

With our problems named, our tension relaxes, in the trust that

        now is the time for pity;
        the appointed time has come (Psalm 102:14).

Emotional release helps us open up to God's grace:

At dawn let me hear of your kindness,
    for in you I trust.

Show me the path I should walk,
    for to you I entrust my life....
Teach me to do your will,
    for you are my God.
May your kind spirit guide me
    on ground that is level.
For your name's sake,...give me life;
    in your justice lead me out of distress (Psalm 143:8-12).

The penitential psalms generally follow a pattern that begins in suffering, then moves to trust and hope. They provide words to voice our personal anguish. We can also pray them in union with desperate, lonely people, with those who are besieged by enemies or oppressors, with sufferers we will never see who are in the grip of illness or depression. When appropriate, we repent, and we pray that we and others may learn to trust in God, "my shelter" (Psalm 32:7).

The "Little Office"

The seven Penitential Psalms have remained standard for centuries. The Office, however, is a more complex prayer and has developed in several formats. Angela suggests that Ursulines *say...at least the Office of the Madonna* (Ch. V:9), the "Little Office," as it is called. Why that version? Probably because it is little. It is shortened. It would have been hard for early Ursulines to acquire the books needed for the full version chanted in monasteries and cathedrals. Many would not have had the time, either, since other people controlled their schedules. The Little Office better suited their lives. It is contained in one small book, with different prayers for the hours of the day, the days of the week and the seasons of the Church year. The Penitential Psalms appeared in an appendix of the edition Angela used.[46]

Angela had her own copy of the Little Office of the Blessed Virgin Mary. Besides the standard Psalms and Scriptures, it contained prayers used when the Church honors Mary. The Little Office was almost a thousand years old when Angela was praying it. Five hundred years before her, Saint Peter Damian had made it popular. In the sixteenth century, many lay Christians were reciting it daily.[47] Angela's office book held a treasure of prayer so precious to her that she promised to bequeath it to Zan Pietro Fontana after her death. He was Barbara's father and had helped the Company.[48]

A lifetime of prayer: that was her bequest to her daughters.

In the aftermath of the twentieth-century liturgical renewal that has restored the Divine Office, would Angela still encourage the Little Office? There is little purpose in trying to answer that question, for she always goes much more to the heart than to the form. What matters is that *by saying the Office one talks with God* (Ch. V:10).[49] Whatever form of the Office one uses, it is the vehicle of that conversation. It is a means to cultivate the fruit of a prayerful life.

Saying the Office, even the Little Office, posed several challenges in the early Company, even for those who could read. For one thing, the prayers were in Latin. The similarities between Latin and Italian allowed the person praying it to understand many words, but special attentiveness was required.[50] One would have to learn certain prayers for seasons of the Church year and special feasts. Instruction is required. Yet learning to pray the Office is not only a matter of language or procedures. More important is learning how to mine its treasures. This involves instruction, but not merely instruction. It is also a process of intimate, sisterly sharing of the Spirit's work in one's heart.

Angela does not tell those who know the Office to teach the others. No, each Ursuline must take responsibility for her own life of prayer. *Those who do not know how to say it will arrange to be taught by the sisters who do know* (Ch. V:11). It is a subtle but meaningful distinction. To become spiritual disciples, we must actively seek out a spiritual teacher.

The Our Father and the Hail Mary

The Rule also accommodates *those who do not know how to read* (Ch. V:12). Probably few could read.[51] To provide benefits like those of the Office, Angela outlines a pattern of vocal prayers, the *Our Father* and the *Hail Mary*. These are to be recited throughout the day in a pattern parallel to the hours of the Office.

12 Now, as for those who do not know how to read, let them want to say every day at Matins thirty-three Our Fathers and thirty-three Hail Marys in memory of the thirty-three years that Jesus Christ lived on this earth because he loved us.

13 Then at Prime say seven Our Fathers and seven Hail Marys for the seven gifts of the Holy Spirit.

14 Similarly, say as many at each of the Canonical Hours, that is at Terce, at Sext, at Nones, at Vespers, and at Compline.

No prayer is more sublime than the Our Father. This is how Jesus taught his disciples to pray (Luke 11:1). He teaches us, too, in words that we both speak and listen to, words that can take a lifetime to learn and live. Like the Psalms, the Our Father lifts us to honor God—"Hallowed be thy name"—and brings us face to face with our sinfulness—"Forgive us our trespasses." It teaches us to ask for what we need—bread, forgiveness, deliverance from evil. It also stretches us to make God's ways our own, as we pray, "Thy will be done" and ask to be forgiven "as we forgive."

In the Hail Mary, we greet Jesus' mother with the words of Gabriel and of Elizabeth (Luke 1:28, 45). We remember how completely human God became by the Incarnation in Mary's womb. Franciscan spirituality fosters devotion to Christ's humanity and surely influenced Angela. Gabriele Cozzano's writings after Angela's death offer an insight into her reverence for Mary. The Company in the world, he said, is akin to the lives of "the first flowers of the holy Church, and especially that of the Madonna."[52] He also wrote, "This is how the Madonna lived…."[53]

The Gospels are the source of both the Our Father and the Hail Mary, which Angela says to pray thirty-three times in the morning, recalling Jesus Christ's humanity. For thirty-three years he *lived on this earth because he loved us* (Ch. V:12). That love becomes the starting point of each day. The *memory of the thirty-three years* (Ch. V:12) evokes reflection upon the saving events of his whole life.

At the hour of Prime, before starting the workday, the members using these prayers are to *pray for the seven gifts of the Holy Spirit* to guide them through the day: wisdom, understanding, knowledge, good advice, courage, devotion, and awe before God (Ch. V:13). Repeating this intention all day, the women would invoke the Father (Our Father), remember the Son (in the Hail Mary) and live by the Holy Spirit (in seeking the gifts). Angela's Trinitarian theology colors daily life. The prayers are very simple. They can anchor a person in the flow of time; they can lead a contemplative soul to lofty places.

Following the *Canonical Hours* of the Divine Office (Ch. V:14), these Ursulines *who do not know how to read* nonetheless join their prayers to those of their sisters and of the entire Church.

The repetitions are not unlike the rosary, with its decades (sets of ten) of Hail Marys, each introduced by the Our Father. Decades are devoted to contemplation of the joyful (also recently the luminous), sorrowful and glorious events in the lives of Jesus and Mary. Though Angela did not speak of this form of prayer, she had a rosary. Repairs to one decade indicate that it must have been well used. In the course of wear, beads had been lost. Among its slightly irregular dark amber beads, strung on a white cord, were seven substituted beads of bone, blackish, a little smaller than the rest.[54] Angela bequeathed her rosary to an Ursuline named Assensa.[55]

Vocal prayer frames the day—one's life—in God-connected words, feelings and thoughts, in relationship with God. In vocal prayer, words give shape to the spirit's movement. Words are the beginning, though not the ending point.

Mental Prayer

The Rule makes a transition to another form of prayer, what Angela terms *mental prayer*. With characteristic energy she says, *we call upon each one...to practice daily....* (Ch. V:15). The Italian verb *essercitarse, to practice*, suggests both effort and regularity. *[W]e...call upon each one to raise her mind to God...in the recesses of her own heart* (Ch. V:15). The general phrase *mental prayer* does not separate the movements of this prayer, which engages not only the mind but also the heart and the will. The chapter touches all of these.

Mental prayer may not involve words at all. Yet, *to give substance and even some direction to mental prayer*, Angela puts words to her own prayer. She is faced with a dilemma. How can she instruct her daughters, teach them to pray in the deep *recesses of [their] heart[s]?* Only by letting them into the recesses of her own heart. Only by letting them overhear the silent exchange that happens there.

15 And to give substance and even some direction to mental prayer, we call upon each one to raise her mind to God, and to practice daily and in the recesses of her heart to say, in this way, or another, or a similar fashion:

The lesson and the beauty of prayer lie not in the words, but in the breath of spirit that carries them. This breath is not visible nor audible. When currents of air course over a lake, we do not see the air, only the birds that float on its currents, high above the water. When incense rises, we do not see the heat from the coals, only the smoke that the heat lifts high above the altar. So it is with prayer.

To teach her daughters how to pray *in the recesses* of their own hearts, Angela let them see words rising on the stream of her spirit, rising toward God. She let them see her with no veils, no formalities, just as she was, intimately face to face with the One she called *my Lover, or rather ours* (Last Counsel:23). With him she entered trustingly into her own depths. Then she followed his lead, stretching out to others, to everyone. As he had given himself, she responded by giving herself. This was their way of being with each other, Jesus Christ and Angela Merici. *In this way, or another, or a similar fashion,* Angela call[ed] upon her daughters to pray *daily* (Ch.V:15). Not in these words, but each one in her own spirit, just as truly and deeply and widely.

And so she gave them her prayer, and she gives it to us in the Rule. She lets us enter her inner experience through the impassioned immediacy of her words. The teenager who had rubbed ashes into her blond hair had matured but had never lost her dramatic intensity. It reveals itself as she gazes on the face of her Beloved and as she anguishes over the results of evil. Once again we observe the polarities so typical of her. They pull in a dynamic tension. Holding everything together is Christ's Passion, accepted out of his love for humanity and symbolized by his blood. The prayer's format reflects the pattern of the Penitential Psalms, moving from lament and contrition to petition and flowing into trust and praise.

Inner Struggle

Having wrestled with her own inner shadow, Angela lets us glimpse her struggle, describing *monstrous and frightening beasts and shapes* (Ch.V:21). Conscious of her share in human sinfulness, she is tormented by *shame...errors...ugliness and blame* (Ch. V:20, 21). Today we might ask whether such internalizing of blame is healthy, but her expressions belong to a long-standing genre of penitential literature. Contemporary religious styles also reinforced Angela's emotional personality. *Devotio Moderna,* with its emphasis on affective prayer, involving the emotions, continued to have an impact. And insofar as she expressed her truth, Angela put it before God for healing.

16 "My Lord, light up the darkness of my heart,

17 and give me grace to die rather than offend your divine Majesty at all today.

18 Keep my affections and my senses safe so that they may not lead me astray, neither to the right nor to the left,....

In any case, a sense of unworthiness never separated Angela from God. Despite the standard phrasing derived from Christ's parable of the tax-collector, *I dare not raise my eyes heavenward* (cf. Luke 18:13; Ch. V:20), she was accustomed *to raise her mind to God...daily* (Ch. V:15). For Angela, it would be worse than death to cut herself off from God. With typical absoluteness she prays, *give me grace to die rather than offend you at all today* (Ch. V:17).

Yearning, she prays, *My Lord, light up the shadows of my heart* (Ch. V:16). Angela knows Jesus Christ as "the light of the world," who has promised that whoever follows him "will not walk in darkness, but will have the light of life" (John 8:12). She acknowledges the shadows not only around her, but also inside her, shadows that obscure parts of her very self. We all have such shadows. Christ can penetrate and dispel them, can show us secret parts of ourselves as he sees them, lovingly. She does not want any part of herself to be apart from him.

No Plaster, No Pedestal

Those who want a plaster saint may find Angela unfit for the pedestal. With striking honesty, she lets us see her lows as well as her highs. Apparently she has sometimes felt helpless and useless. She knows that humanity, herself included, stands in need of redemption. She is well acquainted with temptation and the power it exercises to draw us off the path that leads to God. She recognizes that emotions and senses can turn aside, diverted by so many attractions along the side of the road.

She acknowledges that *the flesh and our sensuality are not yet dead* (Pr.:20). *Sensuality* is over-indulgence of the senses. Angela does not equate the senses, our physical feelings, with sensuality. Her prayer is that the senses be focused aright. *Keep my affections and my senses safe*, she asks, *so that they may not lead me astray, neither to the right nor to the left* (Ch. V:18). [Kept] safe by grace, illumined by light, the senses will not be tricked by deceptive glitter; they will show us reality truthfully.

Your Brilliant Face

19 ...nor turn me away from your brilliant face which soothes every afflicted heart.

Passionately, Angela pleads that nothing may *turn me away from your brilliant face, which soothes every afflicted heart* (Ch. V:19). [Y]our *brilliant face!* Her deeply contemplative spirit has gazed upon Christ, experienced the divine-human brilliance of his face. It was the focal point of her life, her center, her source of joy. His radiance shone on her and through her. It drew others to her and, through her, to him. Angela's contemporaries testified to this grace, also expressed in the obituary written a few days after her death by the Brescian chronicler Pandolfo Nassino, who wrote of the magnetic power of her words as she "used to preach faith in God...to everyone...."[56]

Her prayer shows her coming, in affliction, to Christ. Just to be with him *soothes [her] afflicted heart*. There she rests. (Cf. Psalm 27:7, 8.) And so it is with all who come to him, bringing heavy burdens (Matthew 11:28-30). He himself is their consolation: his *brilliant face!*

Sinfulness: Truth and Trust

In such intimacy with divine goodness, Angela imagines a vast gulf between God's goodness and human sinfulness. The contrast is so clear to Angela that she voices it in her typically emphatic and vivid terms: *while entering into the recesses of my heart, from shame I do not dare raise my eyes heavenward* (Ch. V:20). She feels far from heavenly goodness, *worthy to be devoured alive in hell* (Ch. V:21). She perceives *so many errors, so much ugliness and blame* as *monstrous and frightening beasts and shapes* (Ch. V:21) such as rear up in nightmares. These shadows and unconscious forces may be forgotten in the light of day, but they are not completely extinct.

Thus Angela knew intensely that it is God whose *grace* (Ch. V:17) brings us to

20 Alas! How sorrowful I am that while entering the recesses of my heart, from shame I do not dare raise my eyes heavenward

21 because I am worthy to be devoured alive in hell, seeing in myself so many errors, so much ugliness and blame, so many monstrous and frightening beasts and shapes!

22 So am I forced, day and night, walking, standing, working, thinking, to cry out and shout to Heaven and to beg mercy and time for penitence.

23 O most benign Lord, deign to pardon me so many offenses and each of my omissions that I have ever committed from the day of my holy baptism till now.

24 Deign to forgive my sins, alas, even those of my father and mother and of my relatives and friends, and those of the entire world.

salvation, to goodness, to heaven. No one can climb that ladder by her own strength alone. *So am I forced, day and night, walking, standing, working, thinking, to cry out and shout to Heaven and to beg mercy and time for penitence* (Ch. V:22). Angela's consciousness of human sin never made her despairing or afraid. God's saving love was never in doubt. Nor did she try to excuse or hide herself from God. That would be death! She ran to God, not away. Christ, to whom Angela cries out so fiercely, is not removed from the human condition. She finds him, instead, to be compassionate, gentle, *most benign* (Ch. V:23), offering us *medicine for the wounds of our souls* (Ch. VII:1). She turns to him in complete trust that he will *deign to pardon me so many offenses and each of my omissions that I have ever committed from the day of my holy baptism till now* (Ch. V:23).

What she has done and what she has failed to do she will not minimize. Sin hurts others and hurts the sinner. It offends all of us and the God who created and cares for all of us. It offends the One who gave himself for all of us. Yes, our sins wound our human family. Even from generation to generation we can hurt each other, passing on the results of sin. Through prayer we can also help each other to reach forgiveness and healing. And so Angela also begs that God *deign to forgive my sins, alas, even those of my father and mother and of my relatives and friends, and those of the entire world* (Ch. V:24).

She begs forgiveness through Jesus Christ's *most sacred passion and...precious blood shed for love of us* (Ch. V:25). This line is the turning point of Angela's prayer, because Christ's Passion, blood and love are our source of hope and confidence. In trust she invokes him by his Passion and blood because these are the means through which he has redeemed humanity from the effects of evil. As Saint John tells us, "There is no fear in love, but perfect love drives out fear because fear has to do with punishment, and so one who fears is not yet perfect in love. We love because [God] first loved us" (1 John 4:18, 19). God's love does not depend on our being sinless.

Those who prefer the saint on the pedestal may unwittingly rob Angela. It was actually her sinfulness and need for forgiveness that give her a claim on Jesus. He "did not come to call the righteous but sinners" (Mark 2:17).

Passion = Blood = Love

Passion...blood...love! "Passion" means both suffering and powerful love. Blood is life. Jesus' blood was shed as he poured forth his life, willingly, for love of us, extending life to all. Blood is the emblem

> 25 I beg this of you through your most sacred passion and your precious blood shed for love of us,...

of this life-giving love. Whenever Angela speaks any one of these words, she implies them all: *Passion = blood = love!* Jesus' death is not merely an example. It is redemptive. Truly human and truly divine, he incorporates humanity into his free and faithful relationship with God. In communion with him we are restored to union with God and others, the *merits of [his] passion* (Ch. VI:3).

This fusion was what Angela experienced in the supreme moment of her pilgrimage to the Holy Land. She was blind as she traced the steps of Jesus' sacred Passion along the *Via Dolorosa* in Jerusalem.[57] All the more intensely, therefore, without distraction, her spirit saw the love poured out with his blood shed. On Calvary the impact drove her to her knees. She burst into tears. Again and again she kissed the holy ground.[58] His passionate love for her, for *the entire world* (Ch. V:24)! Calvary was the fountain where her spirit drank, over and over and always: in each day's prayer and in the *sacred Mass* (Ch. VI:3). Calvary draws us to the Company's centerpoint, God's love. Ursulines are *sisters in the blood of Christ* (First Counsel:1). His is the life we share.

Pilgrimage – A Prayer Practice

Angela responded so intensely in that moment on Calvary at least partly because she craved and relished direct experiences. The immediacy of place and presence intensified her spiritual responses. Pilgrimages are rich opportunities for such a person. Her keen emotional reactions involved her whole self. It was not merely a matter of seeing. In fact, when near-blindness descended upon her, outbound to the Holy Land, she rejected suggestions to return home. "Being there" was important to her.

A desire to renew the experience of Calvary led Angela on pilgrimage to the Sacred Mount at Varallo a little before 1530.[59] The Franciscans were in the process of constructing chapels with images of Jesus' life and passion. Completed in the twentieth century, these life-sized statues still allow the faithful to envision the places and retrace the saving events, even those who cannot travel to the Holy Land. In August, 1532, Angela returned to Varallo with fourteen fellow-pilgrims, including Agostino Gallo, his widowed sister Ippolita Dorosini, and probably some of the first Ursulines.

This trip may have been a prelude to the Company's taking shape, coming as it did about the time when Angela moved to St. Afra, decorated the oratory in Isabetta Prato's home and began gathering her followers there. Angela was teaching her daughters to pray. In her Rule, she continues to teach.

Sand, Waters, Stars

Angela teaches her daughters to pray as she did: *through your holy name—may it be blessed beyond the ocean's grains of sand, beyond the drops of the waters, beyond the multitude of stars* (Ch. V:26). How many grains on the sea's shores and sandy bottom? How many drops making up its waters? How many stars in the multitude that stretch from edge to edge of the ocean's horizon? She must have asked herself such questions on shipboard, sailing across the Mediterranean Sea from Venice to the Holy Land. If even creation is beyond our imagining, what of the Creator?

Sand, waters, stars—creatures speak to us of God. We do well to listen, as Angela teaches in her Rule's chapter on obedience. Creation is God's voice. Abraham heard it: "I will bless you abundantly and make your descendants as countless as the stars of the sky and the sands of the seashore" (Genesis 22:17). God offered a covenant. Abraham believed. Faith opens our eyes and ears to God's presence and promises. "It was equally by faith that Sarah, in spite of being past the age, was made able to conceive, because she believed that [the one] who had made the promise would be faithful to it. Because of this, there came from one man...more descendants than could be counted, as many as the stars of heaven or the grains of sand on the seashore" (Hebrews 11:11, 12 – Jerusalem Bible translation).[60]

26 ...through your holy name—may it be blessed beyond the ocean's grains of sand, beyond the drops of the waters, beyond the multitude of stars.

Angela's words remind us of Abraham and Sarah. They remind us that God is the source of our faith, trust and justification. Angela relied on God's promises, too.

Because of God's faithfulness, not ours, there is a new Covenant sealed in Christ's blood.

And so she teaches her daughters to pray, imitating Abraham's and Sarah's faith in the One who is faithful. Faith is the soil of our prayer.

And so she teaches her daughters to pray in awe, in worship: *your holy name—may it be blessed* (Ch. V:26)! The surrounding verses direct this prayer to Jesus Christ, yet the language resonates with Genesis and suggests the Godhead. This mingling alerts us to two pervasive elements of Angela's spirituality. First, her focus on Jesus Christ leads her and us to God. Second, she is keenly consciousness of the Holy Trinity and never far removed from awareness of all the divine persons.

Lament

From the peaceful and poetic interlude of sand, water, and stars, Angela shifts suddenly to lament. She shared with many holy people an intense experience of infinity that puts their human limitations in sharp relief. Whereas others look at them and see only holiness, their yardstick is no longer human. They have come to see everything in light of the divine. Overwhelmed by God's love for them, they long to respond in kind but bump up against their limits.

Urgency colors Angela's language. She laments (to paraphrase), "The more you reveal yourself to me, the more I wish to serve you, yet the more I see how small is my love. Alas! I am slow, meager, disobedient, grudging in my service (Ch. V:27-30)! Your generosity runs ever before me, forever outstrips me. *I lament the fact that I have been so late to begin serving your divine Majesty* (Ch. V:27)." It seems to her, on looking back, that her youth and early adulthood were hardly devoted to God. Forty years have elapsed since her visions had given direction to her life. Perhaps she is computing how long it had taken her to bring the Company of Saint Ursula into existence, four decades later.

Looking upon the crucifix, upon the One who had given his life—poured it out—Angela cries out, *Alas...I have not shed*

27 I lament the fact that I have been so late to begin serving your divine Majesty.

28 Alas, till now I have not shed even a little drop of blood for love of you,

29 nor have I ever been obedient to your divine precepts,

30 and every adversity has been harsh for me because of my little love for you.

even a little drop of blood for love of you (Ch. V:28). Before his complete oblation, she reproaches herself, feeling that she has *not ever been obedient to your divine precepts* (Ch. V:29), has not lived wholly by their direction. Though love should lighten the burdens that we carry for the beloved, *every adversity has been harsh for me because of my little love for you* (Ch. V:30).

Martyrs' Witness

Who has followed Christ so fully as Angela would wish to? The martyrs! Martyrs were Angela's heroes and heroines. She grew up hearing their exciting and idealized stories in the farmhouse kitchen at Le Grezze, with Giovanni Merici reading to his family, probably from *The Golden Legend*. Martyrs shared completely in Christ's Passion—blood—love. Saints Faustinus and Jovita and the other early Christian martyrs of Brescia inspired her. She had moved to an apartment by the Church of St. Afra at least partly to be near the martyrs' relics in the church crypt. She had even petitioned to be buried there, her bones near theirs, her soul with theirs triumphant in heaven (Pr.:31; Ch. XI:36).[61]

The martyrs' deaths bear witness to what gave their lives meaning. (The Greek word *martyr* means "witness.") They repeat the pattern, the good news, of Christ's life and death.[62] Their commitment withstands death and outlasts it. Their blood is the seal of their faithfulness. Angela honored Saint Catherine of Alexandria, who was tortured as a punishment for proclaiming divine truths. According to the account in *The Golden Legend*, many onlookers embraced the truth because of her words and example.[63] Angela chose Saint Catherine's feast day, November 25, to inaugurate the Company. She placed it under the patronage of Saint Ursula, another martyr. *The Golden Legend* tells the story of Saint Ursula and her Companions. It says that pagan antagonism to their example of faith was the motive for their martyrdom.[64]

31 Lord, on behalf of those miserable wretches who do not know you,
32 nor wish to be participants in your most sacred passion,
33 my heart is wrenched,
34 and willingly would I shed my own blood (if I could), in order to open up the blindness of their minds.

The martyrs proclaimed Jesus, who had lived and died to show us God. But there are, Angela recognizes, *miserable wretches who do not know you, nor wish to be participants*

244

in your most sacred passion (Ch. V:31, 32). Perhaps they do not even realize their need for redemption. They do not know where to turn for light and life.

Angela yearns to help these blind *wretches* find enlightenment: *[M]y heart is wrenched for them and willingly would I shed my own blood (if I could) in order to open up the blindness of their minds* (Ch. V:33, 34). She had known darkness and blindness. After her sister's death, so close to their parents', her heart could find no light, until God allowed her to see her sister in heavenly radiance. On the voyage to the Holy Land, sight left her eyes, only to be restored on the return trip. In compassion she longed to reach out to those who stumble blindly, who cannot see God by faith. The heart that is grappled to the heart of Christ loves as he does, in self-emptying for others.

Prayer Rippling Outward

And so Angela teaches her daughters to pray with a zeal that flows into loving action. Jesus is her model. He shed his blood *for love of us;* she regrets not having *shed even a little drop of blood for love of you;* she would *willingly...shed my own blood (if I could)* to lead others to him (Ch. V:25, 28, 34). Intimacy with Jesus means sharing his mission of self-sacrificing love for everyone. Angela's contemplative prayer springs from deep inner experience and flows outward in ever-widening circles. Progressively, it embraces her parents, her relatives, her friends, the entire world, including those who do not know Christ and those who are spiritually blind.

Angela's zeal was not abstract or remote or cool. Her compassionate *heart [was] wrenched* (Ch. V:33). Her willingness to *shed [her] own blood* was not to be realized in martyrdom. Yet she poured out her life for others day by day and year by year. They came to her and left carrying consolation, inspiration, advice, encouragement and reconciliation. Gallo testified about the people who crowded into her rooms at his home seeking advice or consolation, help with a will or a marriage or with a broken relationship.[65] She gave them compassion, solace, wisdom and peace.

She faced danger to seek the lost and lead them home to God. Romano told of how Angela faced the severe nobleman Luigi Gonzaga on behalf of a banished courtier. He also recounted her courageous approach to Filippo Sala and Francesco Martinengo, preparing to duel. The death of either one could have sparked a combustion. Brescia was still shuddering with memories of massacres and retaliations in 1512 and after. No wonder that Duke Francesco Rovere of Urbino had tried to intervene with the enemies![66] But his words had no effect. Who else would dare to confront these violent men? The two men's wives turned to Angela. Her mission of peace was prayer in action.

Offering

The final section of Angela's prayer and of Chapter V is an offering. Angela invites her daughters to offer themselves, as she offers herself, her everything, fully and freely and joyfully (Chs. I:3, 4; IX:2). Her words are addressed to God; they point the way for our actions. We must live the gift, not just talk about it. *Now to the task, with courage!* (Pr.:29). We must *participate in [the] blessed merits* of Christ's Passion (Ch. VI:4). By this prayer we seek to align ourselves with Christ, as he has realigned the universe toward God.

35 However, my Lord, my only life and hope,
36 I beg you to deign to receive this my most vile and unclean heart...

The offering begins with the word *However* (Ch. V:35). Angela was not able to give herself as a martyr. *However*, she wanted to offer herself to God as fully, as completely as she could. No matter her failings and limitations, her changes of mood or fluctuating zeal! Regardless and always, God remains the same. Christ reflects that divine reality. Christ is God's word of *life and hope* (Ch. V:35).

The Divine Goldsmith

37 and to burn its every affection and passion in the blazing furnace of your divine love.
38 I beg you to accept my free will,
39 all of my own will, which of itself, because it is infected by sin, does not know how to discern good from evil.

Once more, Angela's emphatic language takes us by surprise. How could she possibly call her heart *most vile and unclean* (Ch.V:36) as she offers it? A metaphor—*blazing furnace*—explains her words. In shops along Brescia's streets, Angela saw goldsmiths at work over their blazing furnaces, burning away the impurities from ore and refining precious metals. When the miner finds gold, it is muddy and mixed with base elements. Smiths refine the ore, which rests in a crucible over a white-hot fire in the furnace. The heat burns away the base elements till only the purest gold is left, for the gold-smith to fashion into something beautiful.

Our hearts are like this. Of itself, the heart is raw ore. Its emotions and passions can gleam, can radiate. They can reflect God. But only after their dross has been removed. What sort of dross? Affections attached to things unworthy of us, or to hurtful or sinful things. Passions driven by compulsions, or out of control. Infatuations and compulsions are like the dross in the precious ore. When they have been burned away, our affections and passions give us warmth and energy. They attach us to goodness and move us to honorable actions.

Angela had heard the words of the prophet Malachi, heard God promising

...the messenger of the covenant whom you desire.

...he is like the refiner's fire...

He will sit refining and purifying (Malachi 3:1-3).

In her prayer, Angela beg[s] the divine Goldsmith, Christ, to deign to receive...my...heart as it is, raw ore though it is. She sees him take her heart into his own heart, to burn its every affection and passion in the blazing furnace of [his] divine love (Ch. V:35-37). What happens there is his work. He will find the most precious and beautiful elements and make them his own—his and still hers. In such an offering, we do not lose ourselves or become less ourselves. Giving to God does not mean giving away. Not at all! No, we become more truly ourselves and more fully God's.

Angela's prayer of offering acknowledges a realization that may have come to her, as it does to all of us, through experiencing our limitations. Perhaps the teenaged Angela did not yet know that there could be feelings of hesitation. It is easy to take for granted the energy of youthful enthusiasm, as though it would never tire. Learning to recognize the flaws does not diminish the precious gift—the fullness of who we are, all our future, all the possibilities.

God transforms our gift and returns it to us to use in service. The divine Goldsmith burns away impurities from the heart so that we can love fully and truly. To the One who came to set us free from bondage to sin, Angela offers my free will (Ch. V:38). The divine Physician cures the sinful *infect[ions]* of *my own will* so that I may know how *to discern good from evil* (Ch. V:39). God's receiving and accepting are not passive. If we could imagine God as a ruler, at the feet of whose *divine Majesty* we place our gift (Ch. V:42), we would also have to imagine that gift lifted up, cherished, and healed. Jesus did not wait for people to be healed and perfected before he would touch them. As he said, "Those who are well do not need a physician, but the sick do" (Mark 2:17). That is why Angela presents *everything of mine, interior as well as exterior,* all with such complete trust (Ch. V:41-43).

Giving Thoughts, Words, Deeds

All—it takes a lifetime to make that offering complete. It is a partnership between her and her Spouse. She puts herself in the stream of grace that flows from his cross. It is most natural that *everything of mine, interior as well as exterior,* should belong to him. This is the nature of *sacred virginity*, this offering, this consecration. *All.* The offering is not merely an intention. It becomes action as *my every thought, word and deed* (Ch. V:40).

The words are intense, dramatic. Yet in Angela's own life there was nothing dramatic. At home in Desenzano, she worked on the farm and in her vineyard. In Brescia she worked with the other women in the Romano and Gallo households. Ursulines offer to God our ordinary lives, made up of nearly invisible *thoughts, words and deeds.*

Giving our thoughts to God means trying to think in God's way. As Angela describes in the Rule's Chapter IX, "About Virginity," it means opening our minds to God's light, allowing it to dispel *every shadow of envy and ill will* (Ch. IX:8). It means bending our habits of thought toward harmony, not *discord and evil suspicion* (Ch. IX:9). It means cultivating desires for what is truly good, not false lures that would lead us astray. *Instead, be happy, and always full of charity and faith and hope in God* (Ch. IX, 8-11). *[I]ll will...discord...evil suspicion*—how could these habits of thought be offered to God? But harmony, kindness, encouragement—these are beautiful gifts. They also lead us to *be happy.* They nourish

40 Receive my every thought, word and deed,

41 finally, everything of mine, interior as well as exterior,

42 all of which I offer before the feet of your divine Majesty.

43 And I pray that you deign to receive them, although they be unworthy.

44 Amen."

248

charity and faith and hope in God. Selfishness and cynicism, or charity, faith and hope—we can choose what thoughts to cultivate. We can offer them to God.

Giving our words to God means trying to speak always the Word who is Truth, that is, Jesus Christ. His Spirit speaks in Scripture; if we drink deeply from the Bible's inspired words, they will naturally flavor our speech and be useful for our neighbors. People yearn for God's word; they need it. Angela voiced it constantly in Brescia. Accomplished preachers sought her out to consult her about Scripture. So many people had flocked to her during their Cremona sojourn that the Gallos offered her two rooms on their return to Brescia, to accommodate the crowds. Ordinary people came burdened by sorrows or decisions or inner struggles. They needed words of compassion and kindness (Fifth Counsel:12). People suffer just as acutely today. In giving our words to others, we give them to God.

The basket of our offering is woven mostly of ordinary daily conversations, the kinds Angela talks about in the Rule's Chapter IX "About Virginity." We offer God our words of simple honesty, *"yes, yes" or "no, no," as Jesus Christ teaches* (cf. Matthew 5:37). Our words belong to God if we are speaking humbly, *not answering arrogantly*; being whole-hearted instead of grudging; forgiving instead of *staying angry*; being cheerful, *not grumbling*; talking kindly, *not spreading gossip* (Ch. IX:14-19). Breath shapes our words. Breath is spirit (Latin *spiritus*). Words truly given to God will *teach and edify* less by what they say than by the spirit that breathes in them (Ch. IX:21).

And what of our deeds? What does it mean to offer them to God? Acting with integrity is what Angela asks new Ursulines to practice in Chapter III, "About the Manner of Interacting in the World." Make our deeds match our commitment. This is what is demanded by consecration to God in *sacred virginity*. In Brescia's streets Angela could see servants come and go on their masters' business. A servant wore a special color or insignia clearly distinguishing the lord he represented. We belong to Jesus Christ. To offer him our deeds means *not doing anything unworthy of one who has the name of a servant of Jesus Christ* (Ch. IX:20).

We offer to him what he has first given us, and from *the blazing furnace of [his] divine love* he gives it back again! We must use our lives as he did, for God and for others. Belonging to him means radiating his love in our *every thought, word and deed*. We put our selves at his disposal. Like Jesus, then, we become servants and witnesses and lovers.

Sacred virginity is this offering and this life.

Amen.

Reflection

❖ Angela offers us her prayer, as Jesus did. Compose your own psalm or your own prayer of self-offering.

❖ The call to loving intimacy (Prologue) finds its realization in prayer.

❖ A visionary experience had given direction to Angela's life. What prayer experience has profoundly shaped your life? How do you honor that gift?

❖ Do you see any implications of Angela's prayer for healing the family tree? Take time to pray for your family.

❖ Variations in the Divine Office continue to emerge, for example, inclusive-language versions. The language of Scripture is culturally conditioned; some Psalms and readings may distract one from prayer on this account. One approach is to select Psalms that are personally helpful, challenging or comforting and to use them as alternatives. (An occasional return to a troublesome text might reveal material for prayer in different seasons of one's life.)

❖ Angela's contemplative prayer springs from deep inner experience and flows outward in ever-widening circles.

❖ Passion = blood = love. Com-passion is willingness to suffer with another person. Compassion can also lead to action.

Chapter VI, "About Going to Mass Every Day"

Angela sought the closest possible union with Jesus Christ. Her private prayer was intense and intimate. In the Mass Christ brought her into his great action and into himself. In the sacrament, she also joined the entire Church at prayer. In titling Chapter VI "About Going to Mass Every Day," Angela is clearly reflecting her own long practice.

The Entire Mass

Encouraging her daughters to *go* and to *see* the Mass, she uses a common expression (Ch. VII:1).[67] In an era when the congregation was far separated from the altar, the lay faithful tried to *see* the sacred actions. But Angela stresses that mere presence, mere seeing, will not produce an automatic spiritual result. Our presence must be sincere: not for a show of piety, but *with modesty*; not for obligation but *devoutly* (Ch. VI:2).

Why would Angela say to *see at least one entire* Mass (Ch. VI:1)? Why *at least*? Why *entire*? Was she worried that her daughters would come late and leave early? The answer to these questions lies in liturgical misapprehensions of the era. Some Christians considered the Consecration the only part of the Mass that really mattered. Often it was the only moment that they could recognize. A bell rang and the priest, far away and facing away from them, raised the host and chalice over his head, for all to see. Many people came only for that moment, to see Christ's body and blood. Others went from church to church or along the aisle from one side altar to another, where simultaneous Masses were being offered, to be present for the Consecration as many times as possible.

Popular piety had deteriorated to a semi-superstitious cult of magical moments. Angela rejected this fragmented idea of the Mass as a sequence of more holy and less holy events. She affirmed that the Eucharist is one entire action which calls for deep engagement. In the same breath, she responded to those contemporary reformers who were suggesting that the sacrament be discarded

1 Again, let each one go to Mass every day, and see at least one entire [Mass]

2 and attend it with modesty and devoutly,....

altogether. She called for genuine participation, in the fully active sense of "taking part."

To the full sweep of the Eucharistic event, Angela brought all that welled up in her soul throughout each day. She brought sorrow for *my sins, alas, even those of my father and mother and of my relatives and friends and those of the entire world* (Ch. V:23, 24). She brought her attentiveness to Scripture. She brought her *every thought, word and deed, finally, everything of mine, interior as well as exterior, all of which I offer* (Ch. V: 40-42). She brought her hunger for union with Christ.

Taking Part

For all her involvement, Angela recognized that Mass can seem boring and repetitive. Merely to show up would be an empty exercise. Eucharist is not an automatic grace-machine. Nor does our devotion either merit or produce grace. We participate in Christ's *merits*. Therefore she encourages *great attention* and *faith* as the catalysts of our *participat[ion]* (Ch. VI:3,4). *Faith* sheds light on what is happening. Though we do not see, we know that Jesus Christ is present and gathers us into his action. He promised, "Blessed are those who have not seen and have believed" (John 20:29). *Attention* leads us through the Mass so that we can participate in each step: contrition, a desire to live by God's word, offering, adoration, communion, and going forth to give ourselves as Christ has done.

In the sixteenth century, the flow of liturgical action took place at a distance, in Latin. Following word for word would have been difficult. Nonetheless, Latin is close enough to the Italian of the period for even the uninstructed to recognize the biblical passages being read. Angela not only knew Latin but was so well versed in Scripture that the Word entered her understanding and her spirit. Bertolino Boscoli later recounted under oath that one day he and many others saw her rise into the air during the Gospel reading. This marvel occurred in his neighborhood Church of St. Barnabas on a working day. Though he was then a teenager, the sight made such

3 ...since in the sacred Mass are found all the merits of the passion of our Lord.

4 And the more one attends with great attention, faith and contrition, the more one participates in those blessed merits and the greater consolation one receives.

an impression that decades later he could describe the scene at the side altar of St. Nicholas of Tolentino, where the Mass was being offered. He indicated the distance, about a palm's breadth, which he saw her feet rise above the floor.[68] Angela herself put little stock in marvels, as Agostino Gallo testified.[69] But the Good News of the Gospel surely has the power to lift us up!

Communion

Angela speaks of *a communion of the spirit* because actually receiving the sacrament was permitted only infrequently in her day. In a spiritual communion one invites Jesus Christ to enter one spiritually. The Italian term that Angela uses, *un communicarse*, expresses an active and mutual exchange with Christ, a mingling of our spirits with his. We hunger for this communion. We need hunger as much as we need to be fed. Exactly as much. If hunger subsides, we will starve. Angela, a woman of keen desires, must have known this. She had always hungered for sacramental Communion.

> 5 Actually, it will be a communion of the spirit.

In the early 1500s most lay Catholics could receive Communion only on solemn feast days such as Christmas and Easter. Frequent Communion was a rare privilege. Groups like the Third Order of St. Francis were permitted more frequent Confession and Communion than the general population. This opportunity was among the attractions the Third Order held for Angela when she was young, according to the testimony of Agostino Gallo. He also reported that Angela received Communion whenever she could.[70] She hungered for this intimacy with her Spouse, which is at the heart of *sacred virginity*.

Together

Permission for monthly Communion was apparently extended to Ursulines. The Company would gather at a designated church *on each first Friday of the month...and there all together receive communion* (Ch. VII:13). Communion in the Lord's Supper as well as in his sacrifice had a communal significance for *sisters in the blood of Christ* (First Counsel:1). They entered *all together* into this mystery as they could, in their historical moment. Mass was also the setting for the Company's most sacred actions. On November 25, 1535, the Company was founded after Mass at St. Afra Church. The Company continued to receive new members during Mass on that date in subsequent years. The practice had a deep meaning. The things we do together help to define who we are, our common identity. Ursuline identity is to be shaped and experienced in the sharing of Christ's Passion and love.

Eucharist is deeply significant for Ursuline life. Angela could have taken it for granted that the Company's members would naturally attend Mass as a regular part of Catholic life. Instead, she devoted a chapter of her Rule to it. The very nature of this vocation is union with God through Jesus Christ. One lives that union throughout the day. But Eucharist is the privileged place of most directly and fully participating in his divine-human act of love, and of doing so with the whole Church. We unite our lives with his. We bring our sinfulness and our generosity. Across time and space we enter into a sacred event. The more deeply we participate, the more deeply we receive blessing and *consolation* (Ch. VI:4).

The Merits of the Passion

Words such as *blessed merits* and *consolation* echo the long prayer verbalized in Chapter V. There Angela explores the meaning of Christ's Passion. What are the *merits of the passion of our Lord* which she found in the Mass (Ch. VI:3)? The answer comes in her implied equation: Passion = blood = love. The *blessed merits* are, first, the redeeming experience of God's love; and, second, the grace of extending God's love to others (Chapter V:25, 34).

In the Eucharist, Christ again offers his body and blood, as he did at his Last Supper, sharing with his disciples the bread and wine, nourishing them with his body, "which will be given for you" and with his blood, "which will be shed for you" (Luke 22:19, 20). The next day, on Calvary, his body was given, his blood poured out. Passion...blood...love. He told us to do this in memory of him—not just the sacred ritual, but the self-gift in love. While living in Antonio Romano's household, Angela had often attended Mass in Romano's parish church, Santa Agata, where a Crucifixion fresco above the altar made visible the link between the sacrifice of Calvary and the Eucharistic action.[71]

Jesus' Passion includes the suffering he endured and the love that had always kept him faithful to his mission, even to the point of death. His Passion includes the divine power of the love which could not die. The *blessed merits of [his] passion* are Love given, Love dying, Love alive eternally. As we *participate*, we receive and we give, we die and we live, we are loved and we love.

Since the early twentieth century, especially since the papacy of Saint Pius X, reception of Communion has been taken for granted as appropriate participation in the Eucharistic banquet. Now we see the Eucharist as meal—the Lord's Supper—as well as sacrifice—that of Calvary. At a meal we find nourishment. Every part of the celebration feeds our souls. Coming around the table for a shared meal emphasizes the "horizontal" or communal dimension of our experience. We honor Christ present in word and sacrament, in celebrant and community. It becomes imperative to take the experience outside the church in service to others.

In the wake of the Second Vatican Council, our liturgical renewal expands beyond Angela's understanding. Today we situate the Eucharist within the full Paschal Mystery. We celebrate the inextricable unity of Christ's life, death and Resurrection. Resurrection has taken a higher position on our spiritual landscape. Christ is Risen and present in the world around us.

In *going to Mass every day*, we can enter the mystery from any and all of its graced facets. As sacrifice or as banquet, in Passion or in Resurrection, the Eucharist brings us closer than any other religious practice to the One who is the center, the meaning of our life. It puts us with the Spouse in the moment of his greatest act of love. Who would not wish to enter this sacred experience every day? It is the most powerful support to *sacred virginity*. Linked with personal prayer, Eucharist is the essential nourishment for this vocation.

Behavior and Balance

The discourse on the Mass ends with an abrupt shift from the sublime to the mundane. Angela cautions her daughters *not to linger too much in churches* (Ch. VI:6). Back into life's daily round.... An Ursuline's life is in the world, integrated with her responsibilities and relationships. Piety should never be an excuse for neglecting them.

Angela was also well aware that some people used the church as an excuse for liaisons, since young single women had few other opportunities to leave their homes. In the play *Woman of Ancona* (Padua, 1533), a maid and manservant flirt and communicate surreptitiously in church, despite the fact that women and men were seated separately.[72] The diocesan vicar-general Bishop Gian Pietro Ferretti (in 1545) and Cardinal Durante Duranti (in 1551) considered it necessary to reprimand Brescians about wandering around in churches during services and other unbecoming behavior in church.[73]

Finally, Angela is alerting us not to make a display of religious practices. Her words echo those of Jesus, when she says *(if they want to pray longer), let them go into their rooms, and enclosed there, pray...*(Ch. VI:7). Jesus had instructed his followers, "But when you pray, go to your inner room, close the door, and pray to your Father in secret" (Matthew 6:6). As Agostino Gallo observed during the months that Angela lived in his home, she often spent several morning hours in church, praying before the Blessed Sacrament and "hearing the Masses." He also mentions her balanced mixture of hours spent in church, in private prayer and in "good works" for others.[74]

Neither liturgy nor private prayer substitutes, one for the other. The chapter on the Mass concludes with a reference to private prayer, *in the way and as much as the Spirit and conscience will dictate* (Ch. VI:7). Besides the Mass and Divine Office (Ch. V:9-14), Angela urges everyone to enter into daily mental prayer or contemplation. She offers an example in Chapter V (16-44), discussed above. Some might also say the rosary or have other personal devotions. Angela's own rosary was worn by use. She had no desire to regulate the form or content of her daughters' devotions. Rather, she says to follow *the Spirit and conscience* in this regard.

6 But remember not to linger too much in churches;

7 rather (if they want to pray longer), let them go into their rooms, and enclosed there, pray in the way and as much as the Spirit and conscience will dictate.

Let us continue to plunge ourselves into the Eucharist, into God's loving, giving, suffering, saving, healing, nourishing, speaking—raising us to new life! Let us seek the nourishment to live that love in our world!

Reflection

❖ Where do you find Eucharistic nourishment: in sacrifice? In banquet? In the Passion? In the Resurrection? In Christ's transforming presence? In word? In community? In communion?

❖ Imagine a work of art that would express your understanding and experience of the Eucharist.

❖ For what are you hungry?

❖ Catholic women are excluded from following a vocation of priestly service. Does this reality give you pain when you participate at Mass? How do you use this pain?

❖ Consider how the Eucharistic experience helps you to extend God's love to others.

Chapter VII, "About Confession"

When Angela speaks to her daughters about Confession in Chapter VII of her Rule, she says *to make a practice* of it (Ch. VII:1). Confession should be a regular part of Ursuline life.

Medicine, Liberation

Confession, she tells us, is *a necessary medicine for the wounds of our souls* (Ch. VII:1). Jesus is the divine Physician.

Inner wounds can be healed through a ritual that involves exterior actions, *confess[ing] aloud [our] failings to a priest* (Ch. VII:2, 4). The true significance of the ritual is interior. Much of the chapter shows the inter-relationship of actions and dispositions. *Confess[ing] aloud* involves honesty about our sins, honesty with ourselves and with someone else. The One who is Truth, Jesus Christ himself, leads us to this honesty. As we have often noted, "Truth" is one of Angela's favorite names for Jesus, who called himself "the way and the truth and the life" (John 14:6) and promised that "whoever lives the truth comes to the light" (John 3:21). When we *confess aloud*, we take responsibility for our own truth. No running and hiding! Confession is about turning the light of truth on the dark places inside us, letting that light cleanse and heal us (cf. Psalm 32).

Confession is Christ's gift to the Church. *"I will give you the keys of the kingdom of Heaven, and whatever you bind on earth will also be bound in Heaven, and whatever you loosen on earth*

1 Again you are called upon to make a practice of confession, a necessary medicine for the wounds of our souls.

2 Since never will anyone be absolved of sin, if he does not first confess aloud his failings to the priest, as Scripture says: "Dic tu prius iniquitates tuas, ut justificeris"; that is, first say your sins, so that you may be absolved.

3 And Truth says to St. Peter: "Tibi dabo claves regni caelorum, et quodcumque ligaveris super terram, erit ligatum et in caelis, et quodcumque solveris super terram, erit solutum et in caelis"; that is, I will give you the keys of the kingdom of Heaven, and whatever you bind on earth will also be bound in Heaven, and whatever you loosen on earth will also be loosened in Heaven,

4 which clearly shows that a sin cannot be taken away except through the priest and through confession.

will also be loosened in Heaven" (cf. Matthew 16:19; Ch. VII:3). Sin binds us. The result is suffering, individual and communal. Confession can liberate us. We may be bound by the chains of our sinful tendencies or compulsions. How difficult it is to break free! The very act of confessing begins our liberation. We reach out for assistance. Jesus is the divine Liberator. He gave the Church the keys, the capacity to put sinful humanity in contact with the source of wholeness and freedom—himself.

The Priest

Each one should want to present herself before the priest, as if before God, the eternal judge (Ch. VII:7). The priest's presence is a required condition, but if we focus on the priest, we go only part of the way. Angela's concern, as always, is for our sincerity and God's forgiveness. The priest helps us to experience more concretely our connection with God who, as judge, is the source of light and truth. The involvement of another human being also reminds us that our sins affect other people. No sin is without its effect in the human community, even if that effect is subtle or silent.

Priest-confessors of the sixteenth century combined several roles that are now exercised by persons with different skills and training. Spiritual direction and counseling often took place in the confessional. Angela no doubt experienced this combination among the Franciscans of the Island of Garda, whom she met in the church *"della Disciplina"* near her aunt and uncle Biancosi's home in Salò. It would have been natural, when she moved to Brescia, to maintain such a tie with the Franciscan spiritual family there. Toward the end of her life, she chose as her confessor Father Serafino of Bologna, one of the Canons Regular of the Lateran. The Canons were connected with the Church of St. Afra, next to which she made her home. The standard term for a confessor was "spiritual

5 Because in what way will the priest be able to loosen the sin, if he does not know it?
6 And how will he be able to know what has been committed if it is not revealed by one's own lips? In that case, the hidden sin would stay within one's breast.
7 Therefore, each one should want to present herself before the priest, as if before God, the eternal judge,....

father." Angela refers to *spiritual fathers* in other parts of the Rule (Ch. IV:18; Ch. VIII:9).

Today spiritual directors, counselors, therapists and others can be resources for those seeking clarity and inner truth. Angela herself modeled these roles for the many who sought her out, from all walks of life. Agostino Gallo testified to the stream of visitors seeking her advice about family problems and spiritual questions, civic disputes and scriptural interpretations.

Addressing Abuses

Church reformers of Angela's century rightly challenged the many abuses of sacramental Confession, which was sometimes treated as though it were mechanical or magical or were a commercial transaction. Fueled by fear of Purgatory and Hell, the "selling" of absolutions and indulgences financed crusades and cathedrals. Such confessions are empty rituals performed in the hope of paying off spiritual debts. This perversion of the sacrament pretends that we could avoid responsibility for our sinful deeds and neglect conversion of heart.

Amid rampant abuses and harsh critiques of Confession, Angela affirmed the sacramental reality. Our relationship with God is not about accounting, not about ledgers of debits and credits. Sin is not a debt but a wound. God wants to heal us, and Confession is the *necessary medicine*. Just as sin infects our bodies, minds, hearts and spirits, so our healing must involve our whole self. Our bodies perform the ritual, which expresses the mind's truth and the heart's sorrow. The penitent, *sorrowing, totally sincere, and in truth of conscience,...should confess her sin and ask forgiveness for it.* She must take responsibility as she *stay[s] before the confessor* (Ch. VII:8-11). Far from assessing penalties, *God, the eternal judge* offers *medicine, forgiveness* and *absolution* (Ch. VII: 7, 1, 10, 11).

Confession is not an automatic cure. Healing is a process, life-long. That is why Angela calls upon her daughters *to make a practice of* confession, a monthly practice (Ch. VII:1, 12), part of the rhythm of a healthy life.[75]

8 ...and there, sorrowing,
9 totally sincere, and in truth of conscience, she should confess her sin
10 and ask forgiveness for it,
11 and she should always with fear and reverence stay before the confessor till she has received absolution.

Angela's prayer in Chapter V suggests that she engaged in what today might be called a "review of consciousness." She reviewed the action of God in her life and her responses. She found in herself the tendencies that might lead her away from God. This sort of review is not a quick checklist of sinful acts but a deep reflection on life patterns of grace and shadow. Jesus has promised that "truth will set you free" (John 8:32). Gradually the spirit is freed from the sufferings in which sin imprisons us (Ch. VII:3). Gradually the conscience becomes more *purified and clean* (Ch. VIII:15).

Groundwork for Holy Obedience

Inner freedom, a *conscience purified and clean*: these are the essential conditions for hearing and obeying *the counsels and inspirations which the Holy Spirit continually sends into the heart* ("About Obedience," Ch. VIII:14, 15).

12 About this, let it be made known if a place or a certain church has been designated, where a common spiritual father has been chosen, one who is prudent and of mature age, to whom each one may want to confess at least once a month.

13 And then, on each first Friday of the month to gather at this church, and there all together receive communion from this father previously mentioned.

14 In addition to this, we call upon each one to confess and receive communion at her own parish on solemn feastdays.

Confession is a necessary *means and way* to Angela's *holy obedience*, a core value of Ursuline life. This is why Confession is the subject of a whole chapter in the Rule. A person who faithfully and sincerely practices Confession recognizes truth—her own inner truth and God's guidance. She gradually clears away the noisy clamor of sinful tendencies and develops greater sensitivity to *the Holy Spirit...who...teaches us every truth* (Ch. VIII:15, 16).

Sacramental Life

As in the previous chapter, "About Going to Mass Every Day," Angela uses Chapter VII, "About Confession," to encourage her daughters to embrace the sacraments. Ursuline spiritual practices grow out of the Church's liturgical life, experienced mostly by each member *at her own parish* (Ch. VII:14).

This chapter too provides for incorporating sacraments into the Company's shared life. Angela directed the Company to choose *a common spiritual father* for monthly confessions,[76] to designate *a certain church...[a]nd then, on each first Friday of the month to gather at this church, and there all together receive communion* (Ch. VII:12, 13). For many years the Company gathered at the Church of St. Francis on Via S. Francesco d'Assisi in Brescia.[77] As noted above, Communion is essential nourishment for living the *sacred virginity* at the core of the Ursuline vocation. Furthermore, sharing the Eucharistic meal strengthens the unity among Ursulines, who are *sisters...in the Blood of Jesus Christ* (First Counsel:1).

The Reformation was gathering momentum. Certain practices were indeed distorted and deserved criticism. Reformers were calling all sacramental theology into question. Angela's response was consistent with the movement of reform from within the Church. She spoke ardently about the value of Confession and Communion.[78] She grounded Ursuline life in authentic sacramental spirituality. Our call is both deeply personal and deeply rooted in the Church's life.

Reflection

❖ Angela's treatment of the Sacrament of Penance focuses almost completely on one element: confession. God's action is also a part of her picture.

❖ Since the sixteenth century, sacramental renewal has alerted us to the communal dimensions of sin and of healing. Consider your own experiences.

❖ What role can contemporary psychology play in helping us clarify and address the patterns of life that are not life-giving and may lead us toward sin?

❖ What responsibility does an individual have in the face of sinful social systems?

❖ Distinguish between guilt and self-blame, between remorse and shame.

❖ The sacrament may be one in a series of healing moments. Give thanks for the resources, people, or events that contribute to your healing or liberation.

❖ Seek out the resources that you need for healing or liberation.

[1] Pegrari in *Arte, economia, cultura e religione nella Brescia del XVI secolo*, pp. 224, 225. For a discussion of the sorry state of the sixteenth-century Brescian church, see Teresa Ledochowska, OSU, *Angela Merici and the Company of St. Ursula*, trans. Mary Teresa Neylan, OSU (Rome: Ancora, 1968), Vol. 1, pp. 34, ff.

[2] Mariani, Tarolli, Seynaeve, p. 337.

[3] In church politics, monks and bishops often engaged in a tug of war for ecclesiastical authority. Rural towns which were allied with monasteries tended to take the monks' side in conflicts with urban bishops. Charges and counter-charges flew back and forth.

[4] Arnold was active in Rome, however, not in Brescia. [Powell, p. 28].

[5] Gianpietro Belotti, "Umanesimo cristiano e società bresciana fra Quattrocento e Cinquecento nell'esperienza di sant'Angela Merici" in Belotti, ed., p. 35.

[6] Mariani, Tarolli, Seynaeve, p. xxx.

[7] Fossati, p. 19. Erasmus's erudite writings won him admirers among the intelligentsia, including Saint Thomas More. Savonarola, a Dominican, was a fiery street preacher whose sincere but violent extremes were more destructive than reforming and led to his execution. Groote was a preacher, having accepting ordination as a deacon only in order to be able to preach.

[8] Louis Bouyer, Jean Leclerque and François Vanderbroucke, *The Spirituality of the Middle Ages*, Vol. II of *A History of Christian Spirituality*, trans. the Benedictines of Holm Eden Abbey (Carlisle, NY: Seabury Press, 1968), p. 434.

[9] Patricia Ranft, *Women and Spiritual Equality in Christian Tradition* (New York: St. Martin's Press, 1998), p. 190.

[10] Theatines founded by Saint Cajetan of Thiene and Gian Pietro Carafa in Rome, 1523/1524; Barnabites founded by Antonio Maria Zaccharia, Milan, 1530; Somaschans founded by Saint Jerome Emiliani, Somasca, 1531; Capuchins, a reformist Franciscan group, 1529; Company (later Society) of Jesus founded by Saint Ignatius Loyola, Rome, 1540.

[11] Gabriella Zarri, "Living Saints: A Typology of Female Sanctity in the Early Sixteenth Century," in Bornstein and Rusconi, p. 220.

[12] Zarri in Bornstein and Rusconi, p. 221.

[13] Quoted by Zarri, p. 242.

[14] Zarri in Bornstein and Rusconi, p. 226.

[15] Zarri, pp. 239, 294.

[16] Zarri, p. 241.

[17] Zarri, pp. 228, 236.

[18] Mariani, Tarolli, Seynaeve, p. 212.

[19] Zarri, p. 248.

[20] Belotti in Belotti, ed., p. 34.

[21] Belotti in Belotti, ed., p. 34.

22 Bouyer et al., p. 542.

23 Belotti in Belotti, ed., p. 35.

24 King, p. 115.

25 Gallo in *Processo Nazari*, Appendix 16 of Mariani, Tarolli, Seynaeve, p. 601, translation the author's.

26 Cozzano, quoted in Mariani, Tarolli, Seynaeve, p. 160.

27 Caroline Walker Bynum. *Holy Feast and Holy Fast: The Religious Significance of Food to Medieval Women* (Berkley: University of California Press, 1987), pp. 215-227.

28 Bynum, *Holy Feast and Holy Fast*, pp. 166-173.

29 Powell, p. 94.

30 Gallo in *Processo Nazari*, Appendix 16 of Mariani, Tarolli, Seynaeve, p. 601.

31 Mariani, Tarolli, Seynaeve, p. 168.

32 Angela's Rule includes some additional fast times, adding forty days after Epiphany, Saturdays after the Easter octave and after Pentecost, and three days a week between Pentecost and Advent. (Some fasting in this time is implied in the Third Order Rule by the exemptions mentioned for farm workers between Pentecost and the feast of Saint Francis in October.) Yet the Rule of the Company does not list Mondays, Wednesdays, Fridays and Saturdays as general days of abstinence from meat, an element of the Franciscan pattern. The Third Order's Rule also includes references to types and amounts of food and to exemptions. See *Regula Tertii Ordinis: Textus Authenticus Regesti Pontificalis in Seraphicae Legislationes Textus Originales*, a reprint of the text "*Supra Montem*," Constitution of Pope Nicholas IV, 1289 (Florence: Ad Claras Aquas, 1897), Chapter V. There are no such details in Angela's Rule.

33 Chizzola in *Processo Nazari*, Appendix 16 of Mariani, Tarolli, Seynaeve, p. 598, translation the author's. While it must be admitted that Chizzola's report may have been second-hand, it is also worth noting that he lived in the same parish of St. Afra [Belotti in Belotti, ed., p. 139.] and is known to have visited Angela in her home.

34 Gallo in *Processo Nazari*, Appendix 16 of Mariani, Tarolli, Seynaeve, p. 600, translation the author's.

35 In Latin *disciplina* means "learning." It is related to the word disciple.

36 Jesus surely carried out the usual Jewish fasts as part of his people's communal observance. "Do not think that I have come to abolish the law or the prophets. I have come not to abolish but to fulfill" (Matthew 5:17). These fasts were taken for granted by his contemporaries.

37 Gluttony as an allegory for the Original Sin of Adam and Eve's eating the fruit was a common interpretation in Angela's day.

38 All through the Bible, Israelites fast as a way of returning to God and God's ways and as a way of praying for God's help. Jesus taught his disciples to fast sincerely and unobtrusively. He said, "But when you fast, anoint your

head and wash your face, so that you may not appear to be fasting, except to your Father who is hidden. And your Father who sees what is hidden will repay you" (Matthew 6:17, 18).

39 This is a difference between Angela's Rule and Third Order Franciscan practice, which does not prescribe this period of fasting. An old custom of fasting at this time honored Jesus in the desert (Mariani, Tarolli, Seynaeve, p. 168), but Angela's explanation does not allude to this theme.

40 Mary Laven, *Virgins of Venice: Broken Vows and Cloistered Lives in the Renaissance Convent* (New York: Viking, 2002), p. 138.

41 George E. Ganss, S.J., ed., "General Introduction," *Ignatius of Loyola: The Spiritual Exercises and Selected Works*, in the series *The Classics of Western Spirituality* (New York: Paulist Press, 1991), p. 15.

42 In *Holy Anorexia*, cited above, Rudolph Bell identifies sanctity as the pre-eminent medieval ideal, much as thinness prevailed as an idea of feminine beauty among many groups in late-twentieth-century America. [Rudolph M. Bell, *Holy Anorexia*, with Epilogue by William N. Davis (Chicago: University of Chicago Press, 1985).]

43 Bynum, *Holy Feast and Holy Fast*, pp. 191-193.

44 The Rule of the Franciscan Third Order in effect during Angela's lifetime directed members to join clerics in communal recitation or, if that were not possible, to substitute twelve recitations of the "Our Father" and "Glory be to the Father" in the morning and seven recitations at times through the day (*Regula Tertii Ordinis*, Chapter VIII).

45 *Regula Tertii Ordinis*, Chapter VIII.

46 Mariani, Tarolli, Seynaeve, p. 164.

47 *Little Office of the Blessed Virgin Mary*, compiled and ed. John E. Rotelle, OSA (New York: Catholic Book Publishing Co., 1988), p. 7.

48 At the Company's first recorded chapter meeting, in March 1537, Fontana had been asked to be a formal witness. [Mariani, Tarolli, Seynaeve, pp. 239, 274, 293.]

49 For the source of these words, Angela cites *as the blessed martyr Alexander used to say* (Ch.V:10). She doubtless prayed in the Brescian church dedicated to Saint Alexander, as Caterina Patengola's home was in that parish. Angela's uncle Bressanino (on her father's side), a shoemaker, had once lived in the same parish. [Belotti in Belotti, ed., p. 45.]

50 Sixteenth-century Italian and the Bible's Latin (Vulgate translation by Saint Jerome) had many forms in common. If they could hear the reading, lay members of the congregation would have understood most of the ideas. Angela's own understanding of Latin, despite lack of schooling, is attested by Girolamo Chizzola. [Chizzola in *Processo Nazari*, Appendix 16 of Mariani, Tarolli, Seynaeve, p. 598.] It can be seen in her easy use and explanations not only of quotations from the Vulgate but also of occasional Latin phrases, sprinkled through the Rule, Counsels and Testament.

51 Angela had learned to read, probably when she was young. Her father knew how and used to read to the Merici family each night from the lives of the saints. Gallo said that she read many spiritual books, whenever she had time not occupied by works of charity. [Gallo in *Processo Nazari*, Appendix 16 of Mariani, Tarolli, Seynaeve, p. 601.]

52 Cozzano, *Risposta*, Appendix 23 of Mariani, Tarolli, Seynaeve, p. 637 (translation the author's). See also p. 643. Though it is impossible to estimate whether there is any link between Angela's outlook and that of her spiritual director, Fra Seraphino da Bologna, it may be worth noting that he would write a devotional book about Mary, published in 1562. [Ledochowska, p. 81.]

53 Cozzano, *Epistola confortatoria*, Appendix 22 of Mariani, Tarolli, Seynaeve, p. 624 (translation the author's).

54 *Ufficio, corona, disciplina, cilicio: descrizione*, Appendix 10 of Mariani, Tarolli, Seynaeve, p. 586.

55 *Ufficio, corona, disciplina, cilicio: descrizione*, Appendix 10 of Mariani, Tarolli, Seynaeve, p. 588.

56 Mariani, Tarolli, Seynaeve, pp. 176-181.

57 Her sight had inexplicably failed en route to the Holy Land and was later restored, during the return trip.

58 Mariani, Tarolli, Seynaeve, p. 191.

59 In 1528 or 1529. Begun in 1491 by Bernardino Caimi (d. 1499), a Franciscan friar and former Custodian of the Holy Land, the total project of forty-five chapels was completed in the twentieth century. [Mariani, Tarolli, Seynaeve, pp. 213, 214.]

60 The Jerusalem Bible translation of these verses, quoted here, is closer to the Vulgate edition of the Bible that Angela knew than is the New American Bible translation, the source of other biblical quotations in this volume.

61 Mariani, Tarolli, Seynaeve, p. 233.

62 Peter Schineller, "The Challenge of the Martyrs," *America* (Oct. 11, 1980), 207, 208.

63 Jacobus de Voragine, *The Golden Legend*, 2 volumes, trans. Granger Ryan (Princeton, New Jersey: Princeton University Press, 1993), vol. 2, p. 337.

64 de Voragine, 1993 edition, vol. 2, p. 258.

65 Gallo in *Processo Nazari*, Appendix 16 of Mariani, Tarolli, Seynaeve, p. 599.

66 Romano in *Processo Nazari*, Appendix 16 of Mariani, Tarolli, Seynaeve, p. 596.

67 For example, Bertolino Boscoli in his testimony said he had gone to "see Mass" ("*per vedere messa*") in his neighborhood Church of St. Barnabas. [Boscoli in *Processo Nazari*, Appendix 16 of Mariani, Tarolli, Seynaeve, p. 598.]

68 Boscoli in *Processo Nazari*, Appendix 16 of Mariani, Tarolli, Seynaeve, p. 598.

69 Gallo in *Processo Nazari*, Appendix 16 of Mariani, Tarolli, Seynaeve, p 601.

70 Gallo in *Processo Nazari*, Appendix 16 of Mariani, Tarolli, Seynaeve, pp. 599, 601.

71 Painters were actively countering Protestant challenges to the sacrificial dimensions of Catholic Eucharistic theology and practice. Counter-Reformation art became more evident after the Council of Trent. Angela's friend Moretto took an active role in such efforts, repeatedly treating Eucharistic themes and emphasizing "the centrality of Christ, in the Passion, reactualized in the sacrament of bread." His personal commitment was influenced by "figures of the Pre-Tridentine reform," the "lofty spirituality" of Angela Merici and others. [Pier Virgilio Begni Redona, "Gian Girolamo Savoldo, Girolamo Romanino e Alessandro Bonvicino detto il Moretto nella realtà pittorica bresciana" in *Arte, economia, cultura e religione nella Brescia del XVI secolo*," p. 159 (translation the author's).] Moretto had an early commission, with Romanino, in the Blessed Sacrament Chapel of the Church of St. John the Evangelist.

72 Ruzante, p. 125.

73 Mariani, Tarolli, Seynaeve, p. 286, note 6.

74 Gallo in *Processo Nazari*, Appendix 16 of Mariani, Tarolli, Seynaeve, p. 601.

75 At the chapter's end Angela *call[s] upon each one to confess and receive communion at her own parish on solemn feastdays* (Ch. VII:14). The practice of Confession as a necessary preparation for receiving Communion persisted into the twentieth century.

76 The women may have actually elected (*elezzer*, Ch. VI:12) this person to serve them. In any case, the confessor was definitely not imposed by ecclesiastical appointment but chosen by the members. These procedures indicate an unusual degree of autonomy in relation to the clergy.

77 There was a natural affinity through Angela's spiritual kinship with the Franciscan friars who lived in the convent and served in the church of S. Francesco. This site was the local center for Third Order members. Angela would have been buried in its courtyard cemetery, if she had not petitioned to be buried instead at St. Afra, close to the relics of ancient martyrs. [Mariani, Tarolli, Seynaeve, p. 233.]

78 Gallo in *Processo Nazari*, Appendix 16 of Mariani, Tarolli, Seynaeve, p. 601.

Part 6

Saint Ursula

Saint Ursula

"Once upon a time...."

It is almost necessary to speak of Saint Ursula and her companions as the heroines of a grand adventure story, complete with a princess. When Angela Merici chose this patron saint for her new Company in 1535, she harked back to a much earlier epoch. The figure who had inspired countless artworks and multiple legends—and Angela—appears to have suffered martyrdom at Cologne, Germany, around the year 300. Who was this Ursula? And how did her story capture the Christian imagination for centuries?

The History

A group of young Christian women martyred by pagan invaders at Cologne in about 300 were commemorated by local Christians, who constructed a basilica over the cemetery where they were buried, a practice typical of Roman times. Destroyed during a Frankish invasion in 355, the basilica was reconstructed by a man named Clematius sometime between 355 and 450. With an inscribed tablet Clematius marked the site "where holy virgins shed their blood for the name of Christ." This second basilica was altered in the tenth century. A much more elaborate Romanesque basilica was built atop it in the twelfth century, further expanded in Gothic style in the thirteenth century.

Bombed in World War II, this most recent construction required extensive excavation in the 1940s. The process revealed the remains of the previous structures. In the vestiges of the tenth-century building, a tomb was found, containing eleven repositories for exhumed relics. This reliquary tomb bore testimony to the reputed number of martyrs, eleven.[1]

The Legend

By the ninth century devotion to the martyrs had begun to spread beyond Cologne. They received names in the retelling of their story; the leader came to be called Ursula. Whether there was an historic basis for these names is unknown. Perhaps through a misreading of the numeral XI (11), their number multiplied exponentially to 11,000. In 1106, Emperor Henry IV's excavations for fortifications at Cologne turned up an ancient burial site which yielded so many bones—some imbedded with arrowheads—that the inhabitants attributed them to this vast number of martyrs. The citizens held a magnificent funeral for the 11,000[2] and honored the bones as relics. The influential abbess Hildegard of Bingen (1098-1179) composed liturgical texts and music for the Mass and Divine Office of the feast of Saint Ursula and Companions, October 21. The cult reached even farther with the writings of the visionary Elizabeth of Schönau (b. 1123). Her accounts of supposed revelations about the saints expanded the legend with further names and narratives.

German pilgrims spread the cult throughout Europe on the way to Rome or to the Holy Land. Going to Jerusalem, they passed through Venice. There, in the fourteenth century the noble lady Giacobina de Zobi had adapted her house for a group of Augustinian sisters to use as a monastery; it came to be titled the monastery of Saint Ursula.[3] By the same century, a Venetian Confraternity ("*Scuola*") of Saint Ursula had been founded.[4] Brescia's city Council added the feast of "Saint Ursula and her Company," October 21, to the local calendar of observances in 1453.[5]

The basic outline of the legend is this (as recounted by Jacopo da Voragine in *The Golden Legend*): Ursula was the only child of a Christian king and queen in Britain. She dedicated herself to Christ at an early age. A neighboring pagan ruler sought to annex her parents' realm by forcing a marriage between Ursula and his son. Inspired in a dream, Ursula offered a creative plan: delay the marriage three years while she and ten young female companions made a voyage, each accompanied by another thousand girls. Ursula was their captain and their leader in faith. She saw this adventure as an opportunity to lead them, and her suitor as well, to Christ. Another dream invited her to make the journey a pilgrimage to Rome and revealed that she would face martyrdom on the return trip. Her companions unanimously decided to join her in the Christian faith and on the road ahead.

In Rome, Pope Cyriacus was so impressed by Ursula that he resigned from the papacy to join her entourage, along with many others. The Roman clergy struck his name from the list of popes. Having visited the holy places, the company returned by way of Cologne. So powerful was the witness of the women's zeal and faith that "two wicked commanders in the Roman army,...noting that many men and women were hurrying to join them, were afraid that their influence would make the Christian religion flourish overmuch."[6] These two plotted with a barbarian commander to ambush the returning pilgrims at Cologne. There the women and their entourage were massacred, precisely as witnesses of faith in Christ. The chief spared Ursula and sought to make her his wife. When she rejected this offer, he shot her with an arrow.

Told and retold in sermons, this story and its variations received even wider circulation through the printing press, after 1454. The legend appears in one of the first "best-sellers" of the new print technology, *The Golden Legend* by Jacopo da Voragine ("from Verazzo"), O.P. (1228/30-1298), a bishop of Genoa.[7] (The word *legend*, from Latin *legenda*, actually means "readings," as distinct from the visual arts.) Was this work the "spiritual books of Saints and Virgins" that Giovanni Merici read to his family, stories that inspired Angela to imitate their values?[8] Very possibly, since it was printed in Venice in 1474 and circulated in eleven editions in the next twenty-five years.[9]

The Myth

The figure of Saint Ursula came to function as a mythic symbol, i.e., a bridge between the conscious and unconscious.[10] Symbols which arise spontaneously and non-rationally in the communal psyche serve a revelatory function.[11] They have a truth, what Joseph Campbell calls "the penultimate truth," quite apart from history.[12] The true author of legendary material is the people, whose ideals, aims, and dreams are personified in the saints.[13] Ursula took on these mythic proportions in the deepest sense of "stories about the wisdom of life," in Campbell's words, "stories that will connect us with God."[14] She became a prototype of the Church personified as *Virginitas*, longing for Christ her bridegroom. With strong Eucharistic overtones, Hildegard of Bingen expressed the link between the martyrs' bloodshed and that of Christ (cf. Hildegard's liturgical text "*O Ecclesia*" for the martyrs' feast).[15]

Heroic adventures of the Middle Ages ordinarily have masculine protagonists; Ursula's story stands almost alone as a woman's journey of discovery and courage. Its military component, Ursula as captain, provides a leadership role that cultural circumstances did not allow for women (except in cloisters) and which would lie almost completely latent for centuries.

Perhaps because female voices (such as Elizabeth of Schönau's and Hildegard of Bingen's) retold their legend, these holy heroines escaped the fate—worse than death, it would seem—that so many virgin martyrs met in the reframing of their lives and deaths by male authors. Men's versions tend to focus on physical (often quasi-pornographic) tortures, on an other-worldly relationship to God, and on women's frailty. They show the women as passive. They interpret virginity as a renunciation of sexuality and the female body as basically sinful.

Not so with women's versions! Tenth-century playwright Hrotswitha of the Benedictine abbey at Gandersheim, for example, dramatized virgin martyrs as courageous witnesses of the faith, drawing strength and mutual support from fellowship with other women, from sisterhood.[16] Hrotswitha's protagonists are active, engaged in their world. Their self-directed choice of virginity sets them outside patriarchy. Challenged, their commitment holds firm. As martyrs they are not victims but heroines, not tragic but victorious. Their deaths lead to heavenly triumph.[17]

The Art

In countless cities and artistic media, Medieval and Renaissance artists pictured Ursula and her companions, these faith-filled adventurers. Certain conventions prevailed: the palm branch, traditional emblem of martyrdom; the arrows with which they were killed; the ship of their journeying; Ursula's crown; a military standard emblazoned with Christ's cross. Occasionally Ursula is pictured like Mother Church, gathering her companions protectively in her cloak.[18] She is clearly a leader of brave women of faith, loyal to Christ.

German depictions are the most frequent,[19] but many others exist, from England to Italy at least. Naturally, the German depictions reflect Elizabeth of Schönau's influence. Under the paintings of the Master of the Saint Ursula Legend (c. 1495) are verses derived from Elizabeth's "revelations."[20] In Venice, Vittore Carpaccio's nine paintings for the oratory of the Confraternity of Saint Ursula (1490-1500) more closely follow Jacopo da Voragine's *Golden Legend*.[21] In Brescia, Antonio Vivarini (d. 1470? 1484?) painted Ursula and her Companions on the central panel of a triptych for the Church of San Pietro in Oliveto. Around 1530 Alessandro Bonvicino, "Il Moretto," looked to Vivarini's panel as the model for his large painting of Saint Ursula and her Companions in St. Clement, the Gallos' parish church.

The Patron

When Angela Merici initiated *the newly begun life of virgins who are called by the name Company of Saint Ursula* (Pr.:2) under the protection of this fabled heroine-saint, it was the Ursula of legend, not of history, that she knew. She left no explanation of her choice. Yet we recognize in Ursula's story themes that resonate with Angela's own words and deeds: virginity consecrated to Christ; the royal dignity of *spouses of the Son of God* [who] *will become queens in heaven* (Pr.:17); exhortations in the face of dangers: *you must not be afraid of this.... Now to the task, with courage!* (Pr.:22, 29); willingness to *shed my own blood* as a witness of faith (Ch. V:34); devotion to the martyrs of the early Church, exemplified by her desire to be buried near the relics in St. Afra; vivid hope in *celestial glory* (Ch. XI:36); pilgrimages, particularly to Rome; leadership among women; *union and concord* within a company of women (Last Counsel:10). Ursula's features blend into Angela's.

The mythic Ursula embodies the values and spirit that are Angela's bequest to Ursulines down the centuries. Thus the "myth" of Saint Ursula fulfills an important function of mythology articulated by Joseph Campbell, helping individuals integrate the ideals of the group,[22] in this case the Company of Saint Ursula.

The following pages suggest how that integration may have emerged in Angela's own consciousness.

The Model

Ursula, a long-ago-and-far-away heroine, a once-upon-a-time princess, would likely have appealed to the idealistic little girl who first heard the story at her father's knee. As Giovanni Merici read the tale, Angela could imagine the great journey from Britain to Rome. Her appetite for travel, for pilgrimages, would have responded to Ursula's exciting voyage. As she began to feel the tug of God's call to devote herself completely to Christ, the dedicated virgins of the early Church showed her that it was possible to live this *sacred virginity* as lay women in "the world." Cloistered life had not always been the only way. (Only much later would Angela meet Stefana Quinzani and hear of Osanna Andreasi of Mantua, who lived out their consecration as lay women in the Dominican Third Order.)

Of course, many early saints were examples of that dedication in the world. But Ursula had companions. That element too must have appealed to Angela. She had loved her sister so much, her *very dear sister*. Family relationships were precious to her. She was later to envision the Company of Saint Ursula as a spiritual family, bound by deeply personal ties. This new Company would function in Brescia (and eventually around the world) as a community of witness within families and society.

Did Catherine Biancosi Merici sometimes take her children up the coast by boat to visit her family in Salò? Did Angela and her sister ever pretend that they were girls on Ursula's ship, sailing toward holy places and great adventures? Ursula and her companions—so courageous—facing powerful people and great dangers. No matter how they were threatened, they remained faithful to Christ. When the barbarian chieftain would have forced her into marriage and paganism, she refused to abandon her Lord.

Later, orphaned and living in Salò with her aunt and uncle Biancosi, did another part of Saint Ursula's story come to her? Ursula's parents were sympathetic with her choice to dedicate herself to Christ. Nonetheless, when the pressure for her to marry the pagan prince was so great, they saw no alternative. It seemed that she would have to marry him for the sake of her family. But Ursula was inspired to suggest a creative alternative. She proposed the pilgrimage to Rome, with all those companions. Ursula was confident that she would be able to live by her own truth. Angela's aunt and uncle were trying to arrange a marriage for her, trying even harder to persuade her. Did she think of Saint Ursula and pray that she too would be inspired to find a way, a new way to answer her call?

Brescian religious art offered images of Saint Ursula. Furthermore, on her return from the Holy Land in 1524, Angela may have seen Carpaccio's beautiful murals in Venice. They made it seem as though the saint were alive right there on the Adriatic coast. Ursula and her parents greet ambassadors with Venice's San Marco Cathedral in the background. Ursula and her companions seem to live their dedication and face their problems almost as though they are sixteenth-century Italians. Carpaccio took them from the misty past and located them in (Angela's) here-and-now. Their loyalty to Christ, their faith and courage: that was how Angela sought to live, in the midst of her world. These heroines could show the way.

No doubt Angela remembered Saint Ursula when she too made a pilgrimage to Rome, visited its churches and saw the Pope in 1525. Like Ursula, she venerated relics of the early Christian martyrs who had shed their blood for Christ. These holy men and women had trusted that eternal life was theirs. What could be more precious than life itself? What could be worth this sacrifice? Martyrs are willing to accept death rather than to forfeit what gives their lives meaning. Martyrs' deaths are a witness, proclaiming what they believe and whom they love, yes, even more than their earthly lives. Angela recognized the call to bear witness, not by her death but by her life. Her deeds and words would demonstrate what she believed, how she hoped, and whom she loved.

Though Ursula and her companions lived far away in Britain, they traveled to Rome as the center of the Church. Many of Angela's contemporaries damaged, questioned and fractured the Church by abuse, reform and revolt. Countless Church officials were corrupt and more concerned with power than with holiness. Catholic faith was contested and seemingly discredited. Angela reached back into the inspiration of the early Church. She counseled her daughters to *Keep to the ancient way and custom of the Church, established and confirmed by so many Saints under the inspiration of the Holy Spirit. And live a new life.... But pray, and get others to pray, that God not abandon his Church, but reform it as he pleases* (Seventh Counsel:22, 24).

When Pope Cyriacus recognized Ursula's holiness and resigned from the papacy to follow her, the cardinals especially did not understand how anyone could prefer holiness to power, nor how a man could follow a woman. In the sixteenth century, and the twenty-first, there have been Church leaders who prefer power to holiness. Many cannot imagine women as leaders. But Ursula and her companions model a new truth, forge a new way, within the Church. Ursula was a natural leader, who evoked faith and encouraged her companions to greatness. She stood among them, not above them. Her authority flowed from her holiness and zeal. Ursula had shared her spirit with her companions. Following her example, they too had committed themselves to Christ. This sort of leadership Angela entrusted to the colonelle, *teachers and guides in the spiritual life* (Ch. XI:4), instructing them to *live in such a way that your daughters may see in you a model* and *spur themselves to virtuous living* (Sixth Counsel:1, 6).

Ursula's rank as a princess signaled her eminence, but rank does not equal excellence. Greater dignity lay in the calling to be *spouses of the Son of God* (Pr.:17). Angela began and ended her Rule with this royal motif. She spoke to servant girls who *will become queens in heaven* (Pr.:17). She encouraged them to trust that *our sweet and kind spouse Jesus Christ may...bring [them] to celestial glory with the other virgins, crowned with that golden and brilliant virginal crown* (Ch. XI:35, 36).

St. Ursula and her Companions by Alessandro Bonvicino, Il Moretto (1498-1554). In St. Clement Church, Brescia.

The Painting

Alessandro Bonvicino, called "Il Moretto" ("the Moor," perhaps because of having a dark complexion), interpreted Saint Ursula on a canvas for the wall of St. Clement Church in 1530(?).

The Dominicans had taken pastoral responsibility for St. Clement in 1517. They had been redecorating, and they commissioned Moretto, a parishioner at least by 1533,[23] to paint large canvases: Saint Clement for over the altar; Melchizedek with Abraham, offering bread and wine (Genesis 14:18); and some Dominican saints. Moretto's *The Mystic Marriage of St. Catherine of Alexandria* (1543) includes Saint Catherine of Siena, for example; she had belonged to the Dominican Third Order.

One canvas pictures five virgin martyrs of the early Church: Saints Barbara, Cecilia, Agnes, Agatha, and Lucy, saints in whom Angela would have had a particular interest. (This painting was completed in 1540.) Early Christian women recognized how unusual Jesus was in having women disciples. These five chose to shape their lives around their relationship with Christ. They were threatened with death unless they accepted marriage, to fit securely into established roles in their society and state. But they would not trade their own relationship with God for security. Furthermore, women were expected to worship their husbands' gods, and these women would not relinquish Christianity. Women like this made officials nervous. They could not be controlled. So they were killed.

What inspiring models for Angela's daughters, committed to Christ in the world! Our life is not very secure. We are not always understood or approved. We too must be brave and faithful.

Moretto may have painted *Saint Ursula and her Companions, Martyrs* in 1530, the very year when Angela was a guest of the Gallos, a stone's throw away from St. Clement Church. Surely he and Angela could have talked about the subject. They were friends, neighbors and, perhaps by then, fellow parishioners.[24] Moretto was a friend of Agostino and Cecilia Gallo. Their homes were back to back.[25] Moretto and his wife Clara lived at #21 Vicolo S. Clemente.[26] They were such good friends that Agostino Gallo later witnessed Moretto's will, which provided that his children would be entrusted to Agostino if he should die (as he did, a few weeks later) while they were minors.[27]

The dates of Moretto's works for St. Clement are disputed, but it is sure that in 1530 he decorated an altar at the Franciscan church that Angela also frequented.[28] Angela must have seen Moretto there or in St. Clement Church while she lived with the Gallos. She went to daily Mass and often spent part of the morning in prayer before the Blessed Sacrament. He too was deeply religious, deeply devoted to the Blessed Sacrament.[29] He belonged to a Eucharistic society associated with the cathedral, the *Schola del Santissimo Corpo de Cristo*.[30]

Moretto's work incorporated his tutelage by Raphael,[31] demonstrating classical serenity and balance, a sense of weight and substance, but with a more realistic and personal presentation than Raphael favored. In fact, Moretto became an esteemed portraitist.[32] He may have been in Venice just after Giorgione's death, while Titian was still young. Partaking of the rich artistic dialogue between Venice and Lombardy, he studied under Floriano (Fioravente Ferramolo) of the Venetian school,[33] mastering its use of the poetic properties of light. His Lombard predecessors such as Foppa and Savoldo led him toward a distinctively Brescian style, with its silvery tones and realistic, almost domestic manner. Brescian art historian Bruno Passamani describes Moretto's "profoundly religious spirit....pensive pictures....the tragic and sublime style that distinguishes him."[34] Especially when he was preparing to paint a sacred scene, Moretto fasted and prayed to seek enlightenment.[35] His reverence for the Holy Spirit is visible in several of his paintings, where divine light pours down over the canvas from a dove at the top. Attention to the Holy Spirit characterized the Catholic reform, especially before the Council of Trent.

This spirit also characterized Angela Merici, whose influence upon Moretto is indisputable. V. Guazzoni, in his *Moretto: Il tema sacro*, proposes an "'Ursuline inspiration' that is concretized in 'a group of four or five works of Moretto....'"[36] As he prepared spiritually to paint the virgin martyrs, might he not have consulted the wise and holy Madre Suor Angela across the street? Did her insights influence his portrayals?

His artistic model was the earlier painting by Vivarini in Brescia's Church of San Pietro in Olivetto. It has a semi-Byzantine other-worldliness and flat golden background. In contrast, Moretto shows the Venetian influence of his early training. His figures have realistic dimensions. The perspective stretches into the distance. Moretto's luminosity is anchored in flesh and earth. But the difference is in more than style.

Saint Ursula's gentle leadership is at the center of this company of then-contemporary women. She holds firmly in each hand the standard of Christ. Under his banner, the sign of his cross, she will live and die, and go to heavenly glory. She shares that dedication, and that hope, with the women around her. Look at them, bathed in the light of the Holy Spirit! There is an individualized, portrait quality about the faces. Some seem contemplative. Others gaze around at each other and the world. Some hold books, the new communication medium of the modern world. (Vivarini had not included books.) Oral tradition suggests models for two of the faces. Was Moretto portraying his wife Clara when he painted the woman in red on the right? In the woman whose brow almost touches Saint Ursula's, do we see his conjecture of how Angela might have looked years before?

Intriguing questions. The answers escape us. But they do not really matter.

There was once a group of brave Christian women. There was once a woman whom we call Ursula. May she forever be the heavenly friend and model of all who will bear the name Ursuline: companions on life's journey, following Christ together and leading others to him; faithful, courageous, and loving!

---

[1] Ledochowska, Vol. 1, Appendix A. This archeological discussion includes illustrations made by Dr. Eberhard Kuhnemann, who carried out the excavations under the basilica, and the analyses of other historians.

[2] C. M. Kauffmann, *The Legend of St. Ursula* (London: Her Majesty's Stationery Office, 1964), p. 10.

[3] Sergio Pagiaro, *Santuario S. Angela Merici* (Brescia: Centro Mericiano, 1985), p. 102.

[4] Mariani, Tarolli, Seynaeve, p. 267.

[5] Pagiaro, p. 102.

[6] de Voragine, 1993 edition, vol. 2, p. 258. (Variant spellings: de and da.)

[7] As an indication of its wide popularity, *The Golden Legend* was translated into English in 1450 and published in 1483 by William Caxton, the first movable-type printer in England. Another edition came into the hands of Ignatius Loyola in 1521, while he was recovering from a battle wound, and inspired his conversion of life. A nineteenth-century Protestant "de-bunker" of Catholicism, Sabine Baring-Gould, railed against the non-historical character of the Ursula story. [Sabine Baring-Gould, *Curious Myths of the Middle Ages*, ed. Edward Hardy (New York: Oxford University Press, 1978), p. 105.]

[8] Romano in the *Processo Nazari*, Appendix 16 of Mariani, Tarolli, Seynaeve, p. 595.

[9] Mariani, Tarolli, Seynaeve, p. 90.

[10] Introduction to de Voragine (1993 edition), p. 95.

[11] Introduction to de Voragine (1993 edition), p. 105.

[12] Joseph Campbell with Bill Moyers, *The Power of Myth*, ed. Betty Sue Flowers (New York: Doubleday, 1988) p. 163.

[13] Foreword to Jacobus de Voragine, *The Golden Legend*, 2 vols., trans. Granger Ryan and Helmut Ripperger (London: Longmans, Green and Co., 1941), p. x.

[14] Campbell, *The Power of Myth*, pp. 9, 141.

[15] Barbara Newman, *Sister of Wisdom: St. Hildegard's Theology of the Feminine* (Berkley: University of California Press, 1989) p. 225.

[16] Karen Winstead, "Archetypes of Feminine Mastery in Medieval Virgin Martyr Legends," lecture delivered at the 25th International Congress on Medieval Studies (Kalamazoo, Michigan, May 1990).

[17] Mary-Cabrini Durkin, "Art in Brescia, the Spirit of Angela Merici and Women's Leadership Today," address to an inter-Ursuline meeting of superiors general (Rome, May 4, 1991).

[18] Cf. Hans Memling's reliquary paintings for the Hospital of St. John in Bruges, 1488.

[19] Cf. the cycles of Cologne's anonymous Master of 1456—thirty paintings on twenty panels—and Master of the St. Ursula Legend—nineteen paintings.

[20] Kauffmann, p. 12.

[21] Other well-known Venetian depictions came from the brushes of Paolo Veneziano; Vigo di Pieve de Cadore; Tommaso da Modena, [F. Valcanover, *Carpaccio: The Legend of St. Ursula*, trans. Sandra Peterson (Milano: Arti Grafiche Ricordi, 1964), n.p.] and Tintoretto, among others.

[22] Joseph Campbell, ed., *Myths, Dreams, and Religion* (New York: E. P. Dutton and Company, Inc., 1970) p. 141.

[23] His financial report of 1533 records a home in St. Clement parish. [Gyorgy Gombosi, *Moretto da Brescia* (Basel: Ars Docta Band IV, 1943), p. 85.]

[24] After Angela's death, Moretto set up his easel next to her open coffin and painted a lovingly intimate portrait.

[25] Gombosi, p. 85.

[26] Bruno Passamani, *Guida della Pinacoteca Tosio-Martinengo di Brescia* (Grafo: Brescia, 1988) p. 69.

[27] Gombosi, p. 57. Moretto died December 22, 1554; his youngest child, Julia, had been born earlier that year. Moretto's eldest child, Caterina Bonvicino (born 1550 [Gombosi, p. 88.]) would become an Ursuline in 1572. [Mariani, Tarolli, Seynaeve, p. 373, note 48.]

[28] Gombosi, p. 84.

29 Moretto's profound meditative spirit and theological interest were already evident when, in his early twenties, he collaborated with the master Girolamo Romanino. They decorated the Blessed Sacrament Chapel of S. Giovanni Church in Brescia (1521-1524). [Redona in *Arte, economia, cultura e religione nella Brescia del XVI secolo*, p. 158.]

30 Belotti in Belotti, ed., p. 35.

31 "The Brescian Rafael," so called by Redona. [*Arte, economia, cultura e religione nella Brescia del XVI secolo*, p. 145.]

32 *Moretto: Brescian School*, Masters in Art Series, Vol. 9, Part 106 (October 1908), p. 36.

33 *Moretto: Brescian School*, p. 23.

34 Passamani, p. 69. The great critic Giorgio Vasari paid tribute to Moretto as "very delicate in his use of color and so devoted to diligence...." [Quoted by Redona in *Arte, economia, cultura e religione nella Brescia del XVI secolo*, p. 145 (translation by the author).]

35 Moretto: Brescian School, p. 29.

36 Quoted by Belotti in Belotti, ed., p. 118; translation the author's.

Conclusion
The Mystic Marriage of Saint Catherine

The Mystic Marriage of St. Catherine by Girolamo Romanino (1484/87 - after 1559). Memphis Brooks Museum of Art, Memphis, TN; Gift of the Samuel H. Kress Foundation 61.202.

Conclusion

The Mystic Marriage of Saint Catherine

We come finally to a work of art which goes to the heart of the Company of Saint Ursula. It is *The Mystic Marriage of Saint Catherine with Saints Lawrence, Ursula and Angela Merici*, painted by Girolamo Romanino. (This painting appears in Part 3, in the section "Christ at the Center – Sacred Virginity." Some of the following ideas are also expressed there.) What becomes evident as we enter this painting is how vividly it expresses in aesthetic terms the meaning of the Company, as surely as the Rule expresses that meaning in words.

In this conclusion to a book about *The Rule of the Company of Saint Ursula*, we will see how all aspects of the painting converge to visualize the spirit of this new foundation: its genre, composition, light and color, details, background, etc. Its figures personify two keynotes of Angela Merici's spirituality: *sacred virginity* and martyrdom. Its center-point is Jesus Christ, God Incarnate. Through love and witness, the Company of Saint Ursula is called to continue his mission, making God's love present in the world.

The painting's subject has a particular historical connection, clearly marking the Company's birthday. Angela had chosen Saint Catherine's feast, November 25, to found the Company. This was the anniversary of her safe return from the six-month pilgrimage to the Holy Land in 1524, an occasion of great gratitude. Furthermore, since Angela's mother had been named Catherine, perhaps this saint had long been a favorite, whose story would have captured special attention as Giovanni Merici read it by the fireplace in Le Grezze, so long before. November 25 would remain the date for incorporation of new members, "to encourage [them] to imitate Saint Catherine who...was espoused to Christ our Lord, and by his own hands," according to an early Ursuline text.[1]

Romanino was documenting the Company's foundation artistically, either within its first year, i.e., in 1536, or perhaps in the year of Angela's death, 1540.[2] Who commissioned it we do not know. The 60" x 81" canvas was an altarpiece for an unidentified church.[3]

The Context

Art and the Artist

Girolamo Romanino was well suited to his ambitious task. This important work was entrusted to one who may well have been counted Brescia's best, or shared that recognition with Alessandro Bonvicino, Il Moretto (cf. Part 6). They were the leaders of what came to be called the Brescian School of painting. The two had collaborated in 1521.[4] Both painters shared the Venetian masters' fascination with the poetic properties of light, though the Brescians' luminosity tends more toward silver than toward the Venetians' gold.[5]

Girolamo Romanino, called "Il Romanino," was born in Brescia in the mid-1480s.[6] Trained initially in his home town,[7] he later studied in Venice with the great Titian, absorbing the influence of Giorgione as well. Like them he sought the inner significance of a scene.[8] Beginning in 1530, he worked on a commission from the bishop of Trent, in an ecclesiastical court that was "cultured and sensual, humanistic and verging on paganism"; then he executed several fresco cycles in the remote mountainous areas of Pisogne (1534), Iseo and Valle Camonica, where he was inspired by the vibrant religious spirit of the simple brothers and ordinary believers.[9] Romanino enjoyed a successful career in Brescia and environs and produced many religious images and excellent portraits. He held a seat on the city council.[10] His daughter Margharita married into the influential Gambara family, though her husband Lattanzio Gambara was of an undistinguished branch, the son of a tailor, and a disciple of Romanino.[11]

Though portraits were often commissioned as status symbols, Romanino's are more attentive to the sitters' psychology than to their social position.[12] This realism affected his grander subjects, too. He used personalized, naturalistic accents, often rustic, to give a familiar intimacy even to idealized religious scenes. For example, in his *Nativity* (circa 1545), with Madonna and Child at the center, Saint Joseph carries on a conversation with two realistic men on the margin.

A fluid blend of color, light and tone marks Romanino's works. He preferred the pearly gray of twilight to the flat, mundane brightness of daylight. Backgrounds in his paintings often have poetic sentiment reminiscent of Giorgione, with dark skies and dramatic, emotional highlights. In his *Miraculous Catch of Fish and Call of Peter*, dawn just begins to trace rosy edges along layers of cloud and gleams upon the face and form of Christ. Romanino's personal style is expressive and intense.

The Subject: Saint Catherine of Alexandria

Romanino's subject, Saint Catherine of Alexandria, was hugely popular, one of the most-painted saints of the era. Crusaders returning from Egypt had brought her cult to Europe, through Venice.

Catherine's story has exciting elements of holiness, heroism and emotion played out in an exotic setting, ancient Egypt. Now we realize that the account is not historical. That fact in no way diminishes the impact of its meaning when interpreted artistically. The story is a vessel for spiritual truths.

Catherine was said to have been a Christian maiden of Alexandria in the fourth century, daughter of a deceased king, and the mistress of her own large household. One day, as she prayed before an icon of the Madonna and Child, the Christ Child reached out of the picture and placed on her finger a ring of espousal.

Her martyrdom is recounted in the *Golden Legend*. This version was undoubtedly familiar to Angela Merici. When Emperor Maxentius (or Maximinius) began to persecute Christians, Catherine protested the injustice and bore witness to the faith. Well educated in the liberal arts, she engaged in philosophical disputes with pagan scholars. (Alexandria was the center of learning in the ancient Mediterranean world.) She quoted Plato and Greek literature and demonstrated her opponents' errors. She converted them, the queen, the captain of the guard, and 200 soldiers, *open[ing] up the blindness of their minds* (Ch. V:34).

The emperor imprisoned her and threatened her with death but offered marriage as an alternative. Faithful to her divine Bridegroom, she declined. A machine of spiked wheels was used to torture her. When that broke, a sword dispatched her to heaven, victorious.

As a virgin martyr, Saint Catherine resembles other heroines of Angela.

The Painting

No wonder we can link this painting with the Company of Saint Ursula! From the intense portrait of Angela Merici on the right edge, we know that the painter was acquainted with her and meant for the viewer to identify her. Inclusion of contemporary persons in sacred scenes was a frequent element of paintings from the Middle Ages on. Depending on the date of composition, Angela may have been in Romanino's studio (if it was painted in 1536), may well have been involved in planning this work which was to mirror her own lifework. If the painting is dated to the year of her death (1540), Brescia's veneration for her would have called for special fidelity to her spirit.[13]

The Figures

The Mystic Marriage of Saint Catherine with Saints Lawrence, Ursula and Angela Merici brings together personages from different times and places, into a mystic moment shared. The central group of three— Madonna and Child and Catherine—is organized in a triangular composition. Christ places a ring on Catherine's finger. At the far right, dressed in the blood-red that signifies martyrdom, Saint Ursula holds the victory standards associated with the risen Christ. There are two, representing a double victory: virginity and martyrdom.[14]

Under these flags, Angela Merici kneels in prayer. She is recognizable by her resemblance to the funeral portrait done by Moretto and by the garb of a Third Order Franciscan. On the far left, Saint Lawrence can be identified by the grille (instrument of his martyrdom in ancient Rome) leaning against the masonry and by the vestment that marks him as a deacon. It is thought that his presence here acknowledges the assistance of Lorenzo Muzio, Brescia's diocesan vicar, in obtaining diocesan approval for the young Company's Rule (August 8, 1536). Saint Lawrence was Muzio's patron saint. The realistic treatment suggests that this may even be a portrait of the vicar.

The people grouped around Christ shared in what Angela Merici called *sacred virginity* and/or in Christian martyrdom. Exploring these themes will take us into the many meanings of the painting. Though the scene took form under Romanino's brush, it took its spirit from Angela's vision. What was she thinking? What was she seeing?

Christ at the Center

At the heart of the painting itself is Christ.

Christ, always Christ. Christ at the center. He is the centerpoint of the painting itself, in the flesh (Latin *carnis*), God Incarnate. He is the focus of every other person. The different facial exposures of six figures on three planes (quite a *tour de force!*) allow all five others to look at Christ, each with a distinct perspective. His mother gazes with serene absorption, Catherine with her lips slightly parted in ecstasy; Angela focused in contemplative prayer; Ursula in the moment of action; and Lawrence in tenderness.

The centrality of Christ is also subtly reflected by the bridge in the painting's middle ground, says art historian James Clifton. This detail signifies the faith that Christ is "the bridge between heaven and earth, across whom the soul must travel toward God."[15]

Martyrdom

Barely visible, a palm branch in Saint Lawrence's hand traditionally denotes a martyr, much as the ancients used palm and laurel branches to honor victorious generals, poets and athletes. Saint Ursula holds military standards akin to those pictured in the hand of the risen Christ emerging from the tomb on Easter morning: the cross transformed from death to life, from shame to glory. The red cross flutters over the scene.

Catherine too has symbols of martyrdom. Behind her feet we see a wooden wheel and the hilt of a sword, the implements of her torture and death. Hanging from a spike of the wheel is a crown. It may be the earthly crown that she put aside, that of her own position and that of marriage to the emperor. It may be the heavenly crown that she won by her glorious victory. Martyrdom was her avenue to glory. The crown *depends* on it (Latin *dependere*, "hang from").

The painting's composition also speaks of martyrdom. The triangle's left side passes through the touching fingers of Christ and Catherine. The line ascends diagonally from the lower left corner (wheel and sword) to the upper right (victory standards), that is, from suffering to glory. The implements of Catherine's martyrdom present suffering honestly. It can be the price of fidelity, a share in Jesus' Passion, which was the price of his fidelity to his God-given mission. Martyrdom shares in the sacrifice of Calvary. The cross emblem on the standard held by Ursula proclaims the Resurrection. Eternal life is the glorious destination of those who follow his way, the Paschal Mystery, through death to life.

When we envision this painting mounted as it was intended, as an altarpiece, we experience a striking recognition. The Christ figure would stand directly above the crucifix of the altar where Mass was offered. The congregation would see this link among the mystic and historic and sacramental realities. The Eucharist is our participation with Christ in the sacrifice of Calvary, *since in the sacred Mass are found all the merits of the passion of our Lord* (Ch. VI:3).

Mystic espousal draws Catherine not only into ecstasy, but also toward martyrdom. Angela's equation, which we discovered in the Rule's Chapter V, "About Prayer," becomes visible: Passion = blood = love. For Angela, Christ's Passion and death are the supreme evidence of God's love for humanity. Their fruit will be eternal life. The whole Paschal mystery of salvation is here—Incarnation, Crucifixion and Resurrection. God's great act of love for humanity continues in the world. God invites us to embrace it in Eucharist and to imitate it in life.

Sacred Virginity in the Company of Saint Ursula

Saint Catherine's espousal to Christ is the centerpiece of *The Mystic Marriage*. Espousal is a metaphor for a loving, intimate life-partnership with God. The painting demonstrates how and where the Company of Saint Ursula is called to live this vocation. Personages, clothing and setting all provide clues. We will look at each in turn. We will also refer to Angela's words, echoed here.

First of all, God initiates this relationship, in love. Angela described Ursulines as being *chosen to be true and virginal spouses of the Son of God* (Pr.:7). God invites. *Sacred virginity* is Angela Merici's response. This is the heart of the Company of Saint Ursula. As the Rule's Chapter VII, "About Virginity," shows us, *sacred virginity* is her term for a total life, in love with God, in love for others. It includes celibate chastity but is in no way synonymous with it. *Sacred virginity* is not one aspect of our life. It is the integration of every aspect with the One who has invited us.

In this painting the kneeling Angela embodies the Company in prayer. The standing Ursula embodies it in action. They demonstrate that contemplation allows us to see Christ not only when we pray but also when we go about our business, move through the world. With her body poised, her left knee bent, her head turned, her travel cloak about her shoulders, Ursula steps forward. But her eyes are on him.

Like Angela, the whole Company lives under Ursula's banner—Christ's banner—traveling through the world, under the sign of the cross.

Mary's presence corresponds to the traditional story of Catherine's prayer before the icon (recounted above). Mary brings Christ into the world. What is her particular significance for the Company? Angela spoke little about her. Yet she taught her daughters to pray, as she did, *the Office of the Madonna* (Ch. V:9), which expresses special devotion to Mary. She mentioned the Hail Mary in her treatment of vocal prayer and apparently prayed the rosary. She encouraged us to hope for heavenly happiness, the *good news which I announce to them on behalf of Jesus Christ and of our Lady* (Fifth Counsel:24). Mary is our model in bringing Christ's good news to others.

In his writings after Angela's death, Gabriele Cozzano may have been echoing her when he invoked Mary's example. The Company was being compared unfavorably to cloistered religious life. Ursulines are not holy like nuns, it was said. Cozzano defended the Ursuline vocation in the world by saying that it corresponds to the life of the early Church, "and especially that of the Madonna."[16] Cozzano described the apostles and the first Christian saints—"and above all the Madonna"—as following the way of life chosen by Jesus himself.[17] Mary is our model in following Christ.

Many visual details anchor Catherine's mystic experience firmly in the present, that is, in sixteenth-century Brescia. The painting makes a statement about the Company: it embodies a sacred reality, lived in ordinary life in the world.

Contemporary clothing locates the figures. Lawrence's vestment and cross-marked collar demonstrate handiwork of the time. Catherine might be a Brescian noblewoman, with her scoop-necked dress (modestly filled in), elaborate sleeves and tasseled belt. The silky fabric and intricately gold-embroidered hem mark Catherine's high social status as well as displaying the artist's skill with light and detail. This unusual Madonna may be unique in wearing a turban rather than a veil. Her headgear could belong to an early sixteenth-century Brescian matron.[18]

Mary's dress illustrates the *modest and simple* clothing that Angela describes in the Rule's Chapter II, "How They Should Be Attired," with *on top shawls or scarves of cloth such as linen or cotton, not too thin and certainly not transparent* (Ch. II:2). So does Ursula's clothing, with its white shift, *suitably*

295

laced up (Ch. II:2). Any woman might wear a sheer veil such as Angela's outdoors. Her gray-brown dress and white wimple were typical of Third Order lay women who exercised their privilege to wear Franciscan garb.[19]

Landmarks visible in the background place this event solidly in Brescia. They are still recognizable. Atop the Cidnean Hill, the medieval fortress stands today much as Romanino painted it. Citizens gathered here when the city was besieged. Under the shadow of the Mirabella Tower and Visconti Keep, bastions and supply houses provided protection and resources. Angela's mind turned here when she charged the colonelle to foster *union and concord...for I tell you,...thus united in heart, you will be like a mighty fortress, or a tower impregnable against all adversities, and persecutions, and deceits of the devil* (Last Counsel:10, 15-18).

At the foot of the Cidnean Hill we see the city itself. The Broletto towers over Brescia, marking its civic center. The Company of Saint Ursula moves within the swirl of urban events. Angela took an active role in her world. Her Rule's second chapter is "About the Manner of Interacting in the World." She instructed her daughters to *obey the laws and statues of the Lords and governors of the republics* (Ch. VIII:13). Yes, even here in the midst of secular society, intimacy with God allows one to recognize the divine presence and guidance. All is sacred.

Angela intended the Ursulines' presence in their milieu to be other-oriented, to be a good example *for the city and even beyond* (Tenth Legacy:16). The energy of the divine encounter flows outward, *to teach and edify* (Ch. IX:21).

The round Romanesque cathedral (*Rotondo* or *Duomo Vecchio*) pictured to the tower's right was the center of church life in Angela's Brescia.[20] Again and again, Angela located the Company within the Church: Jesus Christ and the saints are our models; sacraments, Scripture and liturgical seasons and prayer are the matrix of Ursuline spiritual practices; the Church's need for reform demands our prayer; its leaders should be listened to.

Romanino's painting belongs to a genre termed *sacra conversazione,* "a sacred interaction." Its contemporary, local setting fuses the sacred with the secular. The Company's core is *sacred virginity,* which shapes an Ursuline's life around her spousal relationship with Christ. Catherine enters this relationship through a mystic experience. She responds to God's initiative, which has been extended to all humanity in the

Incarnation. By placing the event in Brescia, circa 1535, the artist celebrates that this sacred reality is accessible here and now, to Angela and to us. God touches us from within our world, our time, our place.

Incarnation and the Company's Mission

Christ Incarnate was the focus of Angela Merici's spirituality, a focus sharpened by her Franciscan formation. The Company which she formed would show that stamp. It would share Christ's saving mission in the world.

A question sometimes arises: If this scene represents a "mystic marriage," why is Jesus pictured as a baby, rather than as a man? One simple answer is that the traditional story of Saint Catherine involves an icon of the Madonna and Child.[21] The deeper answer is the Incarnation. From the Council of Ephesus (431 C.E.) on, the mother-son image in Christian iconography affirmed Jesus' human nature. History tells us that there were no such images in the fourth century, when Catherine is supposed to have lived. Yet the story's truth is deeper than history. It is not just about looking at a picture. It is about contemplating the Incarnation, through which God reached out in love to humanity, becoming one with us. Catherine experiences this intimacy, this unitive love. It is not about a quasi-sexual attraction to an appealing man. Of course, God engages *everything of [ours], interior as well as exterior* (Ch. V:42), including our sexuality. But "mystic marriage" encompasses much more.

In this painting Girolamo Romanino and Angela Merici tell us, "Look at Jesus! Always! Intently! Contemplatively! Focus on him!" Angela points us to Jesus. Jesus points us to God. In Jesus, God became visible in human terms. Jesus' person, words and deeds reveal the divine presence, historically and irreversibly among us.

God is the ground of all that is, the One in whom, as Saint Paul told the Athenians, "we live and move and have our being" (Acts 17:28). To the eyes of faith, Creation manifests its divine source and center. Faith is a way of seeing that reality. Our eyes see in one way, our minds in another, our spirits in yet another. Faith penetrates to the deepest reality in all that exists. We see the world glowing with the light of God's presence.

Light is an effective tool under Romanino's hand. Like a sculptor's chisel it shapes the surface, creating depth with different planes and prominence—a common Renaissance technique. Light throws the three central figures into strong relief. Brilliant fabrics contribute a shimmering transcendence to the scene.[22] Circlets of light—haloes—represent God's grace. They indicate the saints (not Angela, who was not canonized and may even have been alive when this was painted). Mary's halo is appropriately the most brilliant, as is her clothing. The traditional treatment of Christ shows the light emanating from his head, in cruciform rays. His cross was the culmination of his redemptive mission as the Light of the World. Through the cross he released unbounded grace into the world.

The Company of Saint Ursula too is incarnate in the world. It continues Christ's mission. Ursulines seek to live Godward...*full of charity and faith and hope in God...teaching and edifying* according to the Gospel...dealing justly...*spreading peace.*

The painter communicates this reality with dramatic effects of light, true to his Venetian training. Shining from above left, the light suggests a divine source. It falls fully on Christ and illuminates the women. Lawrence's face is lighted by the reflected brilliance of the divine Child. The twilight gathering over Brescia establishes depth of background but also holds significance. It is darker. We recognize the world's need for Christ's light.

To share Christ's light.... The Company's mission soars across centuries and continents. The setting gives clues to this universality. Suffused with light, the little group clusters among broken columns harking back to the ancient world. Art collapses time and space. A quasi-biblical scene... the early Church... ancient Rome... Egypt... Germany... all flow into contemporary (sixteenth-century) Brescia.

By God's Incarnation the Eternal and Omnipresent One has entered our history and geography. Now a part of Creation, he explodes its limits. In him all times and places find their focus, their spiritual center, brilliant Being—LOVE.

[1] The Company's *Secondo Libro Generale*, quoted in Mariani, Tarolli, Seynaeve, p. 198.

2 Mariani, Tarolli and Seynaeve discuss different theories (pp. 277-279) and conclude for 1535 or 1536. Alessandro Nova and others favor the later date based on linking the painting's style to developments modeled on Romanino's contemporary Savoldo. [Alessandro Nova, "Brescia in the 16th century: Center and Periphery," lecture delivered at the Memphis Brooks Museum of Art (Memphis, Tennessee, September 19, 2003.)]

3 The first extant description dates from 1760. [*The Age of Caravaggio* (New York: Metropolitan Museum of Art, 1985), p. 76.]

[4] They probably exercised mutual influence upon one another. [*Moretto: Brescian School*, p. 241.] They worked together first in the Blessed Sacrament Chapel of the Church of S. Giovanni. Moretto drew his older colleague back into the ambit of Lombard style (established by their predecessor Vincenzo Foppa, 1427/30-1515/16), more realistic than Giorgione or Titian, for example.

[5] In his *Crib* for the Church of San Giuseppe (1525), Romanino had painted a Madonna whose silver cloak, and the play of light upon it, are almost exactly replicated by the cloak in *The Mystic Marriage*, down to the puckered seam. Many other examples illustrate this preference for silver.

[6] Between 1484 and 1487. [*The Age of Caravaggio*, p. 76.] Seventeenth-century Brescian painter Francesco Savanni called him "our Brescian." [Mariani, Tarolli, Seynaeve, p. 246, note 6.]

[7] *The Age of Caravaggio*, p. 76.

8 "The expressive potential," it could be called, with an "unclassical, expressionistic approach." [*The Age of Caravaggio*, p. 76.]

[9] Brescian art historian Pier Virgilio Begni Redona endorses this assessment by his predecessor G. Panazza. [*Arte, economica, cultura et religione nella Brescia del XVI secolo*, p. 155.]

[10] Date uncertain; page 42 of the Memphis Brooks Museum of Art catalogue puts it at 1599, an obvious error.

[11] S. J. Freedberg, *Painting in Italy 1500 – 1600*, third edition (New Haven: Yale University Press, 1993), p. 367. Romanino's son-in-law joined him in his studio and was a distinguished artist himself, who carried Mannerist style to greater lengths than had Romanino. [Redona, "Il Manierismo e Lattanzio Gambara" in *Arte, economica, cultura et religione nella Brescia del XVI secolo*, p. 170.]

[12] Passamani, p. 53.

[13] Pandolfo Nassino, Brescia's chronicler, reported that on January 28, 1540, the day after Angela's death, he saw her body being carried to St. Afra Church "with such solemnity and such a crowd of people as though she were a lord." [Nassino, *Memoria della morte*, Appendix 7 in Mariani, Tarolli,

Seynaeve, p. 582, translation the author's.] Furthermore, Angela's burial was delayed by a dispute between the Canons of the Cathedral and the Canons of the Lateran over her body. Each group wanted the honor of having her remains. [Mariani, Tarolli, Seynaeve, p. 244.]

[14] Two standards appear also in Moretto's depiction of St. Ursula and her Companions, as in his model, Antonio Vivarini's triptych. These traditionally referred to victory over the flesh (virginity) and over the world (martyrdom).

[15] James Clifton, "A Vision of the Catholic Reformation: Romanino's *Mystic Marriage of St. Catherine*," lecture presented at the Memphis Books Museum of Art (Memphis, Tennessee, February 14, 1991, revised April 11, 1991), p. 11.

[16] Cozzano, *Risposta*, Appendix 23 in Mariani, Tarolli, Seynaeve, p. 637.

[17] Cozzano, *Risposta*, Appendix 23 in Mariani, Tarolli, Seynaeve, p. 643.

[18] Cf. Vecellio, 48, cut 71, or the midwife in Moretto's *Adoration by the Shepherds*.

[19] More frequent in this period, however was "grayish," the *beretino* which Angela counseled (Ch. II:3) and in which she was buried. [Nassino, *Memoria della morte*, Appendix 7 in Mariani, Tarolli, Seynaeve, p. 582.]

[20] Both Romanino and Moretto painted works for its chapels, especially for the Blessed Sacrament Chapel. The present Baroque cathedral (*Duomo Nuovo*), built between the seventeenth and nineteenth centuries, now stands next to it.

[21] This is the most frequent but not the only version. Other versions do portray Christ as a boy and as a man. [Clifton, p. 6.]

[22] Clifton, p. 3.

Appendix 1 – Rule of the Company of Saint Ursula

Translated from the text of the Trivulsian manuscript by Nettina Gullo Eckert and Mary-Cabrini Durkin 1997 (revised 2004)

RULE: Trivulsian* Codex

Chapter Index of the Rule of the Company of St. Ursula

[Despite the misnumbering of some chapters in the Trivulsian manuscript, this text uses sequential numbers throughout, shown above.]

* *So named from the Trivulsian Library in Milan, where the manuscript of this text (dating from late 1545 or early 1546) was discovered in the 1980s by researchers Elisa Tarolli of the Company of St. Ursula of Brescia and Luciana Mariani, OSU, and Marie Seynaeve, OSU, of the Roman Union of the Order of St. Ursula.*

[Prologue]

1 In the name of the blessed and undivided Trinity.
2 Prologue about the newly begun life of virgins who are called by the name Company of Saint Ursula.
3 To the beloved daughters and sisters of the Company of Saint Ursula.

4 Since, most beloved daughters and sisters, God has granted you the grace of separating you from the darkness of this poor world and joining you together to serve his divine Majesty,

5 you must give him infinite thanks for having granted such a singular gift especially to you,

6 for how many great persons, and others of every condition, do not have, nor will be able to have, such a grace!

7 For this reason, my very own sisters, I call upon you, actually I beg and entreat you all: having been thus chosen to be true and virginal spouses of the Son of God,

8 first, be willing to recognize what such a thing means and what a new and wondrous dignity this is.

9 Then strive with all your might to keep yourselves as you have been called by God

10 and seek out, and desire all those means and ways that are necessary to persevere and prosper till the end.

11 Because merely beginning is not enough if not carried through. Therefore Truth says, "Qui perseveraverit usque in finem, hic salvus erit"; that is, "He who perseveres till the end will be saved."

12 And once again he says: "Beati qui audiunt verbum Dei et custodiunt illud"; that is, blessed are those into whose hearts God has infused the light of Truth, giving them the desire to long for their heavenly homeland, and then they will try to preserve within themselves this voice of truth and noble yearning.

13 This sort of person will undoubtedly be able to take care of herself: one who will want to embrace the means and ways necessary to such an end,

14 since there is little or no difference between freely saying: "I no longer want to serve God" and not wanting the ways and the rules necessary to be able to keep oneself in this.

15 My very own sisters, it is necessary that we be vigilant, and so much more so, as the undertaking is of such importance that there could be no greater,

16 in which lie our life and well-being,

17 and in which we are called to a life of such glory that we are spouses of the Son of God, and will become queens in heaven.

18 But one needs to be careful and prudent here, for greater labors and dangers may be involved when the undertaking is of greater value.

19 There is no type of evil which is not here to be resisted, considering that we are placed here in the midst of snares and dangers.

20 Indeed, armed against us are water, air, and earth with all of hell, because the flesh and our sensuality are not yet dead.

21 Our adversary, the devil, never even sleeps; he who never rests, but always (as Saint Peter says), like a roaring lion looks and searches for how he can devour any of us with his cunning ways, so many that no one could count them.

22 However, my very own sisters, you must not be afraid of this:

23 because if you strive with all your might for a future of living as indeed is required of true spouses of the Most High,

24 and to observe this Rule which has been composed to be useful to you, indeed as the road for you to walk by,

25 I have this undaunted and firm faith and hope in the infinite divine goodness, that not only will we easily overcome all dangers and adversities, but we will conquer them, and with great glory and jubilation.

26 Actually, we will cross through this momentary life with consolation,

27 and our every pain and sadness will turn into joy and gladness, and thorny and rocky roads we will find flower-strewn for us, paved with finest gold,

28 because the angels of eternal life will be with us insofar as we will partake of the angelic life.

29 Now to the task, with courage! Therefore let us all embrace this holy Rule that God through his grace has offered to us.

30 And, armed with his sacred precepts, let us conduct ourselves courageously, like holy Judith after she boldly lopped off the head of Holophernes, that is the devil, so that we may be able to return gloriously to our homeland,

31 where from all those in Heaven and on earth great glory and triumph will arise.

32 So now, all of you kindly be attentive, with great and longing heart.

ABOUT THE MANNER OF RECEIVING - Chap. I

1 First of all, remember how each one who will be entering or be admitted into this Company ought to be a virgin

2 and should have the firm intention of serving God in this sort of life.

3 Then, she should enter it happily

4 and of her own will.

5 Third, she should not have made a promise to any monasteries nor to earthly men.

6 Fourth, if she has father or mother or other superiors, she should first ask their permission

7 so that the governors of the Company, [women and men] may talk with them so that [they may verify that] they do not have any legitimate cause,

if by chance they should afterwards want to prevent her from entering into this holy obedience.

8 Fifth, she should be at least twelve years of age.

9 Remember, however, that those of a younger age can be received into the group so that they may be taught the truth of this unique way of life.

HOW THEY SHOULD BE ATTIRED - Chap. II

1 Once more remember, indeed, how the apparel and the garb ought to be modest and simple as truly demanded of virginal integrity.

2 Indeed, each one should go about with her bodice suitably laced up, and on top shawls or scarves of cloth such as linen or cotton, not too thin and certainly not transparent; and so should the shawls be.

3 Now, their clothes ought to be of simple cloth or serge, dark in color or dark tan or grayish or a dark blackish color as is convenient for each according to what she can do.

4 But the sisters can wear those same clothes which they are wearing when they enter this rule, but only for as long as these clothes last. However, of course, any type with flounces or braid on the sleeves or of any special cut or with any embroidery or other similar handiwork is never called for.

*5 They ought to wear a cincture cord as a sign of exterior mortification and perfect interior chastity.

6 Silk is not acceptable, even less velvet and silver and gold; no slippers and shoes if they are not black and of a modest style.

7 No colored scarves and kerchiefs, none of silk or any other kind that is too thin and transparent; no gathers on the camisoles.

8 Finally, no styles or varieties or anything at all transparent or other signs of vanity that could mar one's own conscience or that of others

9 and may be contrary to virginal integrity.

ABOUT THE MANNER OF INTERACTING IN THE WORLD - Chap. III

1 In addition to this, remember: first not to deal with a bad sort of woman.

2 Then, not in any way to listen to the private messages of men or of women, especially in secret.

3 Third, not to attend weddings, and even less dances and jousts and other similar displays of worldly pleasures.

4 Fourth, to avoid standing on balconies, even less at doors or in the streets, neither alone nor in the company of others, for many reasons.

5 Fifth, when walking on the roads or streets, to go about with eyes lowered, and wrapped modestly in shawls,

* Verse 5 has been identified as an insertion made after Angela's death.

6 and walk quickly, without dallying or stopping here and there, nor standing about to look curiously at anything
7 because from everywhere come dangers and various traps and diabolic
   snares.
8 Sixth, that if mothers or other worldly superiors should want to pressure
   them into such things or similar dangers
9 or should want to hinder them from fasting or prayer or confession or
   other kinds of good things,
10 be quick to refer this to the lady governors of the Company so that they
   may take care of it.

ABOUT FASTING - Chap. IV

1 Yet again remember that each one should want to embrace bodily fasting
   too as something indeed necessary
2 and as a means and way to the true spiritual fasting through which all
   vices and errors are lopped off from the mind.
3 To this we are invited very clearly by the example of all saintly persons,
4 and above all the life of Jesus Christ, the only way to Heaven.
5 So holy mother Church clearly sings this in the hearing of all the faithful,
   speaking to God thus, "Qui corporali ieiunio vitia comprimis, mentem
   elevas, virtutem largiris et praemia"; that is to say, God, you who rein in
   vices through bodily fasting, [who] exalt the mind [and] give virtue and
   rewards;
6 since gluttony was indeed the origin of all our evils, so may fasting and
   abstinence appropriately be the beginning and the means of our spiritual
   goods and benefits.
7 But the sacred canonists, too, say: "Indictum est ieiunium abstinentiae, lex
   a Domino Deo, prevaricatio legis a diabolo"; which is, by the Lord God are
   fasting and the laws of abstinence commanded, and the transgression of
   laws is provoked by the devil.
8 For this reason we call upon each one to fast, especially on these days of
   the year: First, all those days which holy mother Church commands,
   which are all the days of Lent, the four seasons [i.e., Ember Days], and all
   the obligatory vigils.
9 In addition, all of Advent.
10 Thirdly, fast the forty days immediately after the Epiphany to keep in
   check the senses and appetites and lustful desires which lord it over the
   world at this time especially.
11 Also, to ask for mercy before the throne of the Most High for so many
   debaucheries which are committed by Christians during times spent this
   way, as is more than apparent to everyone.

12 Fourth, after the octave of Easter fast three days out of the week, on Wednesdays, Fridays and Saturdays.

13 Fifth, fast the three days of Rogation, or litanies, that the Church celebrates before the Ascension to implore divine help for the Christian people.

14 Sixth, fast every day after the Ascension

15 and together remain in prayer with as much strength of spirit as possible till the day of the sending of the Holy Spirit, that is till the Easter of May,

16 beseeching that great promise made by Jesus Christ to his chosen and well-disposed people.

17 Seventh, after the Easter of May, return to the aforementioned three days of the week till Advent.

18 However, because one does not want anything unreasonable, you are admonished that no one ought to fast without advice, especially that of her spiritual father

19 and of the lady governors of this Company, who may have to relax and diminish these fasts as seems necessary,

20 because he who indiscreetly hurts his body, "Esset offerre holocaustum de rapina"; that is, would be sacrificing stolen goods, so say the sacred canons.

ABOUT PRAYER - Chap. V

1 Remember again that each one be solicitous about prayer, mental as well as vocal,

2 which is the companion of fasting; but Scripture says, "Bona est oratio cum ieiunio"; that is, prayer with fasting is good.

3 And one reads in the Gospel about Anna, daughter of Phanuel, who in the temple day and night continually served God in ieuniis et orationibus [fasts and prayers].

4 Since indeed through fasting one mortifies the appetites of the flesh and one's own feelings, just so, through prayer one beseeches from God the grace of the spiritual life.

5 Although one needs to pray always with spirit and mind on account of the constant need for God's help, and for this reason does Truth say, "Oportet semper orare"; that is, it is necessary to pray always,

6 yet again let us advise frequent vocal prayer

7 through which corporeal sentiments are stirred up

8 and one is disposed for mental prayer.

9 That is why each one should want to say devoutly and attentively at least the Office of the Madonna and the seven penitential psalms every day.

10 Because by saying the Office one talks with God, as the blessed martyr Alexander used to say.

11 Those who do not know how to say it will arrange to be taught by the sisters who do know.

12 Now, as for those who do not know how to read, let them want to say every day at Matins thirty-three Our Fathers and thirty-three Hail Marys in memory of the thirty-three years that Jesus Christ lived on this earth because he loved us.

13 Then at Prime say seven Our Fathers and seven Hail Marys for the seven gifts of the Holy Spirit.

14 Similarly, say as many at each of the Canonical Hours, that is at Terce, at Sext, at Nones, at Vespers, and at Compline.

15 And to give substance and even some direction to mental prayer, we call upon each one to raise her mind to God, and to practice daily and in the recesses of her heart to say, in this way, or another, or a similar fashion:

16 "My Lord, light up the darkness of my heart,

17 and give me grace to die rather than offend your divine Majesty at all today.

18 Keep my affections and my senses safe so that they may not lead me astray, neither to the right nor to the left,

19 nor turn me away from your brilliant face which soothes every afflicted heart.

20 Alas! How sorrowful I am that while entering the recesses of my heart, from shame I do not dare raise my eyes heavenward

21 because I am worthy to be devoured alive in hell, seeing in myself so many errors, so much ugliness and blame, so many monstrous and frightening beasts and shapes!

22 So am I forced, day and night, walking, standing, working, thinking, to cry out and shout to Heaven and to beg mercy and time for penitence.

23 O most benign Lord, deign to pardon me so many offenses and each of my omissions that I have ever committed from the day of my holy baptism till now.

24 Deign to forgive my sins, alas, even those of my father and mother and of my relatives and friends, and those of the entire world.

25 I beg this of you through your most sacred passion and your precious blood shed for love of us,

26 through your holy name—may it be blessed beyond the ocean's grains of sand, beyond the drops of the waters, beyond the multitude of stars.

27 I lament the fact that I have been so late to begin serving your divine Majesty.

28 Alas, till now I have not shed even a little drop of blood for love of you,

29 nor have I ever been obedient to your divine precepts,

30 and every adversity has been harsh for me because of my little love for you.

31 Lord, on behalf of those miserable wretches who do not know you,

32 nor wish to be participants in your most sacred passion,

33 my heart is wrenched,

34 and willingly would I shed my own blood (if I could), in order to open up the blindness of their minds.

35 However, my Lord, my only life and hope,

36 I beg you to deign to receive this my most vile and unclean heart

37 and to burn its every affection and passion in the blazing furnace of your divine love.

38 I beg you to accept my free will,

39 all of my own will, which of itself, because it is infected by sin, does not know how to discern good from evil.

40 Receive my every thought, word and deed,

41 finally, everything of mine, interior as well as exterior,

42 all of which I offer before the feet of your divine Majesty.

43 And I pray that you deign to receive them, although they be unworthy.

44 Amen."

ABOUT GOING TO MASS EVERY DAY - Chap. VI

1 Again, let each one go to Mass every day, and see at least one entire [Mass]

2 and attend it with modesty and devoutly,

3 since in the sacred Mass are found all the merits of the passion of our Lord.

4 And the more one attends with great attention, faith and contrition, the more one participates in those blessed merits and the greater consolation one receives.

5 Actually, it will be a communion of the spirit.

6 But remember not to linger too much in churches;

7 rather (if they want to pray longer), let them go into their rooms, and enclosed there, pray in the way and as much as the Spirit and conscience will dictate.

ABOUT CONFESSION - Chap. VII

1 Again you are called upon to make a practice of confession, a necessary medicine for the wounds of our souls.

2 Since never will anyone be absolved of sin, if he does not first confess aloud his failings to the priest, as Scripture says: "Dic tu prius iniquitates tuas, ut justificeris"; that is, first say your sins, so that you may be absolved.

3 And Truth says to St. Peter: "Tibi dabo claves regni caelorum, et quodcumque ligaveris super terram, erit ligatum et in caelis, et quodcumque
   solveris super terram, erit solutum et in caelis"; that is, I will give you the
   keys of the kingdom of Heaven, and whatever you bind on earth will also
   be bound in Heaven, and whatever you loosen on earth will also be loosened in Heaven,

4 which clearly shows that a sin cannot be taken away except through the
   priest and through confession.

5 Because in what way will the priest be able to loosen the sin, if he does
   not know it?

6 And how will he be able to know what has been committed if it is not
   revealed by one's own lips? In that case, the hidden sin would stay within
   one's breast.

7 Therefore, each one should want to present herself before the priest, as if
   before God, the eternal judge,

8 and there, sorrowing,

9 totally sincere, and in truth of conscience, she should confess her sin

10 and ask forgiveness for it,

11 and she should always with fear and reverence stay before the confessor
   till she has received absolution.

12 About this, let it be made known if a place or a certain church has been
   designated, where a common spiritual father has been chosen, one who
   is prudent and of mature age, to whom each one may want to confess at
   least once a month.

13 And then, on each first Friday of the month to gather at this church, and
   there all together receive communion from this father previously mentioned.

14 In addition to this, we call upon each one to confess and receive communion at her own parish on solemn feastdays.

ABOUT OBEDIENCE - Chap. VIII

1 Again, we call upon each one to observe holy obedience,

2 the only true self-denial of one's own will, which is within us like murky hell.

3 But Jesus Christ says: "Non veni facere voluntatem meam, sed eius qui
   misit me Pater"; that is, I have not come to do my will, but that of the
   Father who has sent me.

4 Because obedience is in man like a great light which makes every work
   good and acceptable,

5 and so one reads: "Melius est obedire, quam sacrificare"; that is, obedience
   is better than sacrifice.

6 And the sacred canons say: "Nullum bonum est extra obedientiam"; that is, it is necessary for everything of ours, if it is supposed to be good, to be done in obedience.

7 For this reason let each one want to obey: first, the commandments of God, since Scripture says: "Maledictus qui declinat a mandatis tuis;" that is, accursed is he who does not observe your commandments;

8 then, that which Holy Mother Church commands, because Truth says: "Qui vos audit me audit, et qui vos spernit me spernit"; that is, "who listens to you, listens to me; who scorns you, scorns me."

9 Third, to obey one's own bishop and pastor, and one's own spiritual father,

10 and the governors [men and women] of the Company.

11 Furthermore, to obey their fathers and mothers, and other household superiors,

12 of whom we advise them to ask pardon once a week as a sign of deference and of preserving charity;

13 again, to obey the laws and statutes of the Lords and the governors of the republics.

14 And above all, to obey the counsels and inspirations which the Holy Spirit continually sends into the heart,

15 whose voice we will hear all the more clearly the more purified and clean our conscience,

16 since the Holy Spirit is he who (as Jesus Christ says): "docet nos omnem veritatem"; that is, teaches us every truth.

17 Now, in conclusion, obey God and each creature for love of God, as the Apostle says,

18 as long as nothing is commanded against the honor of God and of one's own integrity.

ABOUT VIRGINITY - Chap. IX

1 Again, let each one want to preserve sacred virginity

2 not on account of making a vow through any human urging, but voluntarily making a sacrifice to God of her own heart,

3 since virginity (as, again, the canonists say) is the sister of all the angels,

4 victory over the appetites, queen of the virtues,

5 possessing all good things.

6 However, in every situation each one ought to conduct herself in such a manner that she not commit either against herself or in the sight of others anything at all that may be unworthy of spouses of the Most High.

7 Indeed, above all let her keep her heart pure and her conscience clean of every evil thought,

8 of every shadow of envy and ill will,

9 of every discord and evil suspicion,

10 and of every other bad appetite and wish.

11 Instead, be happy, and always full of charity and faith and hope in God.

12 And let interaction with one's neighbor be reasonable and modest as St. Paul says: "Modestia vestra nota sit omnibus hominibus"; that is, let your manners and prudence be evident to all, and let every action and speech be honest and polite.

13 Not naming God in vain.

14 Not swearing, but only saying with modesty "yes, yes" or "no, no," as Jesus Christ teaches.

15 Not answering arrogantly.

16 Not doing things unwillingly.

17 Not staying angry.

18 Not grumbling.

19 Not spreading gossip.

20 Finally, not doing any act, any deed unworthy especially of one who has the name of a servant of Jesus Christ.

21 Instead, let all our words, acts, and conduct always be to teach and edify those who deal with us,

22 having charity always burning in our hearts.

23 Furthermore, let each one be willing to be ready to die sooner than ever consent to stain and profane such a sacred jewel.

ABOUT POVERTY - Chap. X

1 We call upon each one, finally, to embrace poverty,

2 not only that of temporal things

3 but above all true poverty of spirit through which man strips his heart of every affection

4 and hope for created things,

5 and of himself.

6 And in God he has all his wealth and outside of God he sees himself impoverished of everything, being a total nothing, and with God possessing everything.

7 But Truth says: "Beati pauperes spiritu, quoniam ipsorum est regnum caelorum"; that is, blessed are the poor of spirit, because theirs is the kingdom of Heaven.

8 And just so, let each one strive to be stripped of everything

9 and to put all her wealth and love and delight not in material things,

10 not in food and over-eating,

11 not in relatives and friends,

12 not in herself, nor in any of her own attributes and knowledge,

13 but in God alone, and in the kind and ineffable providence that is his alone.

14 But the Gospel says: "Primum quaerite regnum Dei, et haec omnia apponentur vobis"; that is, Seek first the kingdom of God, and all these other things of yours will be placed before you.

15 And it says again: "Nolite solliciti esse quod comedatis, neque quod bibatis: scit enim Pater vester quia his omnibus indigetis"; that is, do not be anxious about seeking what to eat, nor what to drink, since your heavenly Father himself knows well that you need all these things,

16 as if he would clearly say: "Do not be anxious about any temporal need,

17 since God—he alone—knows, can, and wants to provide them.

18 He wants only what is for your good and joy."

ABOUT GOVERNANCE - Chap. XI

1 In order to govern said Company it is provided that four of the most capable virgins of the Company ought to be elected,

2 and at least four widowed matrons, prudent and of honorable life,

3 and four mature men who have led upright lives.

4 These virgins should be like teachers and guides in the spiritual life.

5 And the widows should be like mothers, being solicitous about the well-being and usefulness of their spiritual sisters and daughters.

6 And the four men should be like agents, and yet fathers, in the ongoing necessities of the Company.

8a Now, the four virgins should want especially to have this as their undertaking, that is, to visit, every fifteen days

7 or more or less as seems necessary,

8b all the other sisters, the virgins that are in the city,

9 to comfort and help them if they may be involved in some dissension or in any other trouble, of the body just as of the mind;

10 or to check whether their household superiors may be abusive in any way

11 or may want to hinder them from some sort of good

12 or pressure them into some danger of evil.

13 And if they themselves would not be able to provide for them, they should refer it to the matrons.

14 And if even they cannot take care of things, it may be desirable to call together the four men as well so that all together they may agree to offer a remedy.

15 If it should happen that any one of these sisters, because she is an orphan, would not be able to have what is hers,

16 or, being a housekeeper or a maid or in another station, might not be able to obtain her pay,

17 or some other similar thing should happen so that it would be necessary to go to court, and to seek what is right

18 or arrange an agreement (which is the best that can be done),

19 then these four men, out of charity, like fathers, should want to take hold of this task, and to help according to the need that exists.

20 If one of the positions of the government is vacated either because of death or because of removal from office, then the Company may want to convene and elect some others in order to provide the correct number.

21 Again, if it happened that someone were unable to carry out her [or his] duty or behaved badly, let that person be removed from office.

22 If by God's will and provision it should happen that some money or other material things would be held in common, remember that good management is needed for them,

23 and they should be dispensed prudently,

24 especially to assist the sisters, and according to each need that arises.

25 If there should be just two sisters who are left alone, without father and mother and other superiors, then in charity let a house be rented (if they do not have one), and let them be assisted in their needs.

26 But if only one is left alone, then one of the others should want to take her into her home

27 and offer her the assistance which seems right to those who govern.

28 However, if she would want to go to be a housekeeper or a maid, those that govern ought to take care of this, so that she may be settled where she can live virtuously and well.

29 Should they be so old that they cannot support themselves, they should be graciously willing to be assisted and guided as true spouses of Jesus Christ.

30 Finally remember that if any of the sisters is ill, she should be visited and assisted and guided day and night, if she is in need of this.

31 If she is about to die, let her want to leave some little thing to the Company as a sign of love and charity.

32 When someone dies, then let all the others want to accompany her to the burial place, going two by two in charity and each one with a candle in her hand.

33 And let whoever knows how to read say the Office of the Dead;

34 and let those who do not know how to read say thirty-three Our Fathers and as many Hail Marys

35 so that if that soul should be in the pains of purgatory for any sin, our sweet and kind spouse Jesus Christ may pull her from those punishments

36 and bring her to celestial glory with the other virgins, crowned with that golden and brilliant virginal crown.

Appendix 2 – Regola della Compagnia di Sant'Orsola

REGOLA: Codice Trivulziano*

[Despite the misnumbering of some chapters in the Trivulsian manuscript, this text uses sequential numbers throughout, shown above.]

* So named from the Trivulsian Library in Milan, where the manuscript of this text (dating from late 1545 or early 1546) was discovered in the 1980s by researchers Elisa Tarolli of the Company of St. Ursula of Brescia and Luciana Mariani, OSU, and Marie Seynaeve, OSU, of the Roman Union of the Order of St. Ursula.

[Prologo]

1 Nel nome della beata et individua Trinitade.

2 Prologo sopra la vita de virgine, novamente principiata, che per nome si chiama Compagnia di Santa Orsola.

3 Alle dilette figlie et sorelle de la Compagnia de Sant'Orsola.

4 Poi che, figliole et sorelle dilettissime, Dio vi ha concessa gratia de separarvi dalle tenebre de questo misero mondo, et unirve insiema a servir a sua divina Maiestade,

5 haveti da ringratiarlo infinitamente che a voi specialmente habbia concesso si singular duono.

6 Imperoché quante persone grandi, et altre d'ogni condicione, che non hanno, né potranno haver tal gratia!

7 Onde, sorelle mie, ve essorto, anzi, tutte ve prego et supplico che, essendo state cossì ellette ad esser vere et intatte spose del Figliol di Dio,

8 primo vogliate cognoscer che importa tal cosa, et che nuova et stupenda dignità sia questa.

9 Dapoi, che vi sforzati con ogni vostro potere de conservarvi secondo che da Dio chiamate seti,

10 et cerchare et volere tutti quelli mezzi et vie che necessarie sono in perseverare et prosperare fina al fine.

11 Imperoché non basta a incomminciare, se anche non se sarà perseverato. Onde dice la Verità: "Qui perseveraverit usque in finem, hic salvus erit": chi insino al fine perseverato harà, quello salvo sarà.

12 Et anchor dice: "Beati qui audiunt verbum Dei et custodiunt illud"; cioè: beati sono quelli alli quali Dio harà inspirato nel cuore la luce di Verità, et gli haverà dato sentimento di bramare la lor patria celeste; et da poi cercaran di conservare tal voce di verità in se stesse, et bon desiderio.

13 Quella persona indubitatamente potrà conservarse, la quale anche vorà abrazzare li mezzi et le vie a ciò necessarie,

14 imperoché puoca o nulla differentia è tra il dire liberamente: più non voglio servir a Dio, et il non volere le vie et regole necessarie al poterse in ciò mantenere.

15 Et tanto più, sorelle mie, bisogna che siamo vigilante, quanto la impresa è di tal importantia, che di mazzor esser non potria,

16 dove va la vita et salute nostra,

17 et dove siemo chiamate a tal gloria di vita, che spose del Figliol di Dio siamo, et in ciel regine diveniamo.

18 Però accorte et prudenti qui esser bisogna; imperò che tanto mazzor faticha et pericolo li convien che sia, quanto la impresa che se fa è di mazzor valore;

19 perché non è sorte di male che qui non ce sia per opponersi, considerando che qui siemo poste nel mezzo delli lazzi et pericoli,

20 sì che contra di noi se ha ad armare l'acqua, l'aer, et la terra, con tutto l'inferno, perché già la carne et sensualitade nostra non è morta.

21 Nanche l'adversario nostro, il diavolo, dorme; il qual mai non riposa, ma sempre (come dice San Piero), a modo de leone che rugge, mira et cercha a che modo il possa divorare alcuna di noi, et con tante sue vie et astutie, che nesun le potria numerare.

22 Ma però, sorelle mie, per questo spaventar non ve doveti:

23 imperoché, se vi sforzareti per l'avenire, a vostro gran potere, de viver sì come richiede alle vere spose del Altissimo,

24 et servare questa Regola sì come via per la quale haveti a caminare, et la qual è stata composta per utilità vostra,

25 io ho questa indubitata et ferma fede et speranza nella infinita bontà divina, che non solamente tutti li pericoli et adversitadi di facil superaremo, ma anchora con gran gloria et giubilatione nostra li venceremo.

26 Anzi, trapassaremo questa nostra brevissima vita consolatamente,

27 et ogni nostro dolore et tristezza se voltarà in gaudio et allegrezza, et trovaremo le strate spinose et sassose a noi floride et coperte di piastre de finissimo oro.

28 Imperoché gli angeli di vita eterna saranno cum noi, ciò è tanto quanto participaremo di vita angelica.

29 Horsù valente, adonque, tutte abbraciamo questa santa Regola che Dio per sua gratia ne ha offerto.

30 Et, armate de gli suoi sacri precetti, vogliamosi così virilmente diportare, che ancor noi, a modo de la santa Judith, tronchata animosamente la testa d'Oloferne, cioè del diavolo, gloriosamente nella patria ritornar possiamo,

31 dove da tutti in Ciel et terra gran gloria et triompho ne sia per nascer.

32 Hor tutte adoncha, di gratia, state attente con grande et bramoso cuore.

DEL MODO DEL RICEVER - Cap. I

1 Principalmente: se arricorda come ogn'una che haverà a intrare o esser admessa in questa Compagnia, debba esser vergine

2 et habbia ferma intentione di servir a Dio in tal sorte di vita.

3 Da poi: che la intre allegramente

4 et di propria voluntade.

5 Tertio: che la non habbia fatta promissione a monasterii et mancho a' homini mondani.

6 Quarto: se l'haverà padre, o madre, o altri superiori, essa prima gli domande licentia,

7 sì che le governatrici et governatori della Compagnia anchora essi parleno con loro a cioché non havesseno causa alcuna legitima se poi, per aventura, i volesseno impedirla a intrare sotto questa santa obedientia.

8 Quinto: che la sia almancho di etade de dodeci anni.

9 S'arricorda, però, che le di menore etade pono esser recevude in capitolo, per amaestrarle alla verita di questa singular vita.

COME DEBBANO ANDAR VESTITE - Cap. II

1 Ancora s'arricorda, sì come gli vestimenti et portadure debbano esser honeste et semplici, come veramente richiede la verginal honestade:

2 sì che ogn'una vada vestita con gli busti serrati convenientemente, et sopra con gli veli, over velette di tela, come saria de lino, over bombaso

non troppo sottile et per niente transparente; et di tal sorte siano ancora gli panetti.

3 Hor le veste deno esser come saria di panno, o sarza, et di colore come saria di bruna, o de taneto oscuro, o de beretino, o de morello oscuro, si come a cadauna, secondo la lor possibilità convegnarà.

4 Ma però se pono portare quelle stesse veste, le quale esse sorelle se inbatteno havere quando le intrano in detta Regola; però solamente tanto quanto esse veste duraranno, intendendo però che mai non ricchiede sorte alcuna di balzotti, né de bredoni a le manege, né sorte alcuna di tagliadure, né rechami et altri simili lavori.

5 Et vadino cinti del cingulo de la cintura, in segno de exterior mortificatione et perfetta interior castitade.

6 Non ricchiede seda, et mancho veludo, et argento, et oro; non pantofile et scarpe, se non come sarian negre et de forma honesta.

7 Non velli et panetti coloridi, o di seda, o d'altra sorte, troppo sottili et transparenti; non crespadure alle camise.

8 Non, finalmente, fozze et varietade et transparentie alcune, et altre vanitade che possiano macchiare la conscientia propria o del prossimo,

9 et siano contrarie alla verginal honestade.

DEL MODO DEL CONVERSAR NEL SECOLO - Cap. III

1 Oltra di questo, se arricorda: Primo: che non se habbia pratica con foemine di mala sorte.

2 Da poi: che per niente se ascolteno imbassade de homini o de donne, specialmente in secreto.

3 Tertio: che non se vada a nozze, et mancho a balli et giostre, et altri simili spettacoli de piaceri mondani.

4 Quarto: che fuggano di stare a balchoni et mancho sule porte et nelle strade, né sole, né in compagnia, per molti rispetti.

5 Quinto: che andando per le strade, o vie, vadano con gli occhii bassi et serrate honestamente con gli suoi panetti

6 et vadan prestamente, non induggiando, né fermandose o qui o lì, né stando a mirar curiosamente cosa alcuna.

7 Imperoché da pertutto sono pericoli et varie insidie et lazzi diabolici.

8 Sesto: che, se le madri o altri superiori mondani, le volesseno indure a tali, o simili pericoli,

9 over le volesseno impedire dal digiuno, o oratione, o confessione, o d'altra sorte di bene,

10 esse presto lo referiscano a le governatrici della Compagnia, accioché esse gli provedano.

DEL DIGIUNO - Cap. IIII

1 Ancora se aricorda che ogn'una abbrazzar voglia anche il digiuno corporale, sì come cosa necessaria

2 et come mezzo et via al ver digiuno spirituale, per il qual tutti gli vitii et errori dala mente se tronchano.

3 Et a questo ne invita chiarissimamente l'essempio di tutte le persone sante,

4 et sopra tutto la vita di Giesù Christo, unica via al cielo.

5 Onde la santa madre Giesa questo palesamente nelle orecchie di tutti gli fedeli intona, così a Dio parlando: "Qui corporali ieiunio vitia comprimis, mentem elevas, virtutem largiris et praemia"; ciò è Dio, il qual per il digiuno corporale refreni li vitii, inalzi la mente, dai la virtù et gli premii;

6 imperoché sì come la gola fo origine di tutti li mali nostri, così il digiuno et astinentia convien che sia principio et mezzo de tutti gli beni et profetti nostri spirituali.

7 Però dicono e' sacri canoniste: "Indictum est ieiunium abstinentiae, lex a Domino Deo, prevaricatio legis a diabolo"; ciò è: comandato è sta dal Signor Dio il digiuno, legge de astinentia, et la transgressione della legge e indutta dal diavolo.

8 Per la qual cosa essortemo ogn'una a digiunare, specialmente questi giorni del anno: Primo: tutti quelli che comanda la santa madre Giesa, cio e tutta la quadragesima, li quatro tempori et tutte le vigilie comandate.

9 Da poi: tutto l'advento.

10 Tertio: se digiune subito doppo l'Epiphania quaranta giorni, per domar gli sensi et gli appetiti et lascivie, che allhora specialmente par che signorezzan nel mondo,

11 et anchora per implorar inanzi al throno della divina Altezza misericordia per tante dissolutioni, che in cosi fatti tempi da christiani sono comesse, come è più che palese a tutti.

12 Quarto: doppo l'ottava di Pascha se digiune tre giorni della settimana, ciò è il mercori, il venere e il sabbato.

13 Quinto: se digiune gli tre giorni delle rogationi, over letanie, che la Giesa celebra avanti l'Asscensione, per implorare il divino aiuto per il popol christiano.

14 Sesto: se digiune doppo l'Asscensione ogni giorno,

15 et insiema se stie in oratione, con quanta forza de spirito se poterà, fina al giorno de la missione del Spirito Santo, ciò è fina a pascha di maggio,

16 domandando quella gran promissione fatta da Giesù Christo a gli suo eletti et ben disposti.

17 Settimo: doppo pascha di maggio se ritorne agli tre giorni sopradetti di la settimana fina a l'advento.

18 Ma perché non si vole se non cose discrete, però se admonisse che niuna debba digiunare senza il consilio specialmente del suo patre spirituale

19 et delle governatrici di essa Compagnia, le quale habbiano a relentare et sminuire essi digiunii, secondo che esser bisogno se vedera,

20 perché chi indiscretamente affligesse il suo corpo, "esset offerre holocaustum de rapina"; ciò è sarìa far sacrificio di robbaria, si come dicono ancora gli sacri canoni.

DE L'ORATIONE - CAP. V

1 Se arricorda ancora che ogn'una sia sollecita all'oratione così mentale come vocale,

2 la quale è compagna del digiuno; perho dice la Scrittura: "Bona est oratio cum ieiunio": ciò è: bona è l'oratione col digiuno.

3 Et se legge nel Evangelio di quella Anna, figlia di Phanuel, la quale nel tempio dì e notte di continuo serviva a Dio in ieiuniis et orationibus.

4 Imperoché, sì come per il digiuno se mortifica gli appetiti de la carne et proprii sentimenti, così per l'oratione se impetra da Dio la gratia della vita spirituale.

5 Et benché col spirito et con la mente bisogna sempre orare, per il continuo bisogno che se ha del aiuto di Dio; et per questo dice la Verità: "Oportet semper orare", ciò è: bisogna sempre orare,

6 tutta via consigliemo ancora la frequente oratione vocale,

7 per la quale se excitano li sentimenti corporei

8 et se dispone alla mentale.

9 Per la qual cosa ogn'una voglia ogni giorno dire almancho l'Officio della Madonna et li sette Psalmi penitentiali con devotione et attentione.

10 Imperoché dicendo l'Officio se parla con Dio; come anche diceva il beato Allessandro martire.

11 Et chi nol'sapran dire, sel'faccian insignare dalle sorelle chel saperanno.

12 Hor, quelle che non sapran leggere, vogliano dire ogni giorno a Matutino trentatre Pater Noster et trentatre Ave Maria, per memoria de gli trentatre anni che Giesù Christo visse in questo mondo per amor nostro.

13 Poi, a Prima dica sette Pater Noster et sette Ave Maria per li sette duoni del Spirito Santo.

14 Et similmente tanti ne dica a cadauna delle altre hore canonice, ciò è a Terza, a Sesta, a Nona, a Vespro et a Compieta.

15 Et per dar materia et qualche via ancor all'oratione mentale, essortemo ogn'una ad inalzar le mente a Dio, et per ogni giorno essercitarse et cosi, o ad altro, o simil modo, nel secreto del cor suo dire:

16 "Signor mio, illumina le tenebre del cuor mio,

17 et dammi gratia più presto di morire, che mai hoggi offenda la tua divina Maestade.

18 Et assegura i miei affetti et sensi, che non prevariccheno né a destra, né a sinistra,

19 né me rivoltino dalla lucidissima faccia tua, che contenta ogni cuor afflitto.

20 Haimé dolente che, intrando nel secreto del cuor mio, di vergogna non ardisco levar gli occhii al cielo,

21 che son degna da esser divorata così viva nel inferno, vedendo in me tanti errori, tante brutezze et vituperi, tante monstruose et spaventose fiere et figure.

22 Onde son constretta, di et notte, andando, stando, operando, pensando, di proclamare et gittar cridi al Cielo, et domandar misericordia et spatio di penitentia.

23 Degnati, o benignissimo Signore, di perdonarmi tante offese, et ogni mio fallo che mai habbia comesso fin hora, dal giorno del santo battesmo.

24 Degnati di perdonare gli peccati, haimé, ancora de mio patre et matre, e di miei parenti et amici, et de tutto il mondo.

25 Io tene prego, per la tua sacratissima passione, et sangue precioso sparso per amor nostro,

26 per il tuo santo nome, il qual sia benedetto sopra l'arena del mare, sopra le giozze delle acque, sopra la moltitudine delle stelle.

27 Mi doglio che sia stata tanto tarda a incominciare a servire alla tua divina Maestade.

28 Haimé, fin hora non ho mai sparso pur una giozzetta di sangue per amor tuo;

29 nanche mai son stata obediente a tuoi divini precetti,

30 et ogni adversitade m'e stata aspera per il puocho amore tuo.

31 Signor, in luoco de quelle meschine creature che non te cognoscono,

32 né si curano d'esser participevoli della tua sacratissima passione,

33 mene crappa il cuore,

34 et volentiera (s'io potesse) spargerei il proprio sangue per aprire la cecitade de le lor menti.

35 Però, Signor mio, unica vita et speranza mia,

36 ti prego che tu te degni de recever questo mio vilissimo et inmondo cuore,

37 et abbrusciare ogni suo affetto et passione nell'ardente fornace del tuo divin amore.

38 Ti priego che tu ricevi il mio libero arbitrio,

39 ogni mia propria voluntade, la quale da sé, per esser infetta dal peccato, non sa discerner il bene dal male.

40 Riceve ogni mio pensar, parlar et operare,

41 ogni mia cosa, finalmente, così interiore come exteriore:

42 il che tutto offerisco avanti e' piedi della tua divina Maestade.

43 Et ti priego che tu te degne de riceverlo, benche ne sia indegna.

44 Amen."

DEL ANDAR A MESSA OGNI GIORNO - Cap. VI

1 Ancor ogn'una vada a Messa ogni giorno, et ne vedda almancho una integra,

2 et se gli stie con modestia et devotamente,

3 imperoché nella sacra Messa se ritrovan tutti gli meriti della passione del Signor nostro.

4 Et quanto più se gli sta con maggior attentione, fede et contritione, tanto più se participa de quei benedetti meriti et se riceve mazzor consolatione.

5 Anzi, sarà un communicarse col spirito.

6 Ma perho s'arricorda a non induggiar troppo nelle giese;

7 ma (se voranno piu longamente orare) vadan nelle sue camere, et ivi chiuse, oreno qualmente et quanto il Spirito et conscientia dittaranno.

DELLA CONFESSIONE - Cap. VII

1 Se essorta ancora al frequentare la confessione, necessaria medicina delle piaghe dell'anime nostre.

2 Imperoché gia mai niuno sarà giustificato dal peccato, se egli prima con la boccha non confessarà al sacerdote gli suoi falli, come dice la Scrittura: "Dic tu prius iniquitates tuas, ut justificeris"; ciò è: di tu prima li tuoi peccati, acioché tu sia giustificato.

3 Et la Verità dice a San Piero: "Tibi dabo claves regni caelorum, et quodcumque ligaveris super terram, erit ligatum et in caelis, et quodcumque solveris super terram, erit solutum et in caelis"; ciò è: io ti darò le chiave del reame del Cielo, et qualunche harai legato sopra la terra sarà legato ancora in Cielo, e qualunche harai deslegato sopra la terra sarà deslegato ancor in Cielo.

4 Dove chiaramente se dimostra il peccato non poter esser tolto via se non per il sacerdote et per la confessione.

5 Per che: a che fozza il sacerdote potrà il peccato desligare, se nol lo saperà?

6 Et a che modo il potral sapere, se quello che la comesso, esso non lo manifeste con la propria boccha, conciosia cosa ch'el peccato ascoso stia dentro n'el petto?

7 Ogn'una adoncha voglia presentarsi avanti il sacerdote, sì come avanti Dio eterno giudice,

8 et ivi dolente,

9 schiettamente et in verità di conscientia, confesse il suo peccato

10 et ne domandi perdonanza,

11 et sempre con timore et reverentia stia sotto al confessore, fin che habbia receuta l'absolutione.

12 Sopra questo se fa sapere qualmente se ha a deputare un luoco, o giesa certa, dove se ha da elezzer un commune padre spirituale prudente et maturo di etade, al qual ogn'una voglia almancho una volta il mese confessarsi;

13 et poi, ogni primo vener del mese congregarsi ad essa giesa, et ivi tutte insiema communicarsi da esso prefato padre.

14 Oltra di questo, essortemo ogn'una confessarsi et communicarsi alla propria parochia alle feste solenni.

DELLA OBEDIENTIA - Cap. VIII

1 Se essorta ancora ogn'una a servare la santa obedientia,

2 sola vera abnegatione della propria voluntade, la qual è in noi a modo del tenebroso inferno.

3 Però dice Giesù Christo: "Non veni facere voluntatem meam, sed eius qui misit me Pater"; ciò è: non son venuto per far il mio voler, ma quello del Padre che m'ha mandato.

4 Imperoché l'obedientia è nel homo a modo d'una gran luce, che fa ogni opra esser buona et accetta;

5 onde se legge: "Melius est obedire, quam sacrificare;" ciò è: meglio e l'obedire che il sacrificare.

6 Et gli sacri canoni dicono: "Nullum bonum est extra obedientiam;" ciò è: ogni cosa nostra, se dee essere bona, bisogna che sia fatta sotto obedientia.

7 Per questo ogn'una voglia obedire: primo a gli comandamenti di Dio, imperoché dice la Scrittura: "Maledictus qui declinat a mandatis tuis;" ciò è maledetto è quello che non serva i toi commandamenti.

8 Da poi: a quello che commanda la santa madre Giesa, perche dice la Verità: "Qui vos audit, me audit, et qui vos spernit, me spernit"; ciò è: chi alde voi alde mi; chi sprezza voi sprezza mi.

9 Tertio: obedire al proprio episcopo et pastore, et al proprio padre spirituale.

10 Et alli governatori et governatrice della Compagnia.

11 Più oltra: obedire alli padri et matre, et altri superiori di casa,

12 alli quali consigliemo domandar perdonanza una volta la settimana per segno de suggiettione et conservatione della charità.

13 Obedire ancora alle leggi et statutti de Signori, et alli governatori delle republice.

14 Et sopra tutto: obedire a gli consiglii et inspiratione che di continuo ne manda il Spirito Santo nel cuore;

15 la cui voce tanto più chiaramente aldiremo, quanto più purificata et monda haveremo la conscientia.

16 Imperoché il Spirito Santo è quello il qual (come dice Giesù Christo) "docet nos omnem veritatem"; ciò è: insegna a noi ogni verità.

17 Hor, in conclusione: obedire a Dio, et a ogni creatura per amor de Dio, come dice l'Apostolo,

18 pur che non ce sia comandata cosa alcuna contra l'honor di Dio et della propria honestate.

DELLA VERGINITADE - Cap. IX

1 Ogn'una ancora voglie conservare la sacra virginitade,

2 non già di ciò facciando voto per essortatione homana, ma voluntariamente facciando a Dio sacrificio del proprio cuore.

3 Imperoché la virginitade (come dicono ancora gli canoniste) è sorella de tutti gli angeli,

4 vittoria delli appetiti, regina delle vertute,

5 et che possiede tutti gli beni.

6 Però ogn'una dee cosi in ogni cosa deportarse, che non se cometta né in se stessa, né in conspetto del prossimo, cosa alcuna che sia indegna di spose del Altissimo.

7 Sì che sopra tutto se tenga il cuor puro et la conscientia monda da ogni cativo pensier,

8 da ogni ombra d'invidia et malivolentia,

9 da ogni discordia et mala sospitione,

10 et da ogni altro cativo appetito et voluntade.

11 Ma sia lieta et sempre piena di caritade, et fede, et speranza in Dio.

12 Et la conversatione col prossimo sia ragionevole et modesta, come dice San Paolo: "Modestia vestra nota sit omnibus hominibus"; ciò è: la costumezza et prudentia vostra sia palesa a tutti, sì che ogni atto et parlare sia honesto et costumato:

13 Non nominando Dio vanamente.

14 Non giurando, ma solamente dicendo con modestia: sì, sì; over: no, no, come Giesù Christo insegna.

15 Non rispondendo superbamente.

16 Non facciando le cose malvolentiera.

17 Non stando adirata.

18 Non mormorande.

19 Non riportando cosa alcuna di male.

20 Non, finalmente, facciando atto, ne gesto alcuno, indegno specialmente di chi ha nome di serve di Giesù Christo.

21 Ma tutte le parolle, atti et movimenti nostri sempre sian in amaistramento et edificatione de chi harà pratica con noi,

22 habbiando sempre nel cuore l'abbrasciata caritade.

23 Più oltra, ogn'una voglie esser disposta più presto di morire, che mai consentire a macchiare et profanare cosi sacra gioia.

DELLA POVERTADE - Cap. X

1 Essortemo finalmente ogn'una ad abbrazzare la povertade,

2 non solamente quella del effetto de cose temporale,

3 ma sopra tutto la vera povertà di spirito, per la quale l'homo se spoglia il cuore d'ogni affetto

4 et speranza di cose create,

5 et di se stesso.

6 Et in Dio ha ogni suo bene, et fuora di Dio se vede povero del tutto, et esser totalmente un niente, et con Dio haver il tutto.

7 Però dice la Verità: "Beati pauperes spiritu, quoniam ipsorum est regnum caelorum"; ciò è: beati son gli poveri de spirito, imperoché de lor e il reame del Cielo.

8 Et pertanto ogn'una se sforze spogliarsi del tutto,

9 et metter ogni suo bene, et amore, et delettatione, non in robba,

10 non in cibi et golla,

11 non in parenti et amici,

12 non in si stessa et alcuna sua propria provisione et sapere,

13 ma in solo Dio, et in la lui sola benigna et ineffabil providentia.

14 Però dice l'Evangelio: "Primum quaerite regnum Dei, et haec omnia apponentur vobis"; ciò è: cercate prima il reame di Dio, e queste altre tutte vostre cose vi saran messe inanzi.

15 Et ancor dice: "Nolite solliciti esse quod comedatis, neque quod bibatis: scit enim Pater vester quia his omnibus indigetis"; ciò è: non vogliati esser solleciti in cercar che debbiati mangiar, nanche che debbiati bever, imper-

oché il Padre vostro celeste egli ben sa che haveti debisogno de tutte queste cose;

16 come se chiaramente dicesse: non ve affanati sopra cosa alcuna di bisogno temporale,

17 imperoché Dio egli solo sa, po et vole provedergli;

18 il qual non vole se non il solo bene et gaudio vostro.

DEL GOVERNO - Cap. XI

1 Per governare detta Compagnia se dispone che se debba elezzere quatro vergini delle più sufficiente della Compagnia,

2 et almancho quatro matroni vedove prudenti et honeste de vita,

3 et quatro homini maturi et di vita probata.

4 Le qual vergini siano come maestre et guidatrice nella vita spirituale.

5 Et le vedove sian come matre a esser sollecete circa il bene et utilitade delle sorelle et figlie spirituale.

6 Et gli quatro homini siano come agenti et patri ancora circa l'occurrente necessitade della Compagnia,

8a Hor le quatro vergini vogliano specialmente haver questo per sua impresa, ciò è de visitar ogni quindeci giorni

7 o più o mancho come se vedera bastare.

8b tutte le altre sorelle vergini che sono per la città,

9 per confortarle et aggiutarle, se le fosseno in qualche discordia o in alcun'altra tribulatione, si di corpo come di mente;

10 o ver che gli superiori suoi di casa gli facessen qualche ingiuria,

11 o le volessen impedirle da qualche sorte di bene,

12 o indurle a qualche pericolo di male.

13 Et se lor stesse non potessen provedergli, lo referiscano alle matrone.

14 Et se manche lor potran ripararergli, se voglie convocare anche gli quatro homini, accioché tutti insieme concorrano a dar rimedio.

15 Se l'accadesse che alcuna di esse sorelle, per esser orphana, non potesse haver il suo,

16 o ver, essendo massara, o donzella, o ad altro modo, non potesse haver la sua mercede,

17 o ver accadesse altra cosa simile, onde bisognasse andar per palazzo et per via di ragione,

18 o ver metter d'accordo (il che è il meglio che far se possia),

19 all'hora essi quatro homini per carità, a modo di padri, vogliano pigliar questa impresa, et soccorrere secondo il bisogno che sarà.

20 Se qualch'una delle persone del governo manchasse o per morte, o per esser levata dal officio, all'hora la Compagnia voglia congregarsi, et eleggerne delle altre per supplire il legittimo numero.

21 Ancora, sel vene fusse che non potesse fare il suo officio, o se diportasse male; quella persona sia dal governo rimovesta.

22 Se per voluntà et dispensation di Dio avenesse che in commune se havessen qualche dinari, o altra robba, se arricorda che se gli debba haver bon governo,

23 et prudentemente se habbian a dispensare,

24 specialmente in soventione delle sorelle et secondo ogni occorrente bisogno.

25 Sel fosseno due almancho sorelle rimaste sole, senza padre et matre, et altri superiori, all'hora per carita gli sia tolta una casa a fitto (se elle non haveranno), et siano sovenute ne gli lor bisogni.

26 Ma sel ne sarà rimasta se non una sola, all'hora qualch'una delle altre la voglia ricever in casa sua,

27 et gli sia porzesta la soventione che parerà a chi governarano.

28 Ma perho, se ella volesse andar a star per massara o donzella, essi che governano habbian cura di questo, accioché la sia collocata dove bene et honestamente star possia.

29 Sel ne fussen de così vecchie, che per si stesse non potesseno sostentarsi, queste vogliano di gratia esser sovenute et governate, si come vere spose di Giesù Christo.

30 Finalmente s'arricorda, se alcuna delle sorelle sarà inferma, che la sia visitata, et sovenuta, et governata, de dì et di notte, s'el sarà la necessitade.

31 Et se la fusse per morire, voglie lassare qualche cosetta alla Compagnia, in segno d'amore et charitade.

32 Quando qualch'una sarà morta, all'hora tutte le altre la voglian compagnare alla sepoltura, andando a due a due, con carità et con una candela in mano per una.

33 Et che saperà leggere, dica l'Officio da morti;

34 et chi non saprà lezzere, dica trentatre Pater Noster et tante Ave Maria,

35 acciò che, se quella anima fusse per qualche peccato nelle pene del purgatorio, il nostro dolce et benigno sposo Giesù Christo la cave da quelle pene,

36 et la conduca alla gloria celeste con le altre vergini, incoronata di quella aurea et chiarissima virginal corona.

Bibliography of Works Consulted

Abbott, Elizabeth. *A History of Celibacy: From Athena to Elizabeth I, Leonardo da Vinci, Florence Nightingale, Gandhi, & Cher.* New York: Scribner, 2000.

The Age of Caravaggio. New York: Metropolitan Museum of Art, 1985.

Arte, economica, cultura e religione nella Brescia del XVI secolo, ed. Maurizio Pegrari. Brescia: Società Editrice Vannini, 1988. (A series of essays delivered between Feb. 21 and May 23, 1985, in Seminario VII on the teaching of cultural resources.)

Baring-Gould, Sabine. *Curious Myths of the Middle Ages*, ed. Edward Hardy. New York: Oxford University Press, 1978.

Barsotti, Divo. *La Spiritualité de Sainte Angèle Merici: Une Famille autour de la Mère*, trans. into French and notes by Marie-Bénédicte Rio, OSU. Rome, 2001.

Bell, Rudolph M. *Holy Anorexia*, Epilogue by William N. Davis. Chicago: University of Chicago Press, 1985.

Belotti, Gianpietro, ed. *Angela Merici: La società, la vita, le opere, il carisma.* Brescia: Centro Mericiano, 2004.

Bennet, Judith M. and Amy M. Froide, eds. *Singlewomen in the European Past 1250 – 1800.* Philadelphia: University of Pennsylvania Press, 1999.

Bornstein, Daniel and Roberto Rusconi, eds. *Women and Religion in Medieval and Renaissance Italy*, trans. Margery J. Schneider. Chicago: The University of Chicago Press, 1996.

Bouyer, Louis, Jean Leclerque and François Vanderbroucke. *The Spirituality of the Middle Ages*, Vol. II of *A History of Christian Spirituality*, trans. the Benedictines of Holm Eden Abbey. Carlisle, NY: Seabury Press, 1968.

Breisach, Ernst. *Caterina Sforza: A Renaissance Virago.* Chicago: The University of Chicago Press, 1967.

Bynum, Caroline Walker. *Holy Feast and Holy Fast: The Religious Significance of Food to Medieval Women.* Berkeley: University of California Press, 1987.

Bynum, Caroline Walker. *Jesus as Mother: Studies in the Spirituality of the High Middle Ages.* Berkeley: University of California Press, 1982.

Campbell, Joseph, ed. *Myths, Dreams, and Religion.* New York: E. P. Dutton and Company, Inc., 1970.

Campbell, Joseph with Bill Moyers. *The Power of Myth*, ed. Betty Sue Flowers. New York: Doubleday, 1988.

Clifton, James. "A Vision of the Catholic Reformation: Romanino's *Mystic Marriage of St. Catherine*," lecture presented at the Memphis Brooks Museum of Art (Memphis, Tennessee, February 14, 1991, revised April 11, 1991).

Cohen, Sherrill. "Asylums for Women in Counter-Reformation Italy" in *Women in Reformation and Counter-Reformation Europe: Public and Private Worlds*, ed. Sherrin Marshall. Bloomington, IN: Indiana University Press, 1989, pp. 166-188.

Conroy, Mary, OSU. "Veni Sponsa Christi ... Today." Address to an inter-Ursuline meeting of superiors general (Rome, May 4, 1991).

Contini, Mila. *5000 Years of Fashion*, trans. Olive Ordish. Milan: Arnoldo Mondadori Editore, 1977.

de Voragine, Jacobus. *The Golden Legend*, 2 volumes, trans. Granger Ryan and Helmut Ripperger. London: Longmans, Green and Co., 1941.

de Voragine, Jacobus. *The Golden Legend*, 2 volumes, trans. William Granger Ryan. Princeton, NJ: Princeton University Press, 1993.

Dean, Trevor and K. J. P. Lowe. *Marriage in Italy, 1300-1650*. New York: Cambridge University Press, 1998.

Durkin, Mary-Cabrini. "Art in Brescia, the Spirit of Angela Merici and Women's Leadership Today," address to an inter-Ursuline meeting of superiors general (Rome, May 4, 1991).

Earnshaw, Pat. *Lace in Fashion from the Sixteenth to the Twentieth Centuries*, second edition. Guildford, Surrey: Gorse Publications, 1991.

Firenzuola, Agnolo. *On the Beauty of Women*, trans. and ed. Konrad Eisenbichler and Jacqueline Murray. Philadelphia: University of Pennsylvania Press, 1992.

Fossati, Luigi. *L'Opera e la personalità di S. Angela*. Brescia: Tipografia Opera Pavoniana, 1992.

Fraser, Barbara and Paul Jeffrey. "Women in Latin America: The Gender Gap Kills," Part 7 in the series Latin America: Search for a Future, *National Catholic Reporter* (Oct. 8, 2004), 9-12.

Freedberg, S.J. *Painting in Italy 1500 – 1600*, third edition. New Haven: Yale University Press, 1993.

Ganss, George E., S.J., ed. "General Introduction," *Ignatius of Loyola: The Spiritual Exercises and Selected Works*, in the series *The Classics of Western Spirituality*. New York: Paulist Press, 1991, pp. 10-63.

Gombosi, Gyorgy. *Moretto da Brescia*. Basel: Ars Docta Band IV, 1943.

Guillaume/Linephty, Maur. *Hans Memling in the Hospital of St. John at Bruges or The Shrine of St. Ursula*. Paris: The Marion Press, 1939.

Hellot, Macquer and Le Pileur d'Apligny. *The Art of Dyeing Wool, Silk and Cotton*, trans. from the French, a reissuing of the edition first published in England in 1789 by R. Baldwin. London: Scott, Greenwood and Co., 1901.

Jordan, Constance. *Renaissance Feminism: Literary Texts and Political Models*. Ithaca, NY: Cornell University Press, 1990.

Kauffmann, C. M. *The Legend of St. Ursula*. London: Her Majesty's Stationery Office, 1964.

King, Margaret L. *Women of the Renaissance*. Chicago: University of Chicago Press, 1991.

Klapsich-Zuber, Christiane. *Women, Family and Ritual in Renaissance Italy*, trans. Lydia G. Cochrane. Chicago: University of Chicago Press, 1985.

Köhler, Carl. *A History of Costume*, ed. and augmented by Emma von Sichart and Alexander K. Dallas. New York: Dover Publications, Inc., 1963.

La Chiesa di S. Maria Maddelena in Desenzano del Garda: Guida Storico-Artistica al Duomo de Desenzano. Text by Guiseppe Tosi and Giancarlo Agnolini. Photography by Gianni Lemme and Ugo Allegri. Desenzano: Duomo di Desenzano, 1986.

Laven, Mary. *Virgins of Venice: Broken Vows and Cloistered Lives in the Renaissance Convent*. New York: Viking, 2002.

Ledochowska, Teresa, OSU. *Angela Merici and the Company of St. Ursula*, 2 vols., trans. Mary Teresa Neylan, OSU. Rome: Ancora, 1968.

Leggett, William F. *Ancient and Medieval Dyes*. Brooklyn, NY: Chemical Publishing Co., Inc., 1944.

Lerner, Gerda. *The Creation of Feminist Consciousness from the Middle Ages to Eighteen-seventy*. New York: Oxford University Press, 1993.

Little, Lester K. *Liberty, Charity, Fraternity: Lay Religious Confraternities in Bergamo in the Age of the Commune*, vol. 51 of the series *Studies in History*. Northhampton, Massachussetts: Smith College, 1988.

Little, Lester K. *Religious Poverty and the Profit Economy in Medieval Europe*. Ithaca, NY: Cornell University Press, 1978.

Little Office of the Blessed Virgin Mary, compiled and ed. John E. Rotelle, OSA. New York: Catholic Book Publishing Co., 1988.

Mariani, Luciana, Elisa Tarolli and Marie Seynaeve. *Angela Merici: Contribution towards a Biography*, trans. M. Ignatius Stone. Milan: Editrice Ancora Milano, 1989.

Mariani, Luciana, OSU, and Marie-Bénédicte Rio, OSU. *Against the tide: Angela Merici*, trans. Armida Veglio, OSU. Rome: The Roman Union of the Order of Saint Ursula, 2004.

Marshall, Sherrin, ed. *Women in Reformation and Counter-Reformation Europe: Public and Private Worlds*. Bloomington, Indiana: Indiana University Press, 1989.

McCormick, Mary, OSU. "Interpretation of Angela's Writings," paper presented to the Ursuline Society (Youngstown, Ohio, April 1975).

Merici, Angela. *Rule of the Company of Saint Ursula*, Trivulsian manuscript, trans. Nettina Gullo Eckert and Mary-Cabrini Durkin. Cincinnati, 1997.

Merici, Angela. *Regola: Codice Trivulziano* in Luciana Mariani, Elisa Tarolli and

Marie Seynaeve. *Angela Merici: Contribution towards a Biography.* Milan: Editrice Ancora Milano, 1989, Appendix 1.

Merici, Angela. *Writings: Rule, Counsels, Testament,* Earliest-known Italian Texts and Translation by a team of Ursulines of the Roman Union. Rome: Ursulines of the Roman Union, 1995.

Monson, Craig A., ed. *The Crannied Wall: Women, Religion, and the Arts in Early Modern Europe.* Ann Arbor: The University of Michigan Press, 1992.

Morassi, Antonio. *Brescia: Catalogo Delle Cose D'Arte e Di Antichità D'Italia.* Rome: La Libreria dello Stato (Ministero Generale delle Antichità e Belle Arte), n.d.

Moretto: Brescian School. Masters in Art Series, Vol. 9, Part 106. October 1908.

Newman, Barbara. *From Virile Woman to WomanChrist: Studies in Medieval Religion and Literature.* Philadelphia: University of Pennsylvania Press, 1995.

Newman, Barbara. *Sister of Wisdom: St. Hildegard's Theology of the Feminine.* Berkeley: University of California Press, 1989.

Nova, Alessandro. "Brescia in the 16th Century: Center and Periphery," lecture delivered at the Memphis Brooks Museum of Art (Memphis, Tennessee, September 19, 2003).

Pagiaro, Sergio. *Santuario S. Angela Merici.* Brescia: Centro Mericiano, 1985.

Passamani, Bruno. *Guida della Pinacoteca Tosio-Martinengo di Brescia.* Brescia: Grafo, 1988.

Payne-Bell, LaDoris and Mary Jude Jun, OSU. *The Wisdom of Angela: Circles of Hope.* St. Louis, Missouri: Imani Family Center, n.d.

Pisan, Christine de. *The Book of the City of Ladies,* trans. Earl Jeffrey Richards. New York: Persea Books, 1982.

Powell, James M. *Albertanus of Brescia: The Pursuit of Happiness in the Early Thirteenth Century.* Philadelphia: University of Pennsylvania Press, 1992.

Ranft, Patricia. *Women and Spiritual Equality in Christian Tradition.* New York: St. Martin's Press, 1998.

Regula Tertii Ordinis: Textus Authenticus Regesti Pontificalis in *Seraphicae Legislationes Textus Originales.* Florence: Ad Claras Aquas, 1897, a reprint of the text "*Supra Montem,*" Constitution of Pope Nicholas IV, 1289.

Robinson, Stuart. *A History of Dyed Textiles.* Cambridge, Massachusetts: The MIT Press, 1977; first published in Great Britain by Studio Vista Ltd., 1969.

Old Masters in Context: Romanino's Mystic Marriage of Saint Catherine, IV in the series "Essays on the Collection," ed. Arnold Victor Coonin. Memphis, Tennessee: Memphis Brooks Museum of Art, 2003.

Rossi, Ottavio. *Le Memorie Bresciane: Opera istorica et simbolica.* Brescia: B. Fontan, 1616.

Ruether, Rosemary and Eleanor McLaughlin, eds. *Women of Spirit: Female Leadership in the Jewish and Christian Traditions.* New York: Simon and Schuster, 1979.

Ruzante (Angelo Beolco). *La Anconitana: The Woman from Ancona*, trans. Nancy Dersofi. Berkeley: University of California Press, 1994; first produced in Padua, 1533.

Sachs, Hanelore. *The Renaissance Woman*, trans. Marianne Herzfeld. New York: McGraw-Hill, 1971.

Schineller, Peter. "The Challenge of the Martyrs." *America* (Oct. 11, 1980), 207, 208.

Shahar, Shulamith. *Childhood in the Middle Ages*, trans. Chaya Galai. New York: Routledge, 1990.

Shahar, Shulamith. *The Fourth Estate: A History of Women in the Middle Ages*, trans. Chaya Galai. London and New York: Methuen, 1983.

Sperling, Jutta Gisela. *Convents and the Body Politic in Late Renaissance Venice*. Chicago: The University of Chicago Press, 1999.

Stone, M. Ignatius. *Commentary on the Writings of Saint Angela Merici: Rule, Counsels, Legacies*. England, 1996.

Stocker, Margarita. *Judith, Sexual Warrior: Women and Power in Western Culture*. New Haven, Connecticut: Yale University Press, 1998.

Thorburn, Mary Germaine, OSU. "The Christology of St. Angela Merici." Unpublished paper, 1975.

Valcanover, F. *Carpaccio: The Legend of St. Ursula*, trans. Sandra Peterson. Milano: Arti Grafiche Ricordi, 1964.

Vecellio, Cesare. *Vecellio's Renaissance Costume Book: All 500 Woodcut Illustrations from the Famous Sixteenth-Century Compendium of World Costume*. New York: Dover Publications, Inc., 1977.

Venturi, Lionello and Rosabianca Skira-Venturi. *Italian Painting*, Vol. II, trans. Stuart Gilbert. Geneva and New York: Albert Skira, 1950-1952.

Wernke, Frank J. *Three Women Poets, Renaissance and Baroque: Louise Labé, Gaspara Stampa and Sor Juana Inés de la Cruz*. Lewisburg, Pennsylvania: Bucknell University Press, 1987.

Winstead, Karen. "Archetypes of Feminine Mastery in Medieval Virgin Martyr Legends," lecture delivered at the 25th International Congress on Medieval Studies (Kalamazoo, Michigan, May 1990).

Women and Faith: Catholic Religious Life in Italy from Late Antiquity to the Present, ed. Lucetta Scaraffia and Gabriella Zarri. Cambridge, Massachusetts: Harvard University Press, 1999.

Yarwood, Doreen. *Fashion in the Western World 1500-1990*. London: B. T. Batsford, Ltd., 1992.

Zarri, Gabriella. *Women, Family and Ritual in Renaissance Italy*, trans. Lydia G. Cochrane. Chicago: University of Chicago Press, 1985.

Index of Proper Names